Religion and the New Atheism

Studies in Critical Social Sciences

Series Editor
David Fasenfest
Wayne State University

The titles published in this series are listed at brill.nl/scss.

Religion and the New Atheism

A Critical Appraisal

Edited by

Amarnath Amarasingam

Haymarket Books
Chicago, Illinois

First published in 2010 by Brill Academic Publishers, The Netherlands
© 2010 Koninklijke Brill NV, Leiden, The Netherlands

Published in paperback in 2012 by
Haymarket Books
P.O. Box 180165
Chicago, IL 60618
773-583-7884
www.haymarketbooks.org

ISBN: 978-1-60846-203-2

Trade distribution:
in the US, through Consortium Book Sales and Distribution, www.cbsd.com
in the UK, Turnaround Publisher Services, www.turnaround-psl.com
in Australia, Palgrave Macmillan, www.palgravemacmillan.com.au
in all other countries, Publishers Group Worldwide, www.pgw.com

Cover design by Ragina Johnson.

This book was published with the generous support of Lannan Foundation
and the Wallace Global Fund.

Printed in Canada

10 9 8 7 6 5 4 3 2

Library of Congress Cataloging-in-Publication data is available.

For Harshi, with love

SERIES EDITOR PREFACE

This is the first book in the series "Studies in Critical Research on Religion" published by Brill (hardcover) and Haymarket Books (paperback). We understand the term "critical" in the broadest possible sense and therefore think that this book is appropriate for the series. Some may associate a critical perspective with atheism and therefore be surprised how a book series bearing such a name would publish this. While certain strains of the critical approach (like the Left Hegelians and the Orthodox Marxists) are indeed atheistic, others like the Frankfurt School are more ambivalent. Since as Kant logically argued in his *Critique of Pure Reason*, the existence of God is empirically unverifiable (one way or the other), atheism becomes just another belief system. The essays in this book represent a broad range of perspectives, some of which are closer to a critical perspective. While none of the essays fully embraces the New Atheism, some of them do see validity in some of its claims. We hope that the publication of this book will not only lead to a better understanding of the New Atheism but also help to establish the relationship of a critical perspective to it.

Warren S. Goldstein, Ph.D.
Center for Critical Research on Religion
West Newton, Massachusetts USA
www.criticaltheoryofreligion.org

CONTENTS

ACKNOWLEDGEMENTS

I am grateful to all of those people who made this book possible. First, I would like to thank Warren S. Goldstein, Executive Director of the Center for Critical Research on Religion, and the Studies in Critical Research on Religion Series editor, for his ceaseless support and enthusiasm for the project. I would also like to thank the editors at Brill for their kindness and endurance in patiently answering the dozens of emails and questions I threw their way from the very beginning.

I would also like to thank all of the contributors to this book for releasing their hard wrought chapters into the hands of someone who is just beginning their academic career. You made an enjoyable experience from what could have been a stressful foray into publishing. I am also grateful to Ron Rooth for meticulously copy editing the manuscript.

I would like to thank the students and faculty in Wilfrid Laurier's Religion and Culture department as well as the faculty in the Religious Studies department at the University of Waterloo for their ongoing support. Special appreciation must go to Rory Dickson, Adam Stewart, and Asma Bala.

I am grateful to my thesis supervisor, Lorne L. Dawson, and long-time friend and mentor, Robert A. Campbell, who provided helpful advice gleaned from years of experience.

I would like to thank my parents, who, while often wondering what exactly an academic does, always encouraged my pursuits. Your love is boundless, and I am forever in your debt. I am also grateful to my father-in-law, mother-in-law, and Iyah for their love and endless support.

Finally, I would like to thank my wife, Harshi, who is not only patient and loving, but, as it turns out, also a shrewd editor. This book is dedicated to you.

FOREWORD

In his history of the church in the nineteenth century Alec Vidler pointed out that many of the great Victorian atheists turned against religion not because of the rise of biblical criticism or the rise of science but because what Christianity called upon them to believe with a sense of its moral superiority struck them as morally inferior to their own beliefs and standards. If that is true, as I believe it to be, why then has it taken 150 years for the conviction of a few people then to become the cheering crowds of today. One of the strengths of *Religion and the New Atheism: A Critical Appraisal* is that whatever the strengths or weaknesses of the arguments put forward in the new atheism, it is a truly remarkable phenomenon and therefore needs to be understood from a range of perspectives. This book tries to do just that.

There have of course always been atheists. What distinguishes the attack dogs of the new atheism from their more philosophically inclined predecessors is that they believe religion to be not only untrue, but also pernicious, an evil or poison that needs to be eliminated from the bloodstream of society. The new atheism's predominant tone is one of intellectual righteousness— new atheists like to call themselves 'The Brights'—and it is something of a moral crusade. Such a widespread explosion has only now ignited the fuse lit by the Victorian unbelievers referred to by Alec Vidler, I think, because of two main factors. One is that until fairly recently in the Christian West morality and religion were virtually synonymous. To be a Christian and to be a good person were thought of as the same thing. It was entirely natural, at least in Britain, to strive to be, 'a good Christian' without being a strong believer. It is that nexus that has now been broken and today's atheists bring their own moral critique to religious faith; in doing so they often mimic the religion of the past in claiming the high moral ground.

The second factor in atheism's delayed ignition was the wide acceptance and indeed fashion in the 1960s of making institutions and roles that had previously attracted respect as a matter of course the object of satire, mockery, and abuse. Since then the boundaries of what is regarded as acceptable in the way of mockery have grown ever wider. With the decline in status and prestige of all traditional institutions and roles, it was inevitable that organized religion would become an object of derision. People's negative feelings about religion (who does not have at least some negative feelings?) so long held down, are now allowed free expression.

The new atheists arouse irritation and exasperation on all sides. One distinguished philosopher said that they made him ashamed to call himself an atheist. Liberal religious believers see in the debate only the meeting of two fundamentalist stances. The new atheism and religious fundamentalism seemingly need to feed off one another in order to fuel their polemics. But this book tries to get beyond those feelings to consider the phenomenon in a much wider perspective in relation to Judaism and Islam as well as Christianity; and in relation to science and sociology. I believe many will find this approach fresh and helpful.

Richard Harries

PREFACE

One cold spring day in London, as I crossed the bustling square at Piccadilly Circus, I looked left instead of right (a typical American tourist) and was nearly run down by a careening double-decker bus with a flash of letters emblazoned along its side:

THERE'S PROBABLY NO GOD. NOW STOP WORRYING AND ENJOY YOUR LIFE.

The slogan is now ubiquitous and not only in London. When I first saw it I laughed, amused that atheists in the United Kingdom were miming propaganda techniques perfected by evangelical groups in the United States, whose billboards dot the American landscape ("Having truth decay? Brush up on your Bible!"). I likely would have thought no more of it had not a friend not informed me that the driving force behind the London bus ads was none other than the dean of the so-called new atheists—Darwin's Rottweiler, himself—Richard Dawkins. If you are wondering what an esteemed evolutionary biologist and respected Oxford University professor is doing placing billboards around London proselytizing atheism, this book is for you.

There is, as has often been noted, something peculiarly *evangelistic* about what has been termed the new atheist movement. The new atheists have their own special interest groups and ad campaigns. They even have their own holiday (International Blasphemy Day). It is no exaggeration to describe the movement popularized by the likes of Richard Dawkins, Daniel Dennet, Sam Harris, and Christopher Hitchens as a new and particularly zealous form of fundamentalism— an *atheist* fundamentalism. The parallels with religious fundamentalism are obvious and startling: the conviction that they are in sole possession of truth (scientific or otherwise), the troubling lack of tolerance for the views of their critics (Dawkins has compared creationists to holocaust deniers), the insistence on a literalist reading of scripture (more literalist, in fact, than one finds among most religious fundamentalists), the simplistic reductionism of the religious phenomenon, and, perhaps most bizarrely, their overwhelming sense of siege: the belief that they have been oppressed and marginalized by Western societies and are just not going to take it anymore. This is not the philosophical atheism of Feuerbach or Marx, Schopenhauer or Nietzsche (I am not the first to think that the new atheists give atheism a bad name). Neither is it the scientific agnosticism of Thomas Huxley or Herbert Spencer. This is, rather, a caricature of atheism: shallow scholarship mixed with evangelical fervor.

The principle error of the new atheists lies in their inability to understand religion outside of its simplistic, exoteric, and absolutist connotations. Indeed, the most prominent characteristic of the new atheism—and what most differentiates it from traditional atheism—is its utter lack of literacy in the subject (religion) it is so desperate to refute. After all, religion is as much a discipline to be studied, as it is an expression of faith. (I do not write books about, say, biology because I am not a biologist). Religion, however it is defined, is occupied with *transcendence*—by which I mean that which lies beyond the manifest world and towards which consciousness is oriented—and transcendence necessarily encompasses certain theological connotations with which one ought to be familiar to properly critique belief in a god. One should, for example, be cognizant of how the human experience of transcendence has been expressed in the material world through historically dependent symbols and metaphors. One should be able to recognize the diverse ways in which the universal recognition of human contingency, finitude, and material existence has become formalized through ecclesiastical institutions and dogmatic formulae. One should become acquainted with the unmistakable patterns—call them *modalities* (Rudolph Otto), *paradigmatic gestures* (Mircea Eliade), *spiritual dimensions* (Ninian Smart), or *archetypes* (Carl Jung)—that recur in the myths and rituals of nearly all religious traditions and throughout all of recorded history. Even if one insists on reducing humanity's enduring religious impulse to causal definitions, dismissing the experience of transcendence as nothing more than an anthropological (e.g., Edward Tylor or Max Muller), sociological (think Robertson Smith or Emile Durkheim), or even psychological phenomenon (a la Sigmund Freud, who attempted to locate the religious impulse deep within the individual *psyche*, as though it were a mental disorder that could be cured through proper psychoanalysis), one should at the very least have a sense of what the term 'God' *means*.

Of course, positing a transcendent reality that exists beyond our material experiences does not necessarily imply the existence of a Divine Personality, or God. (In some ways, the idea of God is merely the personal affirmation of the transcendent experience.) But what if it did? What if one viewed the recurring patterns of religious phenomena that so many diverse cultures and civilizations—separated by immeasurable time and distance—seem to have shared as evidence of an active, engaging, transcendent presence (what Muslims call the Universal Spirit, Hindus call *prana*, Taoists call *chi'i*, Jews call *ruah*, and Christians call the Holy Spirit) that underlies creation, that, in fact, *impels* creation? Is such a possibility any more hypothetical than say, superstring theory or the notion of the multiverse? Then again, maybe the patterns of religious phenomena signify nothing. Maybe they indicate little more than a common desire among all peoples to answer similar questions of 'Ultimate Concern,' to use the Protestant theologian, Paul Tillich's famous phrase. The point is that, like any researcher or critic, like any *scientist*, I'm open to possibilities.

The new atheists will say that religion is not just wrong but *evil*, as if religion has a monopoly on radicalism and violence; but if one is to blame religion for acts of violence carried out in religion's name then one must also blame nationalism for fascism, socialism for Nazism, communism for Stalinism, even science for eugenics. The new atheists claim that people of faith are not just misguided but *stupid*—the stock response of any absolutist. Some argue that the religious impulse is merely the result of chemicals in the brain, as though understanding the mechanism by which the body experiences transcendence delegitimizes the experience (*every* experience is the result of chemical reactions). What the new atheists do not do, and what makes them so much like the religious fundamentalists they abhor, is admit that all metaphysical claims—be they about the possibility of a transcendent presence in the universe or the birth of the incarnate God on earth—are ultimately unknowable and, perhaps, beyond the purview of science. That may not be a slogan easily pasted on the side of a bus. But it is the hallmark of the scientific intellect.

Reza Aslan

INTRODUCTION: WHAT IS THE NEW ATHEISM?

Amarnath Amarasingam

The God of the Old Testament is arguably the most unpleasant character in all fiction: jealous and proud of it; a petty, unjust, unforgiving control-freak; a vindictive, bloodthirsty ethnic cleanser; a misogynistic, homophobic, racist, infanticidal, genocidal, filicidal, pestilential, megalomaniacal, sadomasochistic, capriciously malevolent bully.

    – Richard Dawkins (2006, 31)

One must state it plainly. Religion comes from the period of human pre-history where nobody—not even the mighty Democritus who concluded that all matter was made from atoms—had the smallest idea what was going on. It comes from the bawling and fearful infancy of our species, and is a babyish attempt to meet our inescapable demand for knowledge (as well as for comfort, reassurance, and other infantile needs).

    – Christopher Hitchens (2007b, 64)

It is safe to say that almost every person living in New Orleans at the moment Hurricane Katrina struck shared your belief in an omnipotent, omniscient, and compassionate God. But what was God doing while Katrina laid waste to their city? Surely He heard the prayers of those elderly men and women who fled the rising waters for the safety of their attics, only to be slowly drowned there. These were people of faith. These were good men and women who had prayed throughout their lives. Do you have the courage to admit the obvious? These people died talking to an imaginary friend.

    – Sam Harris (2008, 53)

The term 'new atheism' has been given to the recent barrage of anti-religion and anti-God books written by Richard Dawkins (2006), Sam Harris (2004, 2008), Christopher Hitchens (2007b), Daniel Dennett (2006), and others. Statements like those above can be found in abundance throughout their writings. They are characteristically petulant and provocative, challenging yet cranky, urgent but uninformed. The new atheist writers and their respective books have been selling extremely well; they have conducted conferences dealing, largely uncritically, with their own material, and have had a significant media presence discussing and debating their ideas with journalists and other scholars. A rigorous academic treatment of their ideas, however, as well as an exploration of how their arguments are important for larger debates in religious studies and the social sciences, remains wanting. The academic community, with a few exceptions, has largely dismissed their writings as unsophisticated, crude, and lacking nuance. As such, most of the work dealing with the new atheist corpus has tended to be equally crude, mocking, or dismissive. Instead, this book brings together eminent and rising scholars in the fields of religious studies, sociology of religion, sociology of science, philosophy, and theology in order to engage the new atheist literature and place it in the context of larger scholarly discourses and debates. It will serve to contextualize and critically examine the claims, arguments, and goals of the new atheists in order that the scholarly community and educated general reader can become more informed of some of the debates with which the new atheists inevitably and, at times unknowingly, engage.

When I mentioned to colleagues that I was preparing an edited book on the new atheism, there were generally two responses. First, I was told that there was in fact nothing *new* about the new atheism. Everything that is said by the likes of Dawkins, Harris, Hitchens, and Dennett had already been said, and said better, by Russell, Paine, Feuerbach, Marx, Freud, Nietzsche, and others. There is, of course, much truth to this. As Damon Linker (2008, A14) writes, the new athe-ism is "not particularly new. It belongs to an intellectual genealogy stretching back hundreds of years, to a moment when atheist thought split into two traditions: one primarily concerned with the dispassionate pursuit of truth, the other driven by a visceral contempt for the personal faith of others." Although much of the content of the new atheism may have precedents, what *is* original is the newfound urgency in the mes-sage of atheism, as well as a kind of atheist social revival that their writ-ings, lectures, and conferences have produced. In other words, the 'new' atheism is not entirely about new ideas, but a kind of evangelical revival and repackaging of old ideas. One only needs to peruse the Converts' Corner on RichardDawkins.net to get a sense of the influ-ence of the new atheism. The thousands of reader comments posted on the site state ad nauseum that *The God Delusion* had given them the arguments and the courage to confidently profess their atheism (see also Bullivant 2008a). To provide just one example: "Thank you, Dr. Dawkins, for giving me the words to explain, in clear, convicted and coherent voice, that which I have always felt. I have never felt so empowered, so humbled, so awestruck or so electrified as when I read

The God Delusion. All of the pieces, which I had been clumsily trying to fit together for a long time, slid into place with an easy grace."

Second, I was told that the bookshelves are already littered with responses to the new atheism. What is the purpose of yet another? Although there have been more than twenty responses to the new atheism,[1] largely from Christian scholars, there has been little attempt to understand the significance of the movement as a whole. The purpose of this book, for example, is not to provide a defense of theology. This has been done by John Haught (2008), Alister McGrath and Joanna Collicutt McGrath (2007), and others. This book will also not be a traditional response to the new atheism. As McGrath and McGrath (2007, 13) have noted: "Every one of Dawkins's misrepresentations and overstatements can be challenged and corrected. Yet a book that merely offered such a litany of corrections would be catatonically boring." Instead, this book, although containing some corrective chapters, approaches the new atheism more broadly. I also did not want this to be another work dealing with the interplay between religion and science (although this is at times unavoidable), simply because there is already an abundance of literature in this area. Rather, this book places the new atheism within a larger context of debates going on in academia in fields as diverse as cognitive science, sociology of religion, philosophy of religion, and ethics.

So who are the new atheists? Richard Dawkins (1941–) was the Charles Simonyi Professor in the Public Understanding of Science at Oxford University (he is retired as of September 2008). He has gained repute as a prolific author and popularizer of science. His most famous book before *The God Delusion* was *The Selfish Gene* published in 1976. Some of his other books on the topic of religion have been *The Blind Watchmaker* (1986), *Climbing Mount Improbable* (1996), and

---

[1] Some sample titles of these books are: *Atheist Delusions* by David Bentley Hart; *Reason, Faith, and Revolution: Reflections on the God Debate* by Terry Eagleton; *The Truth Behind the New Atheism* by David Marshall; *The Last Superstition: A Refutation of the New Atheism* by Edward Feser; *Deluded by Dawkins?* by Andrew Wilson; *Atheism is False* by David R. Stone; *Darwin's Angel* by John Cornwell; *Is God a Delusion?* by Eric Reitan; *The God Delusion Revisited* by Mike King; *What's So Great About Christianity?* by Dinesh D'Souza; *God is No Delusion* by Thomas Crean; *The Irrational Atheist* by Vox Day; *Delusion of Disbelief* by David Aikman; *I Don't Believe in Atheists* by Chris Hedges; *Answering the New Atheism* by Scott Hahn and Benjamin Wiker; *The End of Reason* by Ravi Zacharias; *Beyond the God Delusion* by Richard Grigg; *The God Solution* by James A. Beverly; *The Godless Delusion* by Joe Egan; *Doubting Dawkins* by Keith Ward; *The Devil's Delusion* by David Berlinski; *The Dawkins Letters* by David Robertson.

Unweaving the Rainbow (1998). Christopher Hitchens (1949–) is a contributing editor to *Vanity Fair* and a visiting professor of liberal studies at the New School. He is the author of seventeen books, and has gained prominence as an acerbic polemicist and critic. He has published biographies of Thomas Jefferson (2005) and Thomas Paine (2006), has called for the prosecution of Henry Kissinger for war crimes in Indochina, Bangladesh, Chile, Cyprus, and East Timor (2001), and has launched a caustic criticism of Mother Theresa under the double entendre title, *The Missionary Position* (1995). Daniel Dennett (1942–) is currently the co-director of the Center for Cognitive Studies, the Austin B. Fletcher Professor of Philosophy, and a University Professor at Tufts University. He has authored many books, including the famous and controversial *Darwin's Dangerous Idea* (1996). Sam Harris (1967–) has a bachelor's degree in philosophy from Stanford University and is currently a doctoral candidate in neuroscience at the University of California, Los Angeles, where he is studying the neural basis of belief with functional magnetic resonance imaging. He is also a Co-Founder and Chairman of The Reason Project, a nonprofit foundation devoted to spreading scientific knowledge and secular values in society.

This book is divided into four parts. The first part contains three chapters, and explores the relationship between the new atheism and Judaism, Christianity, and Islam respectively. Robert Platzner's chapter argues that the Western Enlightenment offers the Jewish community in Europe (and subsequently America) the possibility of a secular revaluation of Jewish values and beliefs. He notes that Baruch Spinoza is the first of a succession of Jewish intellectuals who distance themselves from a traditionalist worldview, and more specifically who undertake a humanistic redefinition of Judaism's God-concept. Platzner argues that the increasing secularization of Jewish discourse in the modern era can be measured by the gradual abandonment of both the personal deity of biblical and rabbinic tradition and the increasing rejection of a teleological view of Jewish history. This pattern of denial and subversion becomes especially clear after the Holocaust in the writings of such figures as Richard Rubenstein and Sherwin Wine, for whom the idea of a beneficent and controlling God is simply incompatible with any intellectually coherent view of human history.

Jeffrey Robbins and Christopher Rodkey begin their chapter by introducing Paul Tillich's argument that the problem with most religious conceptions of God, especially within Christianity, is that they are a form of 'theological theism'—that is, their understanding of God only works as a piece of a metaphysical puzzle within a particular metaphysical system of thought or belief. So given, Tillich concluded, atheism is the proper, if not Christian, response to theological theism. Atheism, however, also errs by itself, trapped within the logic of theological theism whenever it is expressed as a categorical rejection of God and any sense of ontological understanding of the world. In other words, atheism replaces one flawed puzzle for another with different pieces. Consequently, many Christian responses to the new atheism are an argument among and within theological theisms. Their chapter argues that the new atheists are guilty of the same problems that Tillich predicted of future atheism. Robbins and Rodkey propose a radical theological critique employing the theology of the American 'death of God' movement and recent continental philosophy of religion. They argue, in other words, that the new atheists do not go far enough in their critique of traditional Christianity; the new atheism is insufficiently radical and has little argument upon which to stand against a radical Christianity.

Rory Dickson argues that Sam Harris, in *The End of Faith*, presents a woefully inadequate picture of Islam, caricaturing the religion in terms of its most pathological manifestations. Dickson highlights key elements of Islamic history, law, and spirituality that Harris fails to adequately deal with, and concludes that Harris's failure to appreciate these central elements of Islam leads him to provide a two-dimensional presentation of the religion.

The second part of the book, containing two chapters, deals with the relationship between science and the new atheism. The section begins with a chapter by Steve Fuller who notes that until the advent of the new atheists, self-professed atheists have typically opposed religion more on moral than epistemological grounds. Thus, today's new atheism is distinctive in its claim to a scientific and not simply a libertarian basis. But, he asks, what exactly is this scientific basis? In surveying Western intellectual history for an answer, Fuller distinguishes 'atheism,' an anti-clerical philosophy associated with the Enlightenment that basically secularizes key Abrahamic theological concepts in the name of human progress, and 'Atheism,' a more thoroughgoing anti-theistic worldview that descends from Epicurus and denies any cognitive privilege to humanity or, indeed, any purpose to history or the universe. He notes that although the arguments of the new atheists vacillate between these two senses of atheism, their intent is clearly to promote the latter view, which explains the talismanic significance of Charles Darwin. However, Fuller intriguingly argues that had such Atheism been as widespread in history as the new atheists would have it be today, the science on which they base their views would never have developed.

William Sims Bainbridge argues in his chapter that while atheism is often defined as disbelief in God, the recent atheistic school of thought in cognitive science attacks religion's basis more broadly. He argues that this school of thought also debunks the notions of soul and faith, because both concepts are based on naive notions of how human mentality actually functions. His chapter begins with a survey of the origins of cognitive science, an academic discipline that emerged from a multi-disciplinary social movement encompassing cognition-oriented work in philosophy, psychology, computer science, neuroscience, linguistics, and anthropology. Bainbridge then examines how cognitive scientists have critiqued the supposed unity of an individual human mind, stressed the provisional and probabilistic nature of belief, and applied the same scepticism to God's mind and God's own beliefs.

The four chapters in the third section of the book provide a more sociological treatment of the new atheism. In addition to critiques, the chapters in this section explore the movement as a whole and attempt to gauge its social significance. William Stahl's chapter argues that the new atheists are often dismissed as fundamentalists in their own right, and the new atheists just as quickly dismiss this criticism as flawed. His chapter attempts to explore the sociology of this symmetry in more detail. Stahl notes that beneath superficial stylistic similarities lay deeper structural and epistemological parallels. He argues that both the new atheism and fundamentalism (using Creation Science as an exemplar) are attempts to recreate authority in the face of crises of meaning in late modernity.

Stephen Bullivant's chapter argues that, from a sociological point of new, the new atheists' remarkable publishing and media successes are surprising and puzzling. He notes that the socio-religious cultures of neither Britain nor the United States (the new atheism's twin epicentres) seemed to be ripe for such a phenomenon—but for very different reasons. His chapter suggests a number of social and cultural factors, present in either one or both of Britain and the United States, which may cumulatively help to explain the new atheism's rise. More speculatively, Bullivant makes some tentative predictions concerning the phenomenon's lasting effects.

Michael Borer's chapter examines the debates surrounding the rise and decline of the 'secularization thesis' and attempts to show how the emergence of the new atheists provides evidence that both supports and contradicts many precepts of the thesis. Placing the new atheists within the historical and ongoing debates about secularization sheds light on new atheism as a minority 'movement' that aims to show how and why religious faith is an inferior form of knowledge that, in turn, fosters misguided worldviews.

Richard Cimino and Christopher Smith's chapter addresses how the new atheism has created new space for 'freethinkers.' They note that the space for atheism in America has been and continues to be cramped, particularly as many atheist leaders and activists claim that their personal and social identities have carried a fair degree of stigma. The appearance of the new atheism may signal a weakening of the 'atheist taboo' in American society, especially as atheists themselves see the phenomenon as a harbinger of advancing secularism. Cimino and Smith argue that the new atheist books and the responses, debates, and criticisms they have generated create a new space where atheists are empowered and mobilized through their interaction and contention with each other and with their antagonists.

The final section of the book, containing three chapters, explores some of the philosophical arguments put forth by the new atheists. Gregory Peterson's chapter notes that a central plank of the new atheist attack on religion is the claim that religion leads to immoral behaviour and that the atheist accounts of morality provide a superior undergirding of moral norms, including specifically norms of out-group altruism and compassion. However, many of the new atheists' critiques of religious ethics are highly problematic. Peterson argues that there is good reason to believe that support for out-group altruism and compassion is better given in a theological framework than a naturalistic one. Although his chapter focuses on the Christian case, the arguments have more general implications as well.

Jeff Nall draws attention to the recent birth of atheist parenting literature that implicitly challenges the assumption of many in the American public that children are better served when raised in a religious environment. Moreover, he notes, the literature explicitly critiques religious approaches to parenting, a minority of which express concern that religious indoctrination harms children. In particular, Nall's chapter tests the prevailing wisdom about the differences between atheist and Christian approaches to parenting. He argues that while the overarching aim of these parenting approaches is fundamentally different, both Christian and atheist parenting approaches are enthusiastically committed to instilling in their children a deep appreciation of honesty, consideration of others, and honest living. His chapter also shows that emerging leaders within the atheist movement are highly critical of the ridicule and abuse of religion exerted by the new atheists.

Finally, Ryan Falcioni's chapter attempts to demonstrate the fundamental philosophical confusions involved with the methodology of the new atheists. He argues that these same confusions are in play in the works of many contemporary philosophers of religion. The new atheists as well as many 'serious' philosophers of religion tend to treat religious beliefs as putative hypotheses about the world. For them, the existence of God is a broadly 'scientific' hypothesis that is in need of clear, analyzable evidence for its truth to be confirmed. Falcioni attempts to unpack this assumption and show how it is confused. Put simply, it fails to do justice to the nature of religious beliefs. He argues that it is only through paying close attention to the forms of life in which religious claims occur that we can begin to make sense of their meaning and thus understand how best to go about analyzing or critiquing them.

The book ends with an afterword by Mark Vernon, who begins his exploration by asking a broader question, which also runs through all of the new atheist writings: how are we to navigate the plurality of worldviews that is characteristic of the modern, secular, age? For the new atheists, tolerance of intolerance (often presented in the guise of relativism or multiculturalism) is one of the greatest dangers in contemporary society. Disagreements abound, but what cannot be denied about the new atheists, is that they have brought these important discussions into the public sphere with force and vigour. It is my hope that the essays in this book will further contribute to the conversation.

Part I: Religion and the New Atheism

JUDAISM AND ATHEISM: THE CHALLENGE OF SECULAR HUMANISM

Robert L. Platzner

The authors of the Book of Psalms entertained no doubts about either the existence of the biblical God or the status of those who withheld belief in that deity—"The fool [*naval*] says in his heart, there is no God" (Ps14: 1), implying that no rational being would ever question the reality of the Creator and Sovereign of heaven and earth—and not one of the sacred texts of early Judaism even intimates disbelief in the God biblical writers variously designate as YHWH, El, or Elohim. Not even the author of the Book of Job, for all his apparent scepticism regarding the justness of divine decrees, raises any question of God's Being, or his being-in-the-world; on the contrary, the God who answers Job's queries and complaints out of the whirlwind is intimately aware of humankind, and just as clearly beyond the scope of human understanding. Job's God may be a transcendent figure, and morally incomprehensible, but he is certainly not a figment of the human imagination.

Nor are the rabbis of the Talmud capable of conceiving of a world without the "Holy One, Blessed be He." Those who negate God's existence they term *kofer ba-Iqqar*—one who denies a basic principle of faith, or more precisely one who denies the reality of the biblical—but in their various discussions of heresy the issue of *radical* disbelief in any supreme being never arises (Urbach 1987, 26–27). A heretic may be one who rejects the divine source of revealed texts, or one who accepts the existence of multiple deities, but rabbinic discourse appears to lack a category for someone who rejects the 'God hypothesis' altogether. Nor do Jewish philosophers from the Greco-Roman period (e.g., Philo) to the Middle Ages (Saadia or Maimonides) feel the need to defend the existence of a Being whom they perceive as the ground of all material and spiritual realities. In sum, the religio-philosophical tradition in Judaism, from Antiquity through the Middle Ages, is devoted to the elucidation of God's nature and his relation to the world, rather than to a reasoned argument for or against his very existence.

Atheism—understood not simply as disbelief in the biblical Deity, or deities generally, but more broadly as the "rejection of any transcendental or supernatural reality" (Baggini 2003, 3)—has scarcely any impact on Judaism until the modern era, when Jews suddenly find themselves in a position to respond to, as well as interact with, some of the more radical interrogations of faith that increasingly characterize the intellectual life of the West from the seventeenth century to the present. That response, and the trajectory of progressive disbelief that can be traced from Spinoza to contemporary advocates of a 'godless' Judaism, constitutes the focus of this essay. Each of the figures we will consider exhibits both a pattern of growing dissociation from many of the basic assumptions that have sustained Jewish theology over many centuries and a growing interest in a materialist interpretation of religious experience. As such, far from practicing 'blind faith' as the new atheists contend, these thinkers represent a secular counter-tradition within the discourse of Judaism in the modern age that not only preempts but also surpasses the arguments put forth by the new atheists.

It would be a mistake, however, to regard this counter-tradition as nothing more than the end-result of what Charles Taylor (2007, 280) terms modernist 'disenchantment' with the idea of a beneficent and controlling Deity, and with a universe designed to accommodate such a Deity. A more nuanced view of the growth of secularism *within* Judaism would recognize that a traditionalist Jewish worldview carries within itself a potential for cognitive dissonance, and at the very least one can observe, from Spinoza's generation to our own, a growing dissatisfaction among a distinct class of Jewish intellectuals with any teleological interpretation of the human condition, specifically, a messianic view of Jewish history. As we shall see, whenever the normative God-concept of 'orthodox' Judaism is set against a materialist cosmology or historiography that challenges the very notion of a universe governed by a purposeful deity, the cumulative response of this increasingly secularized intelligentsia is one of deepening scepticism and systematic renunciation of core Jewish beliefs.

Spinoza's Revolt

Philosophical modernism, with its signature scepticism that (a la Descartes) calls all things into question, begins to impact Jewish thought no earlier than the 1600s, and in the person of the arch-heretic of that era, Benedict Spinoza (1632–1677). Spinoza's quarrel with the Jewish community of Amsterdam, and his expulsion therefrom, though of vital interest to biographers and historians, are of little relevance to this essay, and we will pass quietly over the cultural and psychological roots of his break with Judaism and focus instead on his rejection of conventional theistic reasoning, for Spinoza is quite candid in his disdain for those who seek evidence of the miraculous and the providential in either nature or human history:

> Hence it happens that one who seeks the true causes of miracles, and is eager, like an educated man, to understand natural things, not to wonder at them, like a fool, is generally considered an impious heretic and denounced as such by those whom the people honor as interpreters of Nature and the gods. For they know that if ignorance is taken away, then foolish wonder, the only means they have of arguing and defending their authority, is also taken away (Spinoza 1996, 29).

Spinoza's tone in this passage is that of an aggressive 'enlightener'—in the eighteenth century such intellectuals were referred to in Hebrew as *maskilim*—and like his Christian predecessor Descartes, he is self-consciously placing himself outside of the normative religious discourse of the community of faith in which he was raised. And while it is customary today to classify Spinoza as a 'pantheist,' it would be more precise to identify his philosophical orientation as that of a monistic materialist, and therefore to see him as an incipient atheist: that is, as someone who ultimately denies any *meta*-physical role to a deity who exists largely as a conceptual abstraction, and whose functions are virtually indistinguishable from the workings of the material universe into which he has been absorbed (see M. Stewart 2006, 178–179).

What is especially problematic, however, about Spinoza's attempt to move beyond the traditional anthropopathic (and to some degree anthropomorphic) Judaic conception of a personal God—or indeed any God-concept at all—is his refusal to abandon a conventionally theistic vocabulary. Repeatedly, throughout the *Ethics* and the *Theological-Political Treatise,* he refers to, or paraphrases, biblical passages that depict a deity who reveals himself to Jew and Gentile alike, and who possesses specific moral qualities that define both his nature and his relation to humankind. However, these observations can be understood as part of a larger phenomenology of theistic belief, demanding what anthropologists today would call a 'thick description' of the culture of faith. But when Spinoza is free to speak in his own voice, he refuses to distinguish his 'God' from Nature, and proceeds to locate that deity at the centre of a deterministic cosmic system. Thus, in Book Four of the *Ethics*, Spinoza (1996, 114) famously (and rather off-handedly) refers to 'God, or Nature,' thereby drawing an equation, at the very least, between the functions of God in the universe and the material 'stuff' of that universe. As the *immanent* cause of all things, Spinoza's God does not intervene in the course of Nature to bring about miracles, nor does he assume human traits or form, nor will he sit some day in judgment on humanity. His principal function in Spinoza's worldview is to establish the necessary (and therefore intelligible) character of all existing processes and things, and it is difficult, at last, to say just how Spinoza's 'God' actually differs from the sum of everything that makes up our world (M. Stewart 2006, 158–159).

In the eyes of his contemporaries, however, Spinoza's 'atheism' consisted of more than the formulation of a naturalistic metaphysic that identifies the Creator with his creation. His even more unforgiveable sin was his attack upon the integrity of the biblical text itself, or more precisely, his close and often sceptical analyses of biblical passages that reveal just how piecemeal (and therefore synthetic) the text of the Hebrew Bible really is. In Spinoza's biblical commentaries we can see the remote origins of what is commonly referred to today as the Documentary Hypothesis, which posits not only multiple authors and distinct literary sources for texts traditionally attributed to Moses or to various prophets, but which also assumes the evolutionary character of the historical process by which the biblical canon came into existence in the first place. By challenging the historicity—as well as the internal consistency—of Jewish Scripture, Spinoza indirectly challenged the very notion of divine revelation, thereby reducing sacred works to the status of human literary creations (Della Rocca 2008, 237). For this act of demythologization alone, he was deemed worthy of excommunication. Seen in long view, then, Spinoza's revolt against Judaism's God and the very sources of Judaism's claim to be a revealed religion represents the earliest stage of an ongoing rejection of all metaphysical claims that lie at the heart of the Judaic faith system.

MORDECAI KAPLAN AND REVISIONIST THEOLOGY

If anyone can legitimately lay claim to being Spinoza's heir in the modern era, it is Rabbi Mordecai Kaplan (1881–1983), whose revisionist theology offers a more nuanced version of 'religious naturalism' than anything one can find in Spinoza's philosophy. In Kaplan's writings we find a form of proto-atheism that has had a more immediate and profound effect on contemporary Judaic discourse than anything one can attribute to a seventeenth century heretic. Deeply influenced by modern social science, and determined to bring Judaism into line with the most advanced systems of thought in his time, Kaplan set to work, deconstructing and reconstructing the traditional theological constructs that had been bequeathed to him by orthodox teachers. Taking his cue from John Dewey and the Pragmatic school of thought, Kaplan (1994, 88–89) asked repeatedly what practical consequence follows from attributing traits of personality or facets of power to the deity when the result is a God-concept that contemporary science cannot sustain:

> Modern science has again reconstructed our picture of the universe... We cannot conceive of God any more as a sort of invisible superman, displaying the same psychological traits as a man, but on a greater scale. We cannot think of him as loving, pitying, rewarding, punishing, etc. Many have therefore abandoned altogether the conception of a personal God, and prefer to think of ultimate reality in terms of force, energy and similar concepts.
>
> Such an attitude, however, is erroneous. It violates completely our sense of the sacredness of life. It is irrelevant to human ideals and the quest for salvation... We do not need to pretend to any knowledge of the ultimate purpose of the universe as a whole, as the theology of the past sometimes claimed for itself. But it is an undeniable fact that there is something in the nature of life which expresses itself in human personality...For such an identification implies that *there is something divine in human personality, in that it is the instrument through which the creative life of the world effects the evolution of the human race.*

Contemporary atheists like Dawkins or Harris would likely argue that, in passages like this, Kaplan wants to have it both ways: he wants to exercise the post-Feuerbach prerogative of rejecting an anthropomorphic deity—whose capricious and often cruel nature stands as a constant reminder of just how illogical monotheism can be—while at the same time retaining the residue of that tradition by positing human ethical qualities that presumably underlie the very processes of human evolution. Ludwig Feuerbach's *The Essence of Christianity* (1841) is the earliest attempt to systematically reduce Christianity—and by implication all monotheistic religions—to a form of inverted humanism: by worshipping God, Feuerbach argues, we are really worshipping a magnified image of ourselves. Dawkins (2006) and Harris (2004) essentially replicate his basic thesis. Thus, Dawkins (2006, 36) dismisses as a tedious and absurd "distraction" the personal deity of the three Abrahamic faiths, insisting that neither he nor his readers believe in an "old bearded man sitting on a cloud." Dawkins (2006, 37) then proceeds to apply his own reductionist methodology to the Hebrew Bible by describing the God of Judaism as "fiercely unpleasant...morbidly obsessed with sexual restrictions, with the smell of charred flesh, with his own superiority over rival gods and with the exclusiveness of his chosen desert tribe," echoing a previously cited observation from Gore Vidal that monotheism is "the unmentionable evil at the center of our culture." For Kaplan, however, these two hypotheses exist in dialectical tension with one another, rather than in a relationship of logical contradiction, and the connecting link between the two lies in the Whiteheadian idea of process (see Lubarsky 1996, 51–57).

As a static concept, the biblical God can be nothing more than the sum of his varied attributes: such a deity possesses whatever fixed traits can be culled from the pages of Jewish Scriptures, or reduced to caricature by those whose purpose is fundamentally satirical. As a dynamic concept, however, the God-idea in Judaism, Kaplan believed, could be appropriated for essentially humanistic ends. Of course, Kaplan (1991, 74–75) can be selective, if not exegetically arbitrary, when deciding which divine attributes he wishes to privilege, but the underlying humanistic character of this entire exercise remains undeniably clear:

> When we say that God is process, we select, out of the infinite processes of the universe, that complex of forces and relationships which makes for the highest fulfillment of man as a human being and identify it by the term "God"... God is the Process by which the universe produces persons, and persons are the processes by *which God is manifest in the individual. Neither term has meaning without the other.*

Like Spinoza, for whom 'God' and 'Nature' were interchangeable terms, Kaplan moves easily and creatively between both sides of this equation, sometimes speaking of a seemingly self-evident 'God-idea' and at other times identifying some variant of that idea with a specific behavioural norm. Thus, he can assert that "God and goodness are one," or that "God and knowledge are identical" (Kaplan1991, 74) without ever really acknowledging that the term 'God' had become functionally redundant, a mere enhancement of an ethical system that was, at its core, a humanistic quest for a worldview grounded in the illusion of transcendent values. For unlike Emile Durkheim, with whom he is often linked, Kaplan was never content to find the source of value judgments or ethical ideals in the sociology of the tribe. His own variety of what he called 'religious humanism' rested on the belief that something called 'God' was made 'manifest' whenever human societies and cultures reached beyond mere animality and displayed elements of moral creativity and 'godliness.'

Yet, though Kaplan (1991, 78) repeatedly insisted that his aim was never to "dissolve the God-idea into ethics," it is increasingly difficult to read his 'reconstruction' of traditional Jewish metaphysics any other way, or to regard his allusions to a 'cosmic urge' as anything more than a rhetorical stratagem designed to sustain a teleological argument free from the philosophical encumbrances of a living, substantive deity. Thus, in place of a philosophical system in which a divine reality defines and determines the meaning of things, Kaplan imagines a universe in which 'what is' is constantly moving towards 'what ought to be,' a place where 'God' can consequently be defined as "the Power that endorses *what we believe ought to be*, and that guarantees that it will be" (1994, 323–324; emphasis added). Little wonder, therefore, that he can insist that belief in such a 'deity'—or more precisely a God-function—is "a necessary concomitant of all idealistic endeavor." Cosmic optimism of this order certainly demands a more than naturalistic body of evidence to support it.

GOD AFTER AUSCHWITZ

Kaplan's philosophical outlook and principal theses were largely formulated within the first three decades of the twentieth century, and consequently his ideas about God were scarcely affected by the tragedy of the Shoah. That can hardly be said, however, of Kaplan's successor in the history of radical humanism in its Jewish context, Richard Rubenstein (1924–), for whom the mass murder of European Jews became the defining event in Judaism's millennial search for a divine reality. And though Rubenstein has since attempted to distance himself from other 'Death of God' theologians of the 1960's, such as William Hamilton and Thomas Altizer, his reflections on the future of Judaism in a post-Holocaust era take a decidedly Nietzschean turn with the publication of his masterwork *After Auschwitz* (1966), which suggests that, like his Christian contemporaries, Rubenstein was so

shocked by the horrors of Nazi genocide that his faith in a God of justice and compassion was shaken to the very core:

> I believe the greatest single challenge to modern Judaism arises out of the
> question of God and the death camps. I am amazed at the silence of con-
> temporary Jewish theologians on this more crucial and agonizing of all
> Jewish issues. How can Jews believe in an omnipotent, beneficent God
> after Auschwitz? Traditional Jewish theology maintains that God is the
> ultimate, omnipotent actor in the historical drama. It has interpreted
> every major catastrophe in Jewish history as God's punishment of a sin-
> ful Israel. I fail to see how this position can be maintained without
> regarding Hitler and the SS as instruments of God's will. The agony of
> European Jewry cannot be likened to the testing of Job. To see any pur-
> pose in the death camps, the traditional believer is forced to regard the
> most demonic, antihuman explosion of all history as a meaningful
> expression of God's purposes. (Rubenstein1992, 171)

In a later edition of this same work, Rubenstein (1992, 171–174)
acknowledges that this earlier philosophical *cri du coeur* overstated
his 'real' theological position, but there is no doubt, from his subsequent writings, that his encounter with radical evil had led him so far
from any conceivable theodicy—or more broadly, any theologically
coherent rationale for human suffering—that it was no longer possible for him to sustain belief in a deity of biblical proportions. "Whatever God may be," Rubenstein concludes, "He/She is not distinctively
and uniquely the sovereign Lord of the covenant and election" (1992,
172).

It is at this point in his argument that Rubenstein's critics pounce on
his putative claim to be doing any form of Judaic theology, and on his
equally improbable claim that his critique of the biblical covenant-idea
amounts to anything more than a definitive rejection of Judaism's
defining perception of the Creator and Lord of History. Rubenstein
(1992, 170–174) defends himself against the latter charge by arguing
that any statements about God's presumptive 'nature,' positive or negative, cannot be invested with metaphysical validity given the finite cognitive capabilities and life experiences of human beings; at most, he
insists, all we can credibly affirm in the present is that the 'death' of
God (or the cessation of belief in a traditional deity) is a measurable
'cultural' fact, and therefore sociologically true, even if God 'exists' in
some inexplicable—or 'mystical-dialectical'—way. That so vacuous a
'deity' can have no necessary influence upon either the individual
moral life or upon the course of history appears not to trouble him
greatly, nor that the universe this shadowy divine presence inhabits

has become, in Rubenstein's words, "cold, silent, unfeeling, [and] unaided by any purposeful power beyond our own resources" (1992, 172). Such is the cosmos that Rubenstein has obviously taken over from his existentialist predecessors, and it is his determination to remain within the philosophical parameters of the world according to Camus and Sartre that finally reduces his plea for a Judaism devoid of both covenant and Creator to historical irrelevancy. Any community of Jews who embraced Rubenstein's agnostic, anti-teleological, and potentially nihilistic worldview would have no compelling reason to regard itself as confessionally Jewish, nor would its theism be distinguishable from the more common forms of atheism. In Rubenstein, the "force that makes for righteousness"—Mordecai Kaplan's favorite humanist euphemism for God—is encountered in a negative inversion as the absence of moral will, or in a still more anguished mutation as divinity's demonic counterpart: the force that makes for evil. And insofar as Rubenstein refuses to accept history's seeming verdict, that madness and cruelty will again and again triumph over goodness and love, he is obliged to reject far more consistently (and even vehemently) than Kaplan the existence of a divine and beneficent purpose underlying the life of things. The metaphysical void he thus leaves behind cannot easily be filled by invocations of human fellowship, or more specifically solidarity on behalf of Israel or of Jewish causes generally.

RABBI SHERWIN WINE AND HUMANISTIC JUDAISM

One of Rubenstein's sharpest critics once observed that his theological position would have been strengthened had he adopted a more straightforward atheistic perspective. William E. Kaufman (1992, 253) sees Rubenstein as an inconsistent nihilist whose invocation of a 'God of Nothingness' reduces the question of God's existence, or the very meaning of the God-concept, to sheer meaninglessness. Ironically, the one figure in contemporary Jewish thought who has consistently advocated for a 'godless' Judaism—the late Rabbi Sherwin Wine (1928–2007)—sounds remarkably like Rubenstein himself:

> From a humanistic perspective, the existence, experience, and survival of the Jewish people hardly demonstrate the existence of a loving, just God who is compassionately involved with the moral agenda of human beings. On the contrary, the very opposite is indicated. In the century of the Holocaust, after twenty centuries of unprovoked Jew hatred, the experience of the Jewish people points to the absence of God...No good

God would arrange or allow a Holocaust of six million victims. A thousand glorious resurrections would never provide moral compensation.

If Jewish history has any message about the nature of the universe, it is that the universe is indifferent to our suffering or happiness, that it cares nothing about the moral concerns of the human struggle. The Jewish experience points to the absurdity of the world. (Wine 1995a, 231)

Yet for all the resemblance between them, for Wine the Holocaust is not the paradigm-shifting event that it is for Rubenstein. Rather, it merely confirms what three centuries of enlightenment philosophy and science have taught us: as Carl Sagan (quoted in Dawkins 2006, 19) put it, "if by 'God' one means the set of physical laws that govern the universe, then clearly there is such a God. [However], this God is emotionally unsatisfying ... it does not make much sense to pray to the law of gravity." Nor does Wine propose praying to gravity or to anything else. Wine's most basic assumption—which he shares with secular humanists who have no connection to Judaism—is that we are alone in the universe; there is no one and nothing to which we can turn in moments of suffering and fear, and the only hope for the amelioration of the human condition lies with humanity itself. The interventionist God of biblical faith, and the equally mythic rabbinic figure of the Messiah are facets, he insists, of an exhausted ideology of redemptive beings. Turning to God, whether out of desperation or nostalgia, is an act of futility that robs human beings of their initiative and moral autonomy. We alone are responsible for our fate, and any faith that preaches reliance on a superhuman will is a betrayal of that conviction; it reduces the 'faithful' to moral passivity and fatalism (Wine 1995a, 231–232).

From these precepts and observations, Wine draws several radical (though not entirely coherent) inferences. Arguing that "Jewish identity is not a belief identity," Wine (1995b, 246–248) dismisses any fears surrounding intermarriage or the demographic plight of the 'vanishing Jew' as regressively tribalistic, and proposes instead that the happiness of individuals is really all that matters (or should matter) to any community. Yet for all his belief in the supreme value of individual liberty and self-realization, Wine (somewhat incongruously) echoes Mordecai Kaplan's belief that 'peoplehood' is the central reality of Jewish life, and then carries that belief beyond anything that Kaplan, or the Reconstructionist movement he founded, would have sanctioned, insisting that Jewish ethnicity will survive even the loss of an informing creed or a distinctive body of rituals. Or, as Daniel Friedman

(1995, 258), one of Wine's rabbinic colleagues and a co-founder of the movement for Humanistic Judaism argues, Jews possess an essential historical identity that precedes, and therefore is independent of, any belief system or body of values that might be identified as 'Judaism.' A Jew is a Jew by virtue of his/her "presence within Jewish history," even if that 'presence' is accidental or involuntary. As for the manner in which that existential participation in Jewish history expresses itself, that is left, once again, to the imagination or volition of the individual. Within an institutional setting, however, humanistic Jews have formed congregations throughout the U.S. that provide a somewhat more concrete setting for what Judith Seid (2001) calls 'God-Optional Judaism,' complete with a liturgy and ceremonies designed to enhance a sense of ethnicity and group identity.

That Wine and his followers have manifested a keen interest in Yiddish language and literature is hardly surprising, given the existence of a thriving Yiddish- based secular culture that existed both in Europe and in the United States at the turn of the twentieth century and during the four decades that preceded the Shoah. Writers like Sholem Aleichem and Isaac Leib Peretz provide latter-day Jewish humanists with a precedent for a type of cultural creativity that feeds off an enlightened, and often agnostic, view of traditional Jewish faith, while at the same time retaining a deep sense of involvement in Jewish life and thought. If it was possible, humanists argue, for a generation twice displaced by political persecution and secular disenchantment with religion to construct an intellectually credible form of Jewish identity under those conditions, then surely we can duplicate that phenomenon today.

A New Age, 'Post-Judaic' Judaism

With the emergence of the movement for Humanistic Judaism, the arc of the humanist challenge to traditional Jewish faith is nearly complete. Kaplan, Rubenstein and Wine chose to remain—however problematically—within the social and cultural context of Diaspora Jewish life, with each retaining, in his own way, a feeling of commitment to the survival of a distinct form of Jewish 'faith,' even if that faith consisted exclusively of a belief in the historical significance of the Jewish experience. With Douglas Rushkoff's work *Nothing Sacred* (2003), the final negation of Judaism—of its people, and particularly of its God—is presented paradoxically as the ultimate and appropriate denouement of Jewish history. As he writes,

> Perhaps our greatest challenge as Jews is to spread the 'bad news' in the least threatening way possible. The bad news is that we may be alone. For all practical purposes, God has receded from human affairs. He is as distant from us as if he did not exist in the first place. At the very least, as Jews, we must behave as if this were the case. We must assume there is no God protecting us and guaranteeing our collective fate and instead learn to take care of one another. (Rushkoff 2003, 173)

Chief among the various renunciations that Rushkoff urges upon his Jewish readers is the idea of the 'chosen people,' which he perceives as not only outmoded, but actually racist. After all, if the God who promised Abraham and his progeny a collective destiny is part of an obsolete 'mythic narrative,' then the ethnic identity that derives from that promise must be equally obsolete. In fact, he goes on to argue, the greatest boon which contemporary Jews can confer upon their children and upon the world is to will the 'dissolution' of Judaism, thereby liberating the moral force of those truly creative ideas that have resided at the heart of Jewish faith for millennia (Rushkoff 2003, 199).

Which ideas? On that subject Rushkoff is often distractingly vague, at times falling back on a Kaplanian view of culture as process, and at other times promoting a very specific anti-traditionalist, anti-Zionist agenda. But on the subject of Judaism's God and the proper worship thereof, Rushkoff (2003, 119) has some detailed—if not entirely consistent—recommendations, as he attempts to move his reader towards what he describes as "radically recontextualized monotheism." Moving beyond the traditional theistic view of the deity as person or being, Rushkoff proposes that we think of God as a kind of energy field, which can be activated by, and among, those who have embraced an evolutionary view of religious precepts and behaviour. Thus, the highest and most evolved form of faith becomes the most iconoclastic, actively resisting any form of stasis or rule-bound behaviour. Ritual, prayer, or any form of collective religious affirmation can only be accomplished authentically as a kind of improvisatory theater, subject (of course) to perpetual revision and redefinition. And most important of all is the recognition, Rushkoff insists, that whatever form of worship we construct or deconstruct must be understood to be self-fulfilling. Whether through our interpersonal relationships or solely within ourselves, the god that we have been searching for is simply self-fulfillment and not some transcendent presence. Anything less or other is really a type of idolatry.

To anyone familiar with some of the dominant themes of New Age spirituality, Rushkoff's potpourri of ideas and social imperatives must have a familiar ring; the same emphasis on autonomy, iconoclasm and self-realization resonates in Rushkoff's post-Judaic Judaism, along with a view of community that is universalist in nature, and therefore devoid of social boundaries or exclusionary ideological sympathies. That such a view of religion—or of any faith-community, not just Judaism—generates opposition to any institutionalized forms or creeds is self-evident. From a more pragmatic perspective, one can only speculate on the historical viability of post-modernist perpetual reinvention that Rushkoff proposes for a Judaism that, as he sees it, has outlived its purposes. At the same time, this worldview reduces the God-idea to a form of interactive mythology, and thus reflective of a non-theistic culture that has taught itself to become, in Nietzsche's words, the God it has just destroyed.

With Rushkoff, our study of Jewish secularism has come full circle. Unlike Kaplan, Rubenstein and Wine, Rushkoff occupies no clerical position or leadership role within the Jewish community, nor does he exhibit that depth of familiarity with traditional texts that one would expect from someone who had received rabbinical training. As a freelance (and largely self-taught) critic of Judaism, and as a self-described 'lapsed' Jew, Rushkoff stands, rather like Spinoza (with whom he frequently compares himself), self-consciously outside of the community of faith whose creed he is attempting to deconstruct. His disaffection from Judaism's God (however that deity is conceived), and his programmatic rejection of the idea of Jewish peoplehood, flow, therefore, from the same philosophically alienated point of view. If the chosen people—or as Kaplan liked to say, the 'choosing' people—and the deity they have chosen to commit to are in error, then it is past time that the centuries-old attempt to eradicate their faith culminate in an act of *self-eradication*. Sam Harris (2004, 94) replicates this obsession when he considers the idea of the 'chosen people' as one of the principal causes of anti-Semitism: "Judaism alone finds itself surrounded by unmitigated errors. It seems little wonder, therefore, that it has drawn so much sectarian fire. Jews, insofar as they are religious, believe that they are the bearers of a unique covenant with God. As a consequence, they have spent the last two thousand years collaborating with those who see them as different by seeing themselves as irretrievably so." Harris's 'blame the victim' logic is almost breathtaking in its perversity, but like Rushkoff he assumes that any resistance to universalism (or at least to cultural assimilation) will be met by largely justifiable demands for the obliteration of that resistant community, and particularly if they happen to be Jews.

There is at last a tragic irony at work here, though it is doubtful that Rushkoff or Harris are fully aware of the implications of the anti-Judaic polemic they have constructed: the ultimate goal of the humanist critique becomes practically indistinguishable from the genocidal fantasies of Nazism, modernity's most barbaric and anti-humanist ideology. For the brave new world of post-theistic spirituality to emerge, Rushkoff and Harris insist, both the Jews and Judaism will have to go.

BEATING 'GOD' TO DEATH: RADICAL THEOLOGY AND THE NEW ATHEISM

Jeffrey W. Robbins and Christopher D. Rodkey

In the span of a few years there was a veritable flood of best-selling books propounding what has come to be termed the 'new atheism.' Taken together in sum, the new atheists tell us religion has been one of the principal causes of human suffering, that it has led to violence, and that it promotes extremism. In addition, the religious mindset thwarts the rationalistic approach to the world and human problem solving, allowing untestable and unsupported mythological stories to serve as explanations for natural phenomena. And even more, when actually examining what religious believers believe when they attest to their faith in God or in sacred scripture, they are riddled with contradictions that should either outrage the mind or offend moral sensibilities. Plain facts told in the most provocative style, the new atheists seized on the cultural angst felt by many of those who felt left out or beaten down by the cultural warriors on the Right and who worried that the two successive terms of President George W. Bush set the United States on a perilous path towards theocracy.

But when examining their central claims—not to mention the public discussion that surrounded their publications—one has to ask whether anyone is really surprised to learn that the historic faiths are guilty of self-contradictions, that religious fanatics are prone to violence, and that all religions have a human origin? There was a time when these observations were truly radical and provocative. But between then and now a gulf of religious scholarship and critique has transpired, heightening our awareness and forcing any religious devotee not only to learn the truths of his or her tradition, but also to rethink the nature of religious truth. Most (with the exception of fundamentalists) would now concede that religions are *true* not in the same way that science or mathematics are *true*, but more in line with the way a Picasso portrait conveys a *subjective* truth that belies the merely representational. For instance, except for the most literal-minded, the Bible is not proven untrue or unreliable because it has two contradictory stories of creation in the first two chapters of the Book of Genesis, or because it has four different portraits of Christ included within the New Testament. On the contrary, an appreciation of these variances—even contradictions—is essential to understanding the particular nature of truth that belongs to the religious.

In this sense, the problem that the new atheists have with religion is not religion *per se*, but with religious literalism—or more technical still, in the words of the Christian philosopher and theologian Paul Tillich, the problem with most religious conceptions of God is that they are a form of "theological theism." That is to say, the new atheists' understandings of God only work as a singular piece of a metaphysical puzzle within a particular metaphysical system of thought or belief. When theological theism is the problem, Tillich went on to argue, atheism is the proper—indeed, *Christian*—response. That being said, atheism can also fall prey to the problem of theological theism whenever it is expressed as a categorical rejection of God and any sense of ontological understanding of the world. In other words, a rigid or dogmatic atheism replaces one flawed puzzle-board with another flawed puzzle-board with different pieces. Consequently, many Christian responses to new atheism are arguments for one theological theism versus another (see, for example, Varghese 2007, 180–183).

This chapter argues that the so-called *new* atheists are guilty of the same problems that Tillich predicted of future atheism, and suggests a radical theological critique of the new atheism. In other words, the argument will be that the new atheists do not go far enough in their critique of traditional Christianity. Put succinctly, *the new atheism is insufficiently radical*. To make this argument we will first draw on the radical theology of the American "death of God" movement, which paradoxically proposes an atheistic Christianity that is *both* atheistic and theistic. Second, we will examine how theology itself has been made radical by passing through the crucible of the death of God. By articulating this radical approach to religion, we hope to show that the idea of a Christian God is not one that is so easy to knock down or simply argue away with atheism, precisely because the concept of God in Christianity is dynamic, contradictory, imprecise, dependent on interpretation, and therefore highly resistant to logical or empirical dismissal. The surprising conclusion, therefore, is that while there will always be some benefit to exposing the contradictions of religious belief and the dangers inherent to religious practice—we might not realize that we are simultaneously establishing the conditions (intellectual and cultural) by which a non-theistic conception of God might be *reborn*, stripped free of the straightjacket of theological theism, no longer the creation of the conceiving mind, but of a radical Other who still has the power to surprise.

PAUL TILLICH AND THEOLOGICAL THEISM

Much of the radical theology in the second half of the twentieth century to the present begins with theologian Paul Tillich and his use of atheism as a tool for doing Christian theology. Tillich saw the great atheistic thinkers of the nineteenth century as "Christian humanists," and believed that Nietzsche's declaration of the "death of God" was an attack upon what he called "theological theism" (Tillich 1996, 32–33; Tillich 1952, 142). By this term, Tillich (1952, 184) referred to a belief system that is based upon theological argument "dependent on the religious substance which it conceptualizes." To this end, most arguments for the existence of God are—as our new atheist writers have demonstrated—easily argued away, usually using some modified forms of the Thomistic teleological and cosmological arguments. These arguments are theological by virtue of the fact that the argument against them—the assumption that God doesn't exist requires the same kind of epistemological and metaphysical assumptions as assuming that God does exist.

For Tillich, any God that can be explained so easily or argued away so easily suggests a "theological theism." *If your God can be killed, it should be*, because any God that can be killed is a God that is an object among other objects, simply a 'thing' or 'place-holder' within an otherwise fragile metaphysical worldview. Beyond this, Tillich (1952, 15; see also Tillich 1951, 1.245) argues, such a view is idolatrous or even "demonic"—that is to say, an ideology that causes evil in the world. The new atheists' moral arguments against God—generally, that religions cause people to do bad things—is thus preempted in Tillich's theology. The reason why religious people do evil is because the religious import of their metaphysical systems is not rooted in the *ground of being*, the *ultimate concern* of all that is. Tillich wrote about this openly as someone who witnessed firsthand the fall of late nineteenth-century German idealism and its antecedents transform into the horror of the Third Reich. As this experience attests, theological theisms are susceptible to being superseded by nationalism, economics, and racism. According to Tillich, the religions of theological theism really do "poison everything." They are religions of idolatry because they are predicated on the God of theological theism, rather than the "God-beyond-God" that is the true object of Christian belief.

It is for this reason that Tillich employs atheism as a reaction against the God of theological theism as a *tool* of religious reform. This atheism is a rejection not of God or religious belief *per se*, but of the particular idolatrous rendering of God accomplished by the dominance of theological theism. As such, Tillich (1952, 185) writes, atheism "is justified as the reaction against theological theism and its disturbing implications." But atheism cannot be a sustainable metaphysic because it cannot provide a ground for a radical self-transcendence; in other words, atheism alone is insufficiently transformative.

What is radically transformative for society in the atheistic shifts of Dawkins and Hitchens, for example, remains to be seen, unless one seriously considers that we would not find an excuse to wage war if it were not for religion. Hitchens' (2007b, 277ff) final chapter to his best-selling *God is Not Great* points toward "the need for a new enlightenment," without really saying what such an enlightenment is or even means (and even forgetting the religious products of the enlightenment, such as John Wesley and the "Methodist" movements). Other than warning us against a 'violence delusion,' what further insight does the new atheism offer? Is it rational to believe that humans will not find excuses to make war? Dawkins (2007b, 310) makes similar rhetoric, proposing an "Atheists for Jesus" slogan, which would hopefully "kick start the meme of super niceness in a post-Christian society" that leads "society away from the nether regions of Darwinian origins into kinder and more compassionate uplands of post-singularity enlightenment," leading away from "supernaturalist obscurantism."

Instead, Tillich (1964, 25) proposed a new, non-theistic paradigm for theological thinking, one which famously requires atheism to occur together with theism: "Genuine religion without an element of atheism cannot be imagined," he wrote; doubt is essential to any conception of faith. Tillich (1951, 1.27) wrote early in his three-volume *Systematic Theology* that atheism is "anti-Christian on Christian terms." Atheism can be a rejection of Christianity on Christian terms: "Nietzsche," he wrote, "acknowledged this when he said he had the blood of his greatest enemies—the priests—within himself." This is "the paradox" of atheistic thinking, that atheism is "the substance of what is Christian" (Tillich 1996, 32). Christianity only stays relevant as a religion so long as it allows itself to be purged by the tool of its own atheistic critique, or as Tillich puts it, by virtue of its ability to sustain "continuous self-negation" (1996, 52). Without this *semper negativa,* he wrote, "Christianity is not true Christianity."

This line of thinking led Tillich to declare that "God does not exist," since 'existence' is an ontological category for objects. God, then, is *being-itself,* an ontological category not only all its own, but implicitly (and pan*en*theistically) projecting and grounding all that is. A God "beyond essence and existence" must be *denied* to be *affirmed:* "to argue that God exists is to deny him" (Tillich 1951, 1.205). By denying the "existence" of God while still affirming faith in the God-beyond-God, Tillich effectively pulls the rug out from beneath the new atheists' respective critiques. That is because his radical conception of God is not a God easily argued away because he not only *anticipated* the atheistic critique but even more, was in general *agreement* with it, and actually *employed* it towards his own ends.

That being said, rather than simply rejecting the idea of God outright, Tillich would insist instead that the task of those seriously grappling with the meaning of religion for the contemporary world was to think God differently—a task that is more difficult and radical than that outlined by the new atheists. When exposing the fallacies and dangers inherent to religious belief, for example, Dawkins and Hitchens argue against a God of theological theism, a big object that is easily knocked down. Tillich points to the fact that this kind of atheism has a Christian function and is an appropriate response to a fundamental theological error within conservative Christianity. Consequently, conservative Christian responses to Tillich are nearly the same as evangelical responses to the New Atheism: Tillich's God is not the God of a literal reading of the Bible and violates an implied, but essential, contradiction between Christianity and science. Tillich's God, as *being-itself,* is a conception of God beyond cosmological, teleological, and moral arguments for or against God; as a radical Christian conception, the new atheists' arguments are not theologically sophisticated beyond their own theological a/theisms to speak for or against the idea.

THOMAS ALTIZER'S GOSPEL OF CHRISTIAN ATHEISM

If Tillich's God as being-itself is an Anselmic "greater-than-can-be-conceivable" being-itself, radical theologian Thomas Altizer's theology takes a different direction. For Altizer the greater-than-can-be-conceivable God *once existed,* but no longer does; God is not pseudonymous with ontology or ontology-itself; rather, "Godhead" reflects an *etiological* ontology, an ontology with an historical or cau`sal aspect. The primordial Godhead—transcendent, bigger-than-may-be-conceivable, pre-Genesis 1—is dead, and died a long time ago. Yet that God continues to die and self-negate through history, and its transcendence is finally and actually poured out and exhausted in the incarnation of Christ: the death of God as an act of kenosis par excellence.

Following the descent into Hell and resurrection of Christ, Altizer writes, the Holy Spirit is radically released into the flesh of all of humanity—Spirit and flesh are finally united.[1] This unity is not static but dynamic and continues the etiology of the primordial Godhead: Godhead may be provoked in the immanence of the present through human self-denial and self-subversion. That is, God continues to die through acts of justice, charity, and negation. Similarly, when humans die or suffer we may also speak of God dying in the present as well. The human body is the temple, as Paul writes in 1 Corinthians 3; it is the residence of God.

It should be noted that Altizer's theology has been rejected as fantastical and fantasy, heresy, and even theological theism. Concerning the latter charge, for instance, the deconstructive philosopher of religion John Caputo has charged that Altizer offers a "Big Story" or "Final Story" in the form of theology that replaces another "Big Story" (that is, traditional Christianity) that is to be rejected as false. Altizer's alternative is, Caputo (2007, 68–69) quips, "quite the Tall Tale." In other words, by Caputo's reckoning, Altizer's death-of-God theology simply becomes another founding narrative, making absolute claims that actually defy, if not contradict, the very iconoclastic logic of the death of God. As Caputo (see 2001, 56–66) argues, when properly understood, the death of God implies the death of the death of God, just as the modern Enlightenment critiques of religion ironically establish the conditions for the postmodern return of religion.

While Caputo offers an important corrective here to the potential excesses of the radical death-of-God movement, Altizer's insistence on

---

[1] Altizer's theology is found in his major works: *The Gospel of Christian Atheism* (1967); *The Descent into Hell* (1970); *The Self-Embodiment of God* (1977); *Total Presence* (1980); *History as Apocalypse* (1985); *Genesis and Apocalypse* (1990); *The Genesis of God* (1993); *The Contemporary Jesus* (1997); *The New Gospel of Christian Atheism* (2002); *Godhead and the Nothing* (2003); and *Living the Death of God* (2006).

the theological nihilism that characterizes the religiosity of the present moment remains a clarion call. By providing a *theological* analysis of this situation, his analysis goes further and remains more radical than the provocations of the new atheists. In contrast to the new atheists, Altizer's atheism contends that the immanental and enfleshed reality of Godhead in the present is not easily quantifiable or defined, and is defined as much by its absence as its presence. In fact, Altizer's theology directly points toward American Evangelical theology as worshipping a dead God, one that ceased to exist years and years ago and is not changing or suffering with human flesh. To the contrary, those Christians worship Satan—and while they deny that God is dead, they themselves worship a dead God and even (to borrow Mary Daly's term) *lust* for death (see Daly 1984, 8ff). Altizer's critique of Evangelicalism is far more sobering than, for example, Sam Harris's claim that American schools have failed "to announce the death of God in a way that each generation can understand" (2008, 91) so that a common enemy might be decided upon Islam.

Beyond this, Altizer's self-subverting Godhead is a conception of God, though radical and perhaps nonsensical to many, that remains standing following a new atheist critique. A dissolving, dismembering, kenoting God is, according to Altizer, implicit in a Biblical Christianity, even if mainstream Christianity [would not only reject such a reading but also harshly implicates Christianity as a source of evil in our culture]. The point here is that a God that is no longer transcendent, totalitarian over all that is, taking sides with political entities with power, or being thought of as a cosmic Santa Claus is not so easy to argue away with traditional arguments against God. To be sure, the vulnerable God is not a foreign concept within other kinds of academic Christian theology and it is as equally ignored by American Evangelicals as the new atheists.

A discourse of a weakening God threatens both Evangelicals and atheists, and reduces their theological theisms to similar tall tales that are chosen by individuals for political and social gain. Altizer, however, offers a vision of Christianity where the individual only has to lose, finding joy in the "eternal death of the crucifixion," requiring of the individual to take up her own cross and carry that curse of Christ to her own depths, following the steps of Christ, into the Hell of humanity (Altizer 2002, 105; 2006, 68; see also Rollins 2006; 2008). This is where Altizer suggests we find the emptying of the Holy Spirit.

THE MAKING OF RADICAL THEOLOGY

Returning to Caputo's reading of the death of God, as many contemporary theologians and philosophers of religion now tell us, the death of God immediately implies the death of the death of God as a movement, or as a dogmatic expression of atheism. In other words, to speak of the death of God need not be an anti-religious rant; rather, it might very well be a religious expression of faith. Gianni Vattimo, a contemporary hermeneutical philosopher from Italy and former member of the European Parliament says this best when he writes, "The end of metaphysics and the death of the moral God have liquidated the philosophical basis of atheism" (2002, 17). In this light, atheism is nothing but the flipside of theism, with neither side understanding the true nature of belief, given that both still rely on absolutist claims characteristic of scientific positivism or transcendent authority (Vattimo 1999, 28). Now that we live in the post-metaphysical age in which there are no absolute truths, only interpretations, the category of belief can again be taken seriously as constitutive of our lived traditions.

On the other hand, there is growing recognition that this postmodern revalorization of religion, which is preconditioned by the deconstruction of traditional forms of theology, has the ironic effect of providing justification for the narrowest and most militant forms of fideism, if not violent fundamentalism. There is an irony here: the death of the moral-metaphysical God, because it effects the correlative demise of absolute truth, makes possible the postmodern return of religion by weakening the strong rationalist reasons for rejecting belief. In the process, the epistemological relativity associated with the postmodern condition becomes an opening for justifying or revalorizing even narrow and uncritical beliefs. The weakening of authority, including religious authority, which has long been associated with the modern processes of secularization and seen as a force for desacralization, has had the converse effect of opening the door to resacralization as evident in the postmodern return of the religious: first, critical knowledge is unhinged or emancipated from faith, then faith is made insusceptible to critique by knowledge.

The problem this raises is that the contemporary resurgence of religion stands bereft of the critical insights and intellectual traditions of theologies past. There are many indications in our world that this forgetfulness has grave consequences, and that the time is ripe for a theological awakening, specifically for a radical theology that refuses to accept ignorance and narcissism masquerading as spirituality or conservatism masquerading as piety. Conversely, an atheism that poses as a radicalism is off the mark so long as it does not acknowledge how contemporary philosophy of religion and theology have been radically transformed *from within* as a consequence of passing through the crucible of the death of God.

In this way, Tillich's critique of theological theism, though it provides our template for radical theology, is in fact just one example of how religious thought has had to come to terms with theistic faith and religion *after* the death of God. Indeed, of the notion that theology would seek to conceptualize the death of God might seem non-sensical. In fact, a brief genealogy of Protestant theology in the middle of the twentieth century shows that when theology is radically conceived, it can absorb the most damning critiques of religion, and thus plunge the depths of human experience while still testifying to our desire for some sense of meaning and purpose. So in addition to Tillich, let us point out three additional genealogical instances in the making of radical theology.

First, in the wake of World War I, the Swiss Protestant theologian Karl Barth emerged onto the theological scene by announcing the moral bankruptcy of modern liberal theology and the impotency of the historical critical method of biblical scholarship. As Barth defined it, whether in his early dialectical or later neo-orthodox stage, the task of Christian theology was to recover and make clear the distinctiveness of the Christian message through a theology of revelation. This strategy of retrenchment coincided well with the prevailing mood throughout Western Europe during this time—namely, that World War I brought a final end to the pretense of Enlightenment optimism. Barth would remain the dominant theological voice throughout the first half of the twentieth century. His theology of revelation can be seen as the necessary counter-point to Heidegger's revamped ontology, as it embodies or fleshes out Heidegger's own cryptic remark to a group of Protestant theologians that if he were to write a theology, the word 'being' would not appear (see Robbins 2003, 13–39).

If the first moment, characterized by the theology of Barth, can be labeled a strategy of retrenchment and can be seen as the final end to the pretense of Enlightenment optimism, then the second moment, which emerges in response to the horrors of the Holocaust, can be seen as a strategy of engagement and as the end to the pretense of Christendom. It is at this point that figures such as Tillich and Rudolf

Bultmann come to the fore, as they helped to accomplish the radical transformation of the *formal* nature of theological thought. For instance, Tillich's method of correlation, which came to its fruition in his theology of culture, relocates the dynamic of faith squarely within an increasingly secularized culture. And it is that secularized culture that raises the questions of urgency and ultimacy to which the theologian must respond. Likewise with Bultmann, his method of demythologization took on the existential and hermeneutical insights he learned from Heidegger and claimed that the biblical language of faith, to which the Christian world was still so stridently attached, was hopelessly out of date and out of touch. The time had long since past when the modern world-picture was determined by an exclusively Christian mindset, yet churches and theologians still used its ancient mythological language of faith to express its truth to a world now determined by a scientific and technological worldview. For Bultmann, this revealed a radical disconnect, which called for a complete translation and remythologization of faith. What is important about this theological innovation, and the reason why someone like Barth refused to go along, is that it conceded the diminished priority of theology by allowing the language and assumptions of contemporary culture and philosophy to establish the agenda and parameters of theology.

Finally, if the second moment transformed the formal nature of theological thought, then the third radically transformed its very content, stripping theology of such supposed fundamentals as God, religion, revelation, and faith. It was Mark C. Taylor who saw this transition and transformation most clearly when he wrote in *Erring* that "deconstruction is the hermeneutic of the death of God." As Taylor understood it, deconstruction, as a formal, methodological hermeneutic, is inextricably tied to the specific proclamation of the death of God, which characterizes the religiosity of late modern and postmodern Western society. This is a religiosity that stands somewhere between faith and suspicion, "between the loss of old certainties and the discovery of new beliefs." It is for those "marginal people [who] constantly live on the border that both joins and separates belief and unbelief"—an "utterly transgressive" site that makes possible a genuinely postmodern a/theology (M. Taylor 1984, 5–6). Or before Taylor, the Anglican Bishop John Robinson, tapping into the cultural spirit of disillusionment in the 1960's, and drawing on the insights of Dietrich Bonhoeffer, Tillich, and Bultmann, argues that for Christian theology to be credible and relevant, it must be honest to God and honest with itself by admitting that the religion, supernaturalism, and mythology upon which its message had long been based, had outlived its usefulness (see Robinson 1963).

A theology after the death of God, between faith and suspicion, and without religion, supernaturalism, and mythology would be a theology unrecognizable to most. Nevertheless, this is the recent history of theology, a tradition of thought that has liberated itself from the revelatory language of God's word, a tradition that has deliberately stripped itself of its privilege and that now acknowledges itself as a strictly human enterprise. This is the tradition of radical theology that still outflanks the new atheists' critique of religion, for it concedes their arguments against religion while simultaneously showing how religion can be radically reconceived from the inside out.

Conclusion

We do not mean to diminish the importance of the new atheists' popularity nor their message, as we have, in fact, shown that atheism is not only healthy for the practice of Christian theology, but that it is *necessary*. At the same time, we must take issue with the "evangelical" nature of the new atheism, which assumes that it has a Good News to share, at all cost, for the ultimate future of humanity by the conversion of as many people as possible. The Good News of the new atheism is a liberation from repressive religion—*but then what?* We would also take up the same issue with what has become "evangelical" Christianity. Although it does offer a liberative message and ethos, it also inspires intolerance and violence in the world (Peters 2008, 164; see also Giannetti 2008). At the same time, evangelical Christianity believes itself to be the answer to the problem of contemporary atheism, just as new atheism poses itself as the answer to the problem of theism. The all-consuming, evangelical nature of both sides encourages endless conflict without progress.

Radical Christian theology offers a new way of thinking about God and atheism as an a/theology, whereby an affirmation of God requires a perpetual denial of false conceptions of God, even from within the system of Christianity itself. The new atheists also ignore the fact that there are actual practicing communities of "religious" atheists within, for example, Unitarian Universalism in the United States and the Ikon Community in Ireland (see Rollins 2006, 77–137; Pomeroy 2008).

Tillich (1996, 60–61) conceived of a radical Christianity confident enough that the *kind of truth* that it offered is deeper than anything literal, to the point that the question of God's existence can joyfully be both a "yes and no." Christianity, then, becomes a cause against systematic claims of certainty from both theistic and atheistic claims, and a dialectic progression *from within itself* that both affirms and betrays God-idols and no-God-idols equally (Rollins 2008, 168–171). More radical than atheism, the death of God is at once an acknowledgement of both the failure and promise of religion.

RELIGION AS PHANTASMAGORIA: ISLAM IN
THE END OF FAITH

Rory Dickson

INTRODUCTION

Ramakrishna, the great nineteenth-century Hindu mystic, reportedly said, "Religion is like a cow. It kicks, but it gives milk too" (quoted in Smith 2003). Ramakrishna's analogy takes into account religion's path-ological manifestations or 'kicks,' while maintaining that, at its core and despite such proclivities, religion is a perennial source of benefit for those in its fold. Sam Harris (2004) could not disagree more. In fact, this sentiment is precisely what he contests in his book. If religion is like a cow, according to Harris (2004, 13–14), its kicks are becoming increasingly dangerous and milk is better found elsewhere: "Our tech-nical advances in the art of war have finally rendered our religious differences—and hence our religious *beliefs*—antithetical to our sur-vival." In an age of nuclear weapons, religious violence may set off an unprecedented conflict that threatens humanity as such. Besides the increasingly dire threat that exclusive religious beliefs pose to the world, Harris believes the benefits or 'milk' religion provides can be more readily accessed through science. For Harris, religion is an increasingly dangerous anachronism. As such, the course of action is clear: the sacred cow must be slaughtered.

The End of Faith is a vivid, provocative assault on religion and its primary mechanism, faith, which Harris (2004, 65) defines as "*unjusti-fied* belief in matters of ultimate concern." Not only are faith's patho-logies diagnosed, Harris takes them as evidence of the inherently pathological nature of faith itself. Lest the faithful dismiss Harris as a twenty-first century Marquis de Sade, a sort of antinomian anarchist, it is important to note that Harris not only condemns religion, but cor-respondingly promotes the rational and scientific pursuit of religion's fruits, such as sound ethical norms and an understanding of the nature of consciousness and spiritual experience. Harris proposes that it is only religion's dogmas, myths, and unsubstantiated beliefs that are to be abandoned. The highest values and spiritual insights of traditional religions need not be discarded but simply updated in light of modern, scientific knowledge; the baby is not to be thrown out with the bathwater (Harris 2004, 43). Indeed, religious leaders such as the Dalai Lama (2005) have made similar arguments regarding religion's need to listen to science (and science's need to listen to religion), and the works of the American philosopher Ken Wilber (2001) attempt just such a synthesis of science and spirituality. However, as I argue in this chapter, Harris's application of science to pursue the meaning of life is, in the case of Islam, abandoned in his analysis of what he opposes.

In the *End of Faith*'s subtitle, Harris places 'religion' and 'terror' side by side, an association that, in post-9/11 America, readily brings to mind Islam. In making his case against faith, Harris pays particularly close attention to Islam, a faith that he deems to be more dangerous than any other. *The End of Faith*'s fourth chapter is entitled "The Problem with Islam". This title is telling, as the problem is not simply an offshoot, sect, or political faction of Islam, or even a set of its laws or tenets, but rather the religion itself, in its entirety. The epistemological pitfalls of speaking simply of Islam—a faith as historically, culturally, and doctrinally varied as it is—are many, and Harris succumbs to them with force. This is not to say that generalizations about Islam are of necessity misguided, but Harris is especially simplistic.

Clearly 'Islam' is not an ontological entity, a thing that can be located 'out there' in the world. However, in spite of this ontological lack, the term 'Islam' has real-world implications as a point of reference, or grammar of meaning, shaping social formations, discursive practices, and material culture. As Talal Asad has cogently observed in discussing the West, there is no "integrated Western culture, or a fixed Western identity, or a single Western way of thinking." However, despite this lack of an essential 'Westerness,' Asad maintains that the West is real insofar as "a singular collective identity defines itself in terms of a unique historicity in contrast to all others." In other words, despite there being no essential, immutable, and static 'West,' a collectivity defines itself in terms of the Western history, in distinction to other histories, and hence the term has real-world implications. In sum, broad historical referents such as Islam and the West are not ontologically or essentially real, but real insofar as they inform social action and discourse. Hence, taking into account important anti-essentialist critiques of terms such as the West and Islam, Asad argues that we can still attempt to make reasonable generalizations about such referents: Islam is monotheistic, its primary sources are Arabic; the West includes a Greco-Roman, Hebrew, and European heritage (Asad 1993, 18–19).

In this sense, generalizations of some sort are necessary to introduce any historical or religious phenomenon, and hence can represent important truths. Yet generalizations, when lacking sufficient basis, can also caricature the phenomenon they represent, failing to account for historical and social complexity. Unfortunately, Harris paints a sophomoric picture of Islam, a picture as wealthy in passion as it is poor in knowledge of its subject. This picture, though provocative, ultimately caricatures the religion, depicting Islam in terms of its most pathological manifestations. Harris's depiction of Islam betrays a profound ignorance of Islamic history and a critical lack of knowledge concerning key elements of the Islamic tradition. In this chapter, I will highlight aspects of Islamic history, law, and spirituality that Harris fails to account for, and will thereby demonstrate the inadequacy of Harris's depiction of Islam. Before considering Harris's treatment of the Islamic tradition in particular, I will first outline his case against faith in general, as his misperception of Islam is part and parcel of his characterization of religion in general.

The Case Against Faith

Since September 11, 2001, the threat of religiously motivated terrorism has contributed to putting religion back on the table as a problematic category of human thought and action in the United States as well as other North American and European countries. For many, terrorism committed in the name of Islam is yet another chapter in the voluminous history of religious bigotry and violence. In response, the new atheists have developed popular polemics against religion and belief, and have attempted to revive reason and rationality in the face of what appears to be ignorance, superstition, and violence resulting from unexamined beliefs assumed *en masse*. In an era of global religious resurgence, Harris and the new atheists seek to ensure that the insights of the eighteenth century Enlightenment are not lost in the twenty-first.

The first three chapters of *The End of Faith* form the core of Harris's critique. The general tone of these chapters is one of bewilderment. Harris is genuinely shocked and dumbfounded that moderns continue to uncritically tolerate beliefs originating in texts written by people who were ignorant of even the most basic knowledge of the universe. He sees the continuing belief in religion as a positively dangerous

abandonment of our creative and critical abilities, with a "mere dilu-
tion of Iron Age philosophy" offered in their stead by the religious
(2004, 21).

Harris argues that an uncritical tolerance of religion shelters faith
from rational critique, a sheltering that is unique, unwarranted, and
increasingly dangerous. In his view, all other fields of human endeavor
base action on knowledge that is intelligible to all. This is the *modus
operandi* of sensible people engaged in an honest inquiry into how
things work in any field. This is how medicine, engineering, and ethics
proceed. So why do we allow religion to propose outlandish claims
about the nature of reality without asking on what verifiable grounds
these claims are made? Perhaps if such claims were ultimately benign,
we'd be forgiven for assenting to them without challenge, yet, argues
Harris (2004, 80–107), these claims have historically caused immense
bloodshed, and continue to do so unabated. What's more, the proliferation of available military technology now means that people can act
on religious sentiments and kill on a categorically more dangerous
scale: that of the destruction of the human species as a whole. In other
words, religious zealots may soon have the means to carry out their
religiously informed desire to destroy opponents of the one true faith,
the fallout of which could end up destroying us all.

Unless humanity is interested in collective suicide, Harris argues
that faith must be exposed to the rational critique it warrants, because
it makes claims about reality that inform action in the world. What
then prevents this warranted (and increasingly urgent) critique? In a
phrase (Harris answers): religious moderates. Harris argues that moderates shelter religion from its otherwise inevitable demise. They give
faith a legitimacy it would otherwise lack if it were merely the preserve
of the fundamentalists, who, he argues, truly represent the essence of
religion. Moderates, on the other hand, preserve religion's respectability by assenting to modern rationality and science, while duplicitously
claiming to abide by the irrationality of their faith. As Harris (2004, 21)
notes, "By failing to live to the letter of the texts, while tolerating the
irrationality of those who do, religious moderates betray faith and reason equally." As such, he argues that religious moderates have no scriptural grounds on which to criticize religious literalism, and no secular
grounds on which to promote a reasonable alternative. Hence they
perpetuate the religious extremism that threatens us all. Harris (2004,
20) contends that moderates are unable to offer religious critiques of
fundamentalists because fundamentalists' "knowledge of scripture is
generally unrivalled."

In claiming that religious moderates betray their faith and have no scriptural grounds on which to challenge extremists, Harris assumes that a) extremists stand on indisputably firm scriptural grounds, whereas moderates do not, and b) extremists, not moderates, truly adhere to and represent their faith, or the reality of what religion really is. This leads Harris to conclude that extremists directly manifest religious teachings, with the consequent conclusion that such teachings are inherently pathological, or violent and irrational. These assumptions and their corresponding conclusions manifest most visibly in Harris's discussion of Islam.

THE CASE AGAINST ISLAM

If religion is by definition irrational and prone to violence, Harris posits Islam as the most exemplary in this regard. He writes, "Islam, more than any other religion human beings have devised, has all the makings of a thoroughgoing cult of death" (Harris 2004, 123). Contrary to statements by North American and European politicians, Harris (2004, 109–110) believes that "We are at war with Islam," with "precisely the vision of life that is prescribed to all Muslims in the Koran, and further elaborated in the literature of the hadith [accounts of the Prophet's life and statements]." In his chapter on Islam, Harris juxtaposes medieval Islamic doctrines on conquest, martyrdom and apostasy with Qur'anic verses condemning unbelievers, Islamist calls to establish a global Islamic state, and survey results showing widespread Muslim support for suicide bombing in defense of Islam. He weaves these elements together in a terrifying narrative meant to illustrate the intolerance, violence, and irrationality of Islam.

By reading the Qur'an, Harris (2004, 130) argues, one can establish with certainty that Muslims are convinced of their cultural superiority and "obsessed with the inferiority of their power." This obsessive inferiority complex makes Muslims prone to political violence against the unbelievers who, in a 'diabolical' overturning of the natural order, reign supreme in the world. Hence, to the degree Muslims subscribe to their faith, they will pose an irreducible threat to others; their faith makes political violence an almost foregone conclusion.

To demonstrate the scriptural roots of Muslim hatred and violence, Harris (2004, 117–123) includes literally pages of verses from the Qur'an that describe the unbelievers' falsehood, and God's resultant punishment of them in this world and the next. He cites verses such as

the following: "Those that deny God's revelations shall be sternly punished" (3: 5), and "We will put terror into the hearts of the unbelievers…The Fire shall be their home" (3: 149–151). In light of such verses,
Harris (2004, 117) concludes, "If you believe anything like what the
Koran says you must believe in order to escape the fires of hell, you
will, at the very least, be sympathetic with the actions of Osama bin
Laden." For Harris (2004, 117), approaching the Qur'an with 'the eyes
of faith' reveals the powerful connection between Islam and terrorism:
the Qur'an makes clear what little compassion is to be wasted on those
whom God is 'cursing,' 'punishing,' and 'mocking,' and hence, killing
them simply provides 'fuel for the fire of God's justice.' With the
Qur'anic roots of Muslim opposition to the religious other in mind,
Harris (2004, 152) concedes that perpetual war with Muslims is likely
the West's only option, that is, unless Islam is radically reformed: "If a
stable peace is ever to be achieved between Islam and the West, Islam
must undergo a radical transformation." Otherwise, Harris (2004, 152)
prophecies, our news headlines may increasingly resemble the Book of
Revelation.

Summing up his perspective, Harris (2004, 31) states, "Muslims hate
the West in the very terms of their faith" and "the Koran mandates
such hatred." The statement merits further examination, as it forms the
core of his argument concerning Islam. This statement consists of three
critical assertions: (1) Muslims hate the West, (2) in the very terms of
their faith, and (3) the Koran mandates such hatred. I will examine all
three assertions. Taken together, Harris's inadequate use of evidence
and his ignorance of much of the Islamic tradition allow him to caricature Islam as a sociopathology represented by its most politically
extreme adherents.

The Case Against the Case Against Islam

1) Muslims hate the West

How exactly does one determine that Muslims hate the West, and furthermore, how does one show this religious 'hatred' is separate from
political or economic issues? Besides the scriptural evidence Harris
presents, he also cites the Pew Research Center's "What the World
Thinks in 2002" survey as evidence of Muslim hatred. The survey
found that, in many Muslim countries, such as Jordan, Lebanon,
Nigeria, and Bangladesh, a majority of those asked responded that

suicide bombing in defense of Islam was justified, at least in dire circumstances (Harris 2004, 126). Harris uses this poll as conclusive evidence of a widespread, Islamic- induced sociopathology. He holds that,
"Muslims have been scientifically polled," revealing that a majority of
Muslims in certain Muslim countries support "the deliberate murder
and maiming of noncombatant men, women, and children in defense
of Islam" (2004, 124). In the same passage, Harris describes the survey's results as hideous and disturbing, a sign of Muslim moral fatuity
and cultural backwardness that clearly results from their adherence to
Islam.

However, there are significant problems with drawing such conclusions from the Pew survey. Besides the obvious problem of determining the moral character of a significant portion of humanity based on
the results of a single survey question, other surveys contradict this
result. The Program on International Public Attitudes (PIPA) survey
conducted in December 2006, found that only 46 percent of Americans
felt that "bombing and other attacks intentionally aimed at civilians"
are "never justified" (Ballen 2007). Alternately, 86 percent of Pakistanis
and 80 percent of Iranians surveyed maintained that deliberate attacks
on civilians are never justified, almost double the number of Americans taking this stance. Replicating Harris's logic in evaluating the 2002
Pew results, we could conclude that Americans have been "scientifically polled," and similarly reveal "hideous numbers" that demonstrate
a complete moral failing; Americans are, apparently, violent, with little
respect for the lives of innocent men, women, and children. Relative to
Americans, Pakistani and Iranian Muslims are paragons of peace and
protectors of innocent life, at least according to the results of the PIPA
survey. Obviously, such specious reasoning should not be taken seriously; a single survey question cannot be used to draw a definitive
conclusion about Americans in general, or the essence of American
culture throughout history. Besides the limitations of surveys, which
can include poorly formulated questions, or questions that unduly
determine the results, we must consider the influence of political events
at the time, and how they may influence survey results. With such
considerations in mind, Harris's conclusions about Muslims or Islam,
with only the results of the Pew Research Center survey question as
statistical evidence, cannot be taken as representative of almost a fourth
of humanity.

Harris's inadequate use of survey results as evidence that Muslims
are sociopaths is further illustrated by John L. Esposito and Dalia

Mogahed's *Who Speaks for Islam: What a Billion Muslims Really Think* (2007). Esposito and Mogahed's (2007, xi) work is based on the Gallup World Poll research study, "the largest, most comprehensive study of contemporary Muslims ever done." The Gallup research study was completed between 2001 and 2007, and included 'tens of thousands' of hour-length, one-on-one interviews with Muslims from 35 nations with majority Muslim populations. Although there are clear limitations in any survey, the Gallup study reveals, somewhat predictably, that Muslims do not differ significantly from others in terms of basic moral and political positions. Where Muslims do express opposition to the West, it is primarily in opposition to specific policies of Western governments, not the principles on which those governments are based, principles for which many of the Muslim Gallup respondents expressed admiration: democracy, human rights, the rule of law (Esposito and Mogahed 2007, 80). Although many Muslim respondents to the survey expressed concern over problems of crime and social fragmentation in Western countries, this is not the result of a hatred of the West, which is demonstrated by the fact that concerns over crime and social fragmentation are shared to a similar degree by Westerners themselves (Esposito and Mogahed 2007, xii). With regard to terrorism, the Gallup study found that "Muslims and Americans are equally likely to reject attacks on civilians as morally unjustified" (Esposito and Mogahed 2007, xii). In sum, this unprecedented project indicates that, contrary to Harris's argument, Muslims differ little from anyone else in basic moral orientations, and that there is much that Muslims respect and admire about Western countries.

If Muslims are equally as likely as Americans to reject attacks on civilians as morally reprehensible, how then do we account for the campaigns of suicidal terror waged by Muslim groups in Palestine and Iraq? To highlight the determinative role Islam plays in these campaigns, Harris (2004, 233) points out that Palestinian Christian suicide bombers are conspicuous by their absence, as are Tibetan Buddhist bombers, examples of which are nowhere to be found despite a "cynical and repressive" Chinese occupation of their homeland. If Christians and Buddhists are not responding to political oppression with suicide bombing, then, Harris reasons, there is something about Islam that fosters it. Careful research demonstrates however, that political circumstances are more closely correlated to suicide bombing than religion. Although the question, as phrased in the Pew survey Harris cites, connects suicide bombing to the 'defense of Islam,' Robert Pape's research on every suicide attack (315 incidents) carried out between 1980 and 2003, whether by Muslims or others, demonstrates that opposition to foreign occupation was the motivating factor in 95 percent of suicide bombings (Esposito and Mogahed 2007, 77). Concrete political realities, not religious principles, are most often at the root of the phenomenon. Only 43 percent of suicide bombers during this period were religious, with the majority representing secular and Marxist organizations. Pape writes:

> The data show there is little connection between suicide terrorism and Islamic fundamentalism, or any one of the world's religions. In fact, the leading instigators of suicide attacks are the Tamil Tigers in Sri Lanka, a Marxist-Leninist group whose members are from Hindu families but who are adamantly opposed to religion. This group committed 76 of the 315 incidents, more suicide attacks than Hamas. (Pape 2006, 4)

Such bombings are, in the vast majority of cases, tactics of the (usually) outgunned opposing the presence of a perceived occupying force. Rather than a simple religious hatred, the logic of suicide bombing is perhaps best expressed in Shabir Akhtar's aphorism that "powerlessness can corrupt as insistently as power does" (quoted in Winter 2007, 382).

2) *In the very terms of their faith*

Harris continues to argue Muslims hate the West 'in the very terms of their faith'—that the tenets of Islamic faith compel Muslim hatred of the West; here he mentions such tenets as jihad, martyrdom, paradise, and infidels. For Harris (2004, 124), the combination of these beliefs makes suicide bombing far from 'an aberration' of Muslim faith, but a positively logical outcome of it. It should be noted, however, that suicide bombing *is* an aberration of Muslim practice, with almost no examples of suicidal attacks among Muslims prior to the twentieth century, the suicidal killings of the Nizari Ismaili assassins, or *hashashin*, in the twelfth century, being the only exception that I'm aware of (see B. Lewis 2003).

The End of Faith's introductory chapter has a subsection on Muslim extremism, in which Harris (2004, 29) writes:

> It is important to specify the dimension in which Muslim 'extremists' are actually extreme. They are extreme in their *faith*. They are extreme in their devotion to the literal word of the Koran and the hadith (the literature recounting the sayings and actions of the Prophet.

It is interesting to note that Harris defines Muslim faith as an uncom-
plicated literalism, with extremism being simply the logical outcome
of this literal approach to sacred texts. Implicit in this definition is the
assumption that Muslim extremists are not extreme in terms of Islam;
they simply practice the faith as it is in its actuality. Further, Harris
assumes that those claiming to literally follow religious scriptures are
actually literalist, which is, in fact, not the case; so-called literalists
choose certain verses to follow as against others, and particular interpretations are pursued at the expense of other possibilities. Furthermore,
contrary to Harris's thesis, a basic understanding of political, historical, and sectarian developments among Muslims during the past two
centuries reveals that contemporary political extremism among Muslims, as manifested in suicidal terrorism, is rooted first and foremost in
recent Islamic movements and the historical, political circumstances
that have made them possible.

The theological roots of contemporary extremist ideology amongst
Muslims can be convincingly traced to the more xenophobic and militant aspects of the thought of Ahmad Ibn Taymiyyah, (d. 1328 CE).
Ibn Taymiyyah was a staunch opponent of Sufism and was famous for
his *fatwa* that permitted fighting Muslim rulers if they failed to abide
by Islamic law. However, Ibn Taymiyyah's thought fell into near irrelevance in the Islamic intellectual tradition for nearly five hundred years,
until it was resurrected by the Arabian reformer Muhammad ibn Abd
al-Wahhab (d. 1792 CE). Followers of Ibn 'Abd al-Wahhab successfully
captured the hijaz, or area encompassing Mecca and Medina, in 1805.
As Mecca and Medina are the most important pilgrimage sites of Islam,
'Wahhabi' control of them ensured that their narrow interpretation of
Islam and anti-Sufi polemics reached Muslims around the world,
thereafter influencing nineteenth-century revivalist movements from
Africa to India. It should be noted that Shi'a Muslims often share a
particular opposition to Wahhabism, as the followers of Ibn Abd al-
Wahhab "sacked the Shi'i city of Karbala in 1802 and massacred the
inhabitants" (Denny 1994, 326).

Besides Wahhabi theology, twentieth-century Islamism has shaped
extremist movements. Olivier Roy (1994, vii) defines Islamism as consisting of "the activist groups who see in Islam as much a political ideology as a religion." Islamism's ideological roots can be traced to the
writings of Sayyid Qutb (d. 1966) and Abul Ala Maududi (d. 1979),
both of whom contributed to the current conception of the Islamic
state, and the activism necessary to achieve it. Osama bin Laden is

paradigmatic here, for he was reared in Saudi Arabia, where the Wahhabi interpretation of Islam is the official doctrine of the state, and was later influenced by Ayman al-Zawahiri, who, as a leader of a radical offshoot of the Muslim Brotherhood in Egypt, was influenced by the writings of Sayyid Qutb.

We should note that Wahhabi theology and Islamist ideology are necessary but not sufficient conditions for the formation of extremist *jihadi* groups. Wahhabism is the theological base of the Saudi kingdom and yet very few Saudis actively support terrorist groups. As well, there are many Islamists who support democracy, human rights, and peaceful means.

That being said, the radical re-casting of Islam as political ideology rather than spiritual path and law, is the hallmark of extremist movements, including Al-Qaeda, Al-Muhajiroun, and Hamas. This transformation effects how Islam is understood, which elements are emphasized, and what sorts of political actions legitimated, and thus constitutes a recent re-formulation of Islam in terms of the modern state. This re-formulation stands in contrast to the pre-modern polyvalent tradition. Moreover, radical political movements do not exist in a vacuum, and require the necessary socio-structural conditions within which to flourish. The breakdown of traditional religious authority, and the economic challenges and strained political circumstances emerging out of the colonization of much of the Muslim world in the nineteenth and twentieth centuries, have provided these conditions amply (see Roy 2004, 158–167). Unless one appreciates the influence of these recent, and often anomalous, strains of Islamic theology and political ideology, and the post-colonial crisis in religious authority and political legitimacy that has allowed for their growth, one cannot appreciate the novelty and exceptionality of contemporary Muslim extremism within the greater Islamic paradigm, and one is left assuming, in ignorance, that it is based on Islam as such, or the Qur'an itself.

Not only does Harris fail to appreciate the historical circumstances, political contexts, and sectarian developments that underlie contemporary Muslim extremism, he falsely concludes that militant extremists represent the traditional essence of Islam. Quite ignorant of Islamic history, he seems oblivious to the formative role that Sufism has played in the Islamic tradition. Sufism, often defined as Islamic mysticism or Islamic spirituality, is renowned for its poetry and music, its emphasis on ecstatic love and tolerance, as well as its exploration of the polysemous possibilities of the Qur'an (Heck 2007). Although Sufism has been at the centre of Muslim belief and practice for much of Islamic history, Harris makes mention of Sufism only in a footnote in *The End of Faith*. In this footnote, Harris (2004, 294) inaccurately states that Sufism "has generally been considered a form of heresy in the Muslim world." Though some Muslims have clearly opposed Sufism as heretical—as illustrated by the rare but legendary Sufi martyrs executed at the behest of the orthodox—elements of Sufism were, until the late 1700s, taken for granted amongst most Muslims as integral to orthodox Islam. It is no exaggeration to say that for the majority of its history orthodox Islam has been wedded to the practice of Sufism (Schimmel 1975; Ernst 1997).

Medieval Muslim societies were remarkably hospitable to Sufism, a fact best illustrated by the proliferation and patronage of Sufi orders between the twelfth and eighteenth centuries (Dickson 2008; Trimingham 1971). In certain parts of the Muslim world, such as pre-modern Chechnya as well as parts of Africa, almost every adult male had some affiliation with a Sufi order. Following Abu Hamid al-Ghazzali's (d. 1111 CE) successful synthesis of Sufi spirituality with Sunni law and theology in the eleventh century (with his remarkable *Ihya 'Ulum ad-Din*, or "The Revival of the Religious Sciences"), Sufism became an increasingly integral part of Muslim religiosity. Medieval Muslim rulers, including those among the Seljuk, Ayyubid, Mamluk, and Ottoman dynasties, patronized Sufi teachers and institutions with official and material support (Dickson 2008). Sultans built Sufi lodges alongside theological schools, and Sufi teachers were sometimes employed by Muslim rulers as diplomatic 'go-betweens,' negotiating complex relationships between sultans and caliphs, and between Muslim and Christian kings. What is more, sultans were frequently themselves devout students of Sufi teachers. Notable *'ulama*, or religious scholars, were also students of Sufis, or were even Sufis themselves. Carl Ernst (1997, xiii) writes, "as recently as the eighteenth century, and for much of the previous millennium, most of the outstanding religious scholars of Mecca, Medina, and the great cities of the Muslim world were intimately engaged with what we today call Sufism." Under the Seljuks for example, universities of Islamic law and institutions of Sufi practice were overlapping networks of religiosity; students freely moved between studies of sacred law at universities and studies of the spiritual path at Sufi lodges (Safi 2006, 99). For much of its history, orthodox, official Islam has been deeply Sufic in orientation. This is not to say that Sufis have not come into conflict with the powers that be. However, as Omid Safi (2006, 158–200) has shown, conflicts between Sufis and sultans were frequently political rather than religious. With regard to the Sufi martyr 'Any al-Qudat Hamadani (d. 1131), it wasn't the perception that Hamadani was a heretic that led to his execution, but rather it was his vocal opposition to the Seljuks and their system of land-grants (in which Seljuk leaders took land from its owners and gave it to their generals), along with Hamadani's association with an opponent of the vizier. Still, such conflict is exceedingly rare.

Since the proliferation of anti-Sufi reform movements such as Wahhabism in the eighteenth and nineteenth centuries, however, Sufism has been radically marginalized within Islamic discourse, and Sufi teachers and teachings have come under sustained attack in many parts of the Muslim world (Dickson 2008; Sirriyeh 1999). Ernst (1997, xiii) observes,

> Ironically, as a result of strategic successes by fundamentalist movements in certain key regions like Arabia, and the massive oil wealth that fell into the lap of the Saudi regime, many contemporary Muslims have been taught a story of the Islamic religious tradition from which Sufism has been rigorously excluded.

Assuming this anti-Sufi narrative of Islam as accurate, Harris fails to appreciate the centrality of Sufism in the classical Islamic tradition, and the many signs of Sufism's flourishing and revival today in the Muslim world (see van Bruinessen and Howell 2007). As Ernst (1997, xiii) notes, Sufism continues to infuse the fabric of social and religious life in countries like Morocco, Senegal, Egypt, and Pakistan, and the veneration of "the Sufi saints is found as a major theme in every Muslim country from China to Morocco." In underestimating Sufism's historically normative position within Islam, and its continuing relevance in many parts of the Muslim world, Harris is able to write off Sufis, along with their traditions of spirituality and tolerance, as insignificant and 'not-really-Islamic,' thereby centring extremists as the true representatives of Islam.

3) *The Koran mandates such hatred*

Harris argues that the Qur'an is at the root of violent political action undertaken by Muslims, or, at the very least, the Qur'an provides more resources than other religious scriptures to justify violence. Discussing suicide bombing, Harris (2004, 233) writes, "As a Buddhist, one has to work extremely hard to justify such barbarism. One need not work nearly so hard as a Muslim." Although this might appear plausible based on a survey of verses in the Qur'an that can be used to justify violence, with this argument Harris reveals both his ignorance of the historical context within which the Qur'an emerged, and the role of Islamic law in mediating Muslim interpretations of scripture and regulating possibilities of action.

Sherman Jackson (2007, 395) follows Fred Donner in noting the critical importance of historical circumstances in shaping both the Qur'an's representation of war, and later Muslim jurisprudence on armed conflict. Seventh century Arabia functioned in a continuous state of tribal warfare; a 'state of war' was assumed as normal (Jackson 2007, 396). In this context of tribes competing for dominance, the early Muslim community, in breaking with the old tribal solidarities, faced an almost constant threat to its existence. Jackson (2007, 398) notes,

> ...the Qur'anic injunction to fight was clearly connected with the very specific necessity of preserving the *physical* integrity of the Muslim community at a time and place when fighting, sometimes preemptively, sometimes defensively, was understood to be the only way to do so.

Jackson notes that not only seventh-century Arabia, but the pre-modern world as a whole was characterized by an almost constant 'state of war.' In a context of perpetual conflict among and between the peoples of various religions/ethnicities, jihad was understood as a necessary means with which to secure a realm safe for the practice of Islam.

> Indeed, the "Abode of Islam/Abode of War" dichotomy, cited *ad nauseam* by certain Western scholars as proof of Islam's inherent hostility towards the West, was far more a *description* of the Muslim peoples of the world in which they lived than it was a *prescription* of the Islamic religion per se (Jackson 2007, 401).

During the medieval period, there generally were two realms for Muslims, one ruled by them, and the other in which they were fighting their opponents. This was not simply because Muslims sought conflict, but that conflict was a fact of life, and the free practice of Islam was generally limited to Muslim lands. Today however, Muslims are free to practice their faith in most non-Muslim countries, and the pre-modern 'state of war' has been, officially at least, replaced by a 'state of peace,' regulated by international law and its protection of national sovereignty; the medieval dichotomy of the Abodes of Islam and War no longer applies as it once did (Jackson 2007, 402–403). Both Qur'anic verses on fighting and the medieval jurisprudential tradition's ruling on fighting must be understood then, as Jackson notes, not simply as prescriptions for Muslims, but as reflective of this conflictive state of affairs. With the importance of pre-modern historical contexts in mind, we can consider some relevant elements of Islam's jurisprudential tradition, a tradition that Harris neglects to consider in his claim that the Qur'an mandates hatred.

Islamic jurisprudence or *fiqh* (literally "understanding") has guided Muslim behaviour since its formation and systematization in the first three centuries of Islam (see Hallaq 2005). Its methods arose out of attempts to understand the Qur'an in a comprehensive and contextual manner, so as to secure its correct application, in other words, to follow God's commandments and prohibitions accurately. Surely, as Harris notes, the Qur'an is believed by most Muslims to be the literal word of God. The Qur'an is hence analogous not to the Christian Bible, but to Christ, as the *logos*, or divine word. However, Muslim belief in the Qur'an's wholly revealed nature does not mean that traditional religious authorities have read the Qur'an literally, without concern for the plurality of semantic possibilities in the Qur'an, or without consideration for the historical contexts in which various verses were believed to have been revealed. Nor have Muslim jurists assumed that verses can be utilized in isolation from the whole of the Qur'an. In particular, Muslim jurists have traditionally functioned on the principle that one cannot discern the legal regulation concerning a given issue, say war for example, without taking into account all of the texts from the Qur'an and Prophetic traditions (hadith) deemed applicable to said issue, nor can this be done without understanding the historical context, the semantic, grammatical implications of the verses in consideration, and how these relate to the basic principles and aims of the law (See Keller 2006 for a traditionalist critique of the *salafi* approach to Islamic law).

To illustrate some of these principles, I will refer to the Malaysian Shafi'i jurist Shaykh Muhammad Afif al-Akiti's recent ruling (*fatwa*) against terrorism (2005), or the targeting of civilians. In discussing Qur'anic verses on fighting, Al-Akiti notes that one of the most severe Qur'anic verses ordering war—"Slay the unbelievers wherever you find them" (9: 5)—was revealed in reference to a historical episode, the breach of the Treaty of Hudaybiya, by the Meccans opposed to Muhammad in 630 CE. Considering the verse's reference to this historical episode, al-Akiti (2005) writes, "no legal rulings, or in other words, no practical or particular implications can be derived from the Verse on its own." As the verse is historically specific in its genesis, general rulings cannot be made from it. What is more, al-Akiti (2005) notes jurisprudential rules dictate that even if the verse (9: 5) was not subject to an historical episode, the verse is "of the general type ['amm]" and "will therefore be subject to specification [takhsis] by some other indication [dalil]." In other words, as a general statement, it would require corroboration by a more specific verse in the Qur'an, or hadith text, should it be applied as a ruling. This example indicates just some of the legal complexity involved in applying a verse from the Qur'an within the Islamic legal tradition.

In terms of suicide bombing specifically, al-Akiti (2005) relates that jurists have condemned it as categorically forbidden, and as a serious crime, as suicide bombing violates three undisputed norms of the law: (1) it targets civilians, (2) it is military action taken outside the bounds of legitimate state authority, and (3) it is suicidal, which itself is forbidden. Al-Akiti provides an in-depth account of the nature of the violation of these three norms, referencing Qur'an, hadith, and the principles of the Shafi'i school of law. Some may object that although the elite scholars of Islam may perpetuate and practice attempts at contextual and comprehensive interpretations of sacred texts, the average Muslim has little understanding of these sophisticated hermeneutical methods, and instead simply reads the Qur'an literally. Contrary to such an impression, Saba Mahmoud's (2005, 100–106) study of women's piety movements in Cairo, Egypt, illustrates well how non-scholars involved with the piety, or da'wa, movement understand and apply scholarly interpretive principles in their local Qur'an classes, and how students of these classes also demonstrate a familiarity with elements of Islamic legal reasoning.

Interestingly, Harris (2004, 123) acknowledges that Muslim jurists have condemned suicide bombing as contrary to the tenets of Islam, yet he minimizes this condemnation by rhetorically asking, "where are these jurists, by the way?" and writes that theirs is a minority opinion. It should be said that Harris's lack of knowledge concerning the whereabouts of these scholars does not mean they do not exist. Besides al-Akiti's learned fatwa cited above, in 2005 the Fiqh Council of North America released a fatwa condemning suicide bombing (terrorism) and forbidding Muslim support for any involved in it. Similar fatwas, of varying detail, have been issued around the globe, including in Saudi Arabia, Egypt, Lebanon, England, and Australia. Secondly, these opinions are by no means in the minority; a strong case can be made that they in fact represent the majority opinion within the Islamic legal tradition.[1]

To illustrate the depth of the Islamic prohibition against targeting civilians, we need only note that even committed jihadists have adamantly opposed it. The father of the Arab jihad movement in the Afghan war against the Soviets, and the forefather of Al-Qaeda, Abdullah Azzam (d. 1989)—whose oft-repeated motto in relations with non-Muslims was "Jihad and the rifle alone: no negotiations, no conferences, and no dialogues" (Suellentrop 2006)—disagreed strongly with bin Laden on targeting civilians, a disagreement which precipitated their split, and perhaps even Azzam's assassination shortly thereafter. Hence, bin Laden's opinion on the legal permissibility of targeting civilians was rejected even among die-hard jihadists like Azzam. Notably, Azzam, unlike bin Laden, was educated in Islamic law, receiving his doctorate in *usul al-fiqh* (sources of the law) from Al-Azhar University in Cairo (1973), and he adamantly refused to allow jihadist funds to go towards operations that involved civilian targets. He even released a *fatwa* stating that to use jihadist funds to train in terrorist tactics would violate Islamic law, as Muslims should avoid targeting non-combatants (Gunaratna 2002, 22).

CONCLUSION

Harris's portrayal of Islam as a death-cult and Muslims as sociopaths demonstrates that Harris suffers from a profound unfamiliarity with the traditions, beliefs, and culture of its followers. Harris's assumption that scriptural literalists and militant extremists represent the essence of Islam betrays his ignorance of the richness and complexity of Islamic law and spirituality, and the everyday lives and beliefs of the vast majority of Muslims. In failing to acknowledge a) the historical context in which Qur'anic verses on war emerged, b) the nature of Islamic law and its regulatory role in interpreting the Qur'an, c) the formative influence of Sufi spirituality on Islam and its wide-ranging presence throughout the Muslim world, and d) political and sectarian

---

[1] See "Muslims Condemn Terrorist Attacks," (November 2, 2006). Available at: http://www.muhajabah.com/othercondemn.php, for a series of links to fatwas by Muslim scholars and jurists condemning terrorist attacks, and various other articles by Muslim authors, lay or otherwise, in the same vein.

developments in recent Islamic history and their importance in shaping contemporary extremist ideology, Harris is able to draw the conclusion that Islam is coeval with the suicidal violence of the politically desperate.

While Harris perhaps writes an accurate analysis of a pathological offshoot of the Islamic tradition, he mistakes the pathology for the phenomenon itself when he mistakes Islam's most radical representatives for the religious tradition in its entirety. Unfortunately, Harris's conclusion—that religion is best represented by literalists, fundamentalists, and extremists—allows him to marginalize and exclude the vast majority of Muslim beliefs and practices from his overall account of Islam. In piecing together de-contextualized scriptural verses, elements of the political vision of radical Islamists, medieval Islamic doctrines on conquest, and the results of a single survey question on suicide bombing from 2002, Harris presents them as a final, accurate, and complete representation of the Islamic tradition as a whole. His 'death-cult' vision of Islam amounts to little more than the lantern-projected ghosts and demons of eighteenth-century French phantasmagoria theater shows—crude fictions that played on people's fears and credulity, and based on appearance rather than reality.

Part II: Science and the New Atheism

WHAT HAS ATHEISM EVER DONE FOR SCIENCE?

Steve Fuller

WHAT'S NEW ABOUT ATHEISM? ITS RECENT EPISTEMIC TURN

What has atheism ever done for science? After all, it's one thing to admit that religious dogmatism has periodically halted the march of scientific progress, but it's quite another to argue that atheism has actually advanced science. The difference matters. Richard Dawkins, the original professor of Public Understanding of Science at Oxford, is spending his retirement spearheading a foundation bearing his name that aims to be the evil twin of the John Templeton Foundation. Where Templeton supports projects that aim to build a spiritual consensus among scientists and religious believers, Dawkins supports activities that aim to maximize the difference between the two groups. In this evangelical atheism, Dawkins finds several fellow travelers in the recent non-fiction best-selling lists, including journalist Christopher Hitchens, philosopher Daniel Dennett, and neuroscientist Sam Harris. Their confidence in atheism has extended to suggesting—and not in jest—that religious instruction is so potentially corrosive to the mind that it should be left exclusively to certified secular authorities.

To be sure, open declarations of atheism have never been more fashionable among scientists. A recent poll of members of the U.S. National Academy of Sciences found that 85 percent claim that they do not believe in God. But again, it is one thing for scientists to deny the existence of God and quite another for atheism to actually advance science. It may also be that 85 percent of the National Academy's membership is male or members of the Democratic Party. So the question returns: What has atheism ever done for science? Moreover, given the institutional history of Christianity, it is difficult to know what to make of the poll's findings. After all, people of strong and informed faith have been labeled 'atheists' simply for refusing to profess dogma, respect clerical authority and/or pass judgment on the beliefs of others. Indeed, such people are probably overrepresented in the history of science. This embarrassing fact leads to no end of attempts by philosophers of science to excuse, if not undermine, this persistent theological trace as a personal eccentricity or a regrettable atavism that can nevertheless be conveniently deployed to explain anything strange or unacceptable about the behaviour of an otherwise exemplary scientist. Michael Ruse (1999) is the past master of this style of science apologetics.

So far I have interpreted my opening question as "What has *atheism* ever done for science?" And it shall be the focus of the rest of this chapter. However, for Americans the stress might be better placed on "What has atheism ever done for *science*?" This version has particular resonance in the United States, where the legal opposition to religion in public life has until quite recently been about morals, *not* science. There the label 'atheist' continues to evoke widespread dislike and distrust, since atheism has been traditionally associated with a radical libertarianism, which to unsympathetic eyes looks like 'loose morals'. A highbrow version of such libertarianism was originally associated with the great British philosopher Bertrand Russell, who took on numerous book contracts, speaking engagements and teaching assignments in the US to make ends meet. Although Russell was one of the most scientifically literate people of his time, his objection to organized religion was mainly based on its irrational inhibition of what he judged to be matters of harmless personal expression, such as sex between two consenting adults out of wedlock. But on the specific matter of God's existence, Russell (1957) remained studiously agnostic.

But much more popular and effective, at least from a legal standpoint, was Madalyn Murray O'Hair, who in the midst of a tumultuous personal life (eventuating in her murder) managed to extend constitutional protection of civil liberties by removing the state from the business of moral improvement. The end of compulsory daily prayers in state-supported schools in the 1960s was O'Hair's breakthrough achievement. According to a 1964 story in *Life* magazine, this achievement made her 'America's most hated woman'. O'Hair's presidency of American Atheists from 1963 to 1995 also coincided with many of the religiously inspired 'creationist' court challenges to the exclusive teaching of evolution in public high schools. Yet O'Hair did not figure significantly in this debate. Creationists were generally defeated on the simple grounds that the Bible is itself not a scientific text, alleviating any requirement that the judge pronounce on the conduct of science in terms of a biblically informed mindset.

Atheism became salient in legal debates over science only when it became clear that a significant number of creationists were themselves reputable scientists, or at least holders of reputable degrees in science. At that point, atheism entered its current phase, known as the new atheism by friends and foes alike. Since the late 1980's, such new atheists have targeted creationist-friendly organizations whose publications, including textbooks, are written by people with scientific credentials who make no reference to the Bible or even to God. In this context, the phrase 'intelligent design' has increasingly been used. However, the objections to evolution—specifically Darwin's version—have remained and have been bolstered by close readings of the relevant technical literature.

In particular, these 'neo-creationists' discovered that belief in a very old Earth (as of this writing, 4.5 billion years) runs much deeper than a reasonable empirical inference from the decay rate of atoms in ancient rocks, which just so happens to refute 'young earth' accounts inspired by Biblical chronology. Rather, belief in a very old Earth is an outright conceptual requirement of Darwin's theory of evolution, which explains organic change by nothing more intelligent than random variation and natural selection. From a Darwinian standpoint, the older the Earth the better, since it allows that much more time for undirected chance-based processes to work themselves out in nature.

Neo-creationists had thus found their scientific marching orders: Cast aspersions on the methods used to justify a very old Earth. One might attack the radiometric techniques used to date rocks, the computer simulations used to replay the Earth's natural history, or even the background cosmological assumptions that incline one to expect a very old Earth in the first place. In essence, the more zeros that can be knocked off the Earth's age, the more Darwinism looks like a secular version of miracle-mongering, in which the frequency of 'beneficial mutations' that flourish in spite of their significantly altered genetic makeup becomes too good to be truly products of chance. It is perhaps no accident that in 1940, just as various syntheses of evolutionary theory and experimental genetics were jostling to become what we now recognize as biology's research paradigm, the maverick geneticist Richard Goldschmidt recast such mutations in the old religious language of miraculous births by calling them 'hopeful monsters,' a phrase that subsequently resonated with Karl Popper's self-styled 'evolutionary' account of the growth of human knowledge and Donna Haraway's (1990) account of the emergence of the cyborg as a cultural hybrid that blurs heretofore inviolate distinctions between human and non-human.

ENLIGHTENMENT 'ATHEISM' AS MERE ANTI-CLERICALISM

But even granting the new atheists' success in shifting public interest in atheism from ethical to epistemic matters, the espousal of atheism as a positive worldview is not as pervasive as either its defenders or its opponents think. Indeed it never has been. Of course, it is understandable why the new atheists might wish others to think that people rather like themselves have been a major force in intellectual life. But it is much less clear why theists would want to follow suit. Perhaps an excessive generosity of spirit moves theists—especially monotheists— to overestimate the historic presence of atheism. Maybe theists do not wish to underestimate the force of their opponents. At least this would explain why they use the term 'atheist' for people who were no more than religious non-conformists who happened to make a point of openly defying church authority.

A striking example of this practice appears in Alister McGrath's widely reviewed *The Twilight of Atheism* (2004), which includes deists like Thomas Paine and Humanists like Ludwig Feuerbach in the ranks of atheists. To be sure, McGrath's inclusive definition of atheism has the immediate advantage of establishing common ground between himself and Christopher Hitchens (2007d), who, faced with a shortage of genuine intellectual antecedents, is eager to claim the likes of Paine and Feuerbach for the atheist side. Nevertheless, this ironic convergence of interests masks what really is at stake between so-called theists and atheists, namely, the standing of the church as a source of religious authority. Put more pointedly: Should any institution be allowed to authorize one's relationship with the ultimate source of their being? This is the question that divides a church historian like McGrath from a civil libertarian like Hitchens. It is not about the belief in God, let alone the truth of that belief, but about how that belief is validated.

I raise this point because behind the recent resurgence of atheism is Christianity's unresolved relationship to the Enlightenment. A still popular version of Western intellectual history identifies 'secularization' with the transition, often presented as a radical break, from religion to science—or superstition to reason—as the final epistemic court of appeal in society. This transition supposedly occurred during the period that, after Kant, has been called the 'Enlightenment,' roughly, 1650–1800. However, from a sociological standpoint, 'secularization' simply refers to the institutional separation of church and state. Thus, earthly governors become mainly accountable to the governed, not to some higher-order governors who have been empowered to speak for God. It would be difficult to overestimate the significance of this reversal in the arrow of legitimation, especially in terms of enabling greater democracy in public life, most notably in the shift from royal to parliamentary rule (Schneewind 1984). I adopt the sociological definition of 'secularization' because it best captures the spirit of the Enlightenment's relationship to organized Christianity, which was anti-Church without being anti-God, and that in turn problematizes the new atheists' attempt to mobilize the Enlightenment for their cause.

At the same time, it is worth underscoring that to deny the epistemic and political privilege of a particular church in its access to God is by no means to deny the significance of religion in public life. On the contrary, the separation of church and state opened the public sphere to greater opportunities for religious expression, as alternative routes to God implied different ways of organizing civil society. This was the spirit in which the U.S. Constitution was drafted—to encourage evangelism and proselytism, but understood as a state-licensed market activity, one epitomized in the non-profit legal status still enjoyed by churches. In this respect, the rational choice approach to religion championed in Stark and Bainbridge (1987) captures exactly the melding of religious and commercial sensibilities that secularization was designed to foster as the ultimate convergence of, in Max Weber's memorable phrase, the 'Protestant Ethic' and the 'Spirit of Capitalism'.

Bluntly put, in a secular environment, the balance of power in the market for religious goods shifts from the producer to the consumer. Thus, religious promoters (evangelists) must make direct appeals to the interests of potential converts, which may include creating a sense of urgency in the need to make a decision on a specific brand of faith. Under the circumstances, the religious promoters—and what they promote—appear to be more like their would-be converts and what they already want. The shift in the balance of market power towards the consumer of religious goods appears in the nineteenth century with the distinction between 'high' and 'low' church Protestantism designed to contrast the style of the Church of England, whose clerics enunciate edifying words from a pulpit above the faithful, and that of the non-established churches, whose clerics speak in roughly the same register, while standing at roughly the same level as the faithful.

In this respect, secularization amounts to a purification—not a corruption—of religious life, the divestiture of atavistic social formations and modes of thought that inhibit direct encounters with the numinous. Notwithstanding their perennial reputations as 'snake oil artists,' evangelists certainly have driven home that we encounter God in our daily lives by being who we normally are. That a transatlantic 'Great Awakening' in Christianity coincided with the Enlightenment should be seen as alternative attempts to bring to fruition the revolution in the human spirit that was begun by the Protestant Reformation. A bellwether figure here is the Unitarian preacher, experimental chemist and confidant of the U.S. Founding Fathers, Joseph Priestley, who is comfortably included in both trends: He denounced and deconstructed the pretences of historical Christianity on behalf of the purer encounter with God that Newton had made possible and whose central sacrament was the scientific experiment (S. Johnson 2008).

It is worth recalling that the Enlightenment gave us the generic term 'monotheism' to capture the common biblical lineage of Judaism, Christianity and Islam (Masuzawa 2006, 49–51). The force of this term focused on the nature of the privilege that humans enjoy in Creation by virtue of having been made in the image and likeness of God. (Let us set aside for the sake of argument the rather Christianized understanding of Islam that this move entailed, since the Qur'an tends to portray humans, not least Muhammad, more as vehicles of divine agency than as free-standing agents.) The capacity for reason—often capitalized as 'Reason'—was proposed as a suitably secularized version of the divine *logos*. A proper genealogy of this turn of events would begin in the fourteenth century with John Duns Scotus' analytic separation—Feuerbach might put it 'alienation'—of divine attributes from their divine lineage, so that the sense of 'power' implied in God's 'omnipotence' is the same as that which humans possess in diminished but corrigible form (Brague 2007).

This rather literal reading of humans as creatures *in imago dei* subsequently led to the construal of natural law with the formality, explicitness and binding character of human legislation. As this conception created an overarching expectation of stability in the conduct of both nature and society, it also cast increasing doubt on the veracity of claims about God's past miraculous interventions that had provided a unique basis for religious knowledge (Wootton 1988). It is worth noting that Thomas Hobbes, perhaps the exemplar of this development, followed his mentor Francis Bacon in believing that the shift away from a superstitious church to a scientific state was simply an extension of the Reformation of Christianity. As the Enlightenment was taken forward into the nineteenth century, other theological terms acquired secular meanings: 'conscience' became 'consciousness,' 'spirit' became 'mind,' etc. A good way to appreciate the seamlessness of this transition is to observe the various provisos and excuses that translators routinely give to their renderings of words like *Geist* and *l'esprit* in such authors as Hegel and Comte: Did they or did they not believe in God?

NEW ATHEISM AS A NEW THEOLOGY?

If atheism is to go beyond the mere denial of certain religious authorities, so to earn its right to capitalization as a positive faith called *Atheism*, then it must be something more than a position that retains all the key metaphysical assumptions of monotheism—including the eschatology, soteriology, and theodicy—and sometimes even its institutions, as in Comte's post-Catholic positivist religion. Hegel and Comte may have been 'atheists' but they were not 'Atheists.' The same might be said of most of the people throughout the modern period that since the nineteenth century have been classified as 'freethinkers' (Robertson 1929), and it applies most noticeably today to the smug pockets of amnesiac secularists who call themselves 'humanists,' who in reality are throwbacks to the period, roughly 1870 to 1930, when it was still scientifically literate to portray 'evolution' as a progressive organic development with humans at the helm. In contrast, Atheists give up the theological game entirely; they do not continue trying to draw the rational wheat from the superstitious chaff of religion.

Historians have already figured this out. The studied refusal to make professions of faith or to engage in religious rituals are regularly invoked as evidence for someone's Atheism, a practice that has been long observed of pagans and even Jews living in Christian and Muslim lands (Hecht 2003b, 279–282). The Atheist then simply passes life quietly and benevolently but without contesting the beliefs of others, since their beliefs are not the sort of thing about which the Atheist feels strongly: If there is no God, then what is there to argue about? This criterion neatly distinguishes Atheists from *heretics*, who are so deeply invested in their religion that they would risk their lives to contest its authorities (Evans 2003). Indeed, the French social historian Lucien Febvre (1982) famously questioned whether anyone could have been an Atheist in the Renaissance, given the preponderantly polemical use of 'unbelief' to bait heretical Christians: A true heretic would rather die for his/her beliefs than be associated with those whose mere indifference to the orthodoxy leads them *inadvertently* into sacrilege.

Of course, any positive characterization of Atheism raises a problem for today's new atheists, since they are clearly in conflict—and perhaps even promoting conflict—with religious believers, especially mono-theists. What then is the source of this animus, if they are not heretics? In which case, perhaps the likes of Hitchens, Dawkins, and Dennett are no more than overheated and dumbed-down versions of Hegel and Comte, mere 'atheists' who each in his own way would recast theology for scientific purposes. A principled case for this interpretation could be made at least for Dawkins, especially if we stick to the version of modern evolutionary theory that he defends, shorn of any anti-theo-logical polemics. In this context, many of Dawkins' fellow biologists have criticized him for extreme 'adaptationism,' the view that most, if not all, of an organism's evolutionarily relevant traits are naturally selected (see chapter six of Segerstrale 2000).

To be sure, this interpretation of Darwinism has been very popular throughout the movement's history as the source of endless 'just so stories' of why animals look and behave as they do, sophisticated exam-ples of which can still be found in the evolutionary psychology litera-ture. Their popularity, albeit unspoken, is that they can be accepted without deviating much from the familiar script of arguments for design in natural theology, except that now Nature—more precisely, Natural Selection—replaces God as a 'blind watchmaker' (Dawkins 1986). Indeed, Dawkins (1983) attributes his rhetorical success in con-verting William Paley's oxymoron 'design without a designer' into a literal description of natural selection to just this point.

Moreover, Dawkins is hardly the sole beneficiary of this move. On the one hand, Dawkins provides protective colouration for gun-shy theistic evolutionists who wish to admit the reality of design in nature without having to enter the public minefield of theorizing about what-ever intelligence might be informing it. This is the spirit in which Cambridge's Professor of Palaeobiology, Simon Conway Morris, has expressed his grudging admiration for Dawkins (Morris 2003, chap. 11). On the other hand, and perhaps more importantly, Dawkins pro-vides licence for atheistic evolutionists to make glib assertions, in both popular and technical forums, about 'suboptimal' features of organ-isms and their parts that purport to demonstrate the lack of intelligent design in nature. Such assertions presuppose that one already knows, or can imagine how, a superior intelligence would design nature, so that by nature failing to bear the relevant signatures, it can be inferred that no such intelligence is to be found.

Given the centuries of dispute among theologians and other religious believers about how to (if at all) second-guess God's moves, the seriousness with which the public takes pronouncements about nature's suboptimality by theologically illiterate atheists is nothing short of amazing. It testifies to more than simple public tolerance for scientific incursions into theological turf. Indeed, whatever light was shed on the nature of evolution from the heat generated by the quarter-century feud between Dawkins and his American nemesis, the late Stephen Jay Gould, rested on evolutionists being able to discuss *amongst themselves* the degree to which nature is optimally designed (Sterelny 2001). Gould found nature so suboptimal that he attributed virtually every complex organ or function to by-products of evolution. Like Darwin, he personally could not believe in a deity whose modus operandi verged on trial-and-error, even if over a sufficient amount of time it might yield stable and interesting biological structures. The amount of suffering and death that would be allowed in the process prohibited worship on moral grounds alone. Consequently Gould (1999) promoted the politically correct idea that science and religion are 'non-overlapping magisteria.' He meant to provide space for people to interact with a sense of reality not fulfilled by a life of science that satisfied their emotional need for meaning. I suppose Gould the scientist saw this as a case of noblesse oblige to potentially disenchanted religious folk. It would be easy to call it condescension, if so many believers did not embrace his idea, as if to prove his point.

For his part, Dawkins sees enough optimality in nature produced in the normal evolutionary fashion to make a belief in God unnecessary—or so it seems. In the notorious but revealing final scene in Ben Stein's pro-intelligent design film, *Expelled* (2008), Dawkins is caught musing that, in light of the complex logic on display in the genetic code, it is entirely possible that it was seeded by an alien life-form. While hardly a confession of faith, Dawkins' admission touch-kicks the question of life's origins into a zone where the theologians and physicists trying to peer into the mind of God rub shoulders with earthbound biologists and seekers for extraterrestrial life. Implicit in Dawkins' admission is a reluctance to accept the standard Darwinian line that life boot-strapped its way out of the primordial soup.

DARWIN AS NEW ATHEIST ICON

If instead we take the rhetoric of the new atheists literally—that is, *not* as crypto-theology—then they are best understood as attempting to elevate a previously suppressed worldview to social respectability. As Dawkins (1986, 6) once again put it, "Darwin made it possible to be an intellectually fulfilled [A]theist." While it is easy to understand why in religious societies Atheists have had to remain, so to speak, 'in the closet,' it might not be so clear why they have been also intellectually unfulfilled. It seems that here Dawkins is alluding to Atheism's historic affinity with chance-based philosophies of nature, what the U.S. pragmatist philosopher Charles Sanders Peirce called 'tychism.' In the Western tradition, this tendency is most clearly represented by Epicureanism, with its radical indeterminism based on the endless recombination of material atoms, any stable version of which is always bound to be temporary. Darwin's theory of evolution constituted a significant improvement over Epicureanism because of the path dependency of its chance-based processes. Genetic mutations may arise randomly but they are not all equally ephemeral, as natural selection determines which survive long enough to reproduce so as to propagate lines of organic descent. Moreover, reproductive success across a few generations may be all that is required for a new variant to sustain a stable population if not dominate a niche in its ecology (Sober 2008, 122–125).

In effect, Darwin gave Atheists reasons for believing that, at least in principle, a durable sense of order could indeed arise from disorder. This meant that Atheists could re-orient their attitude towards theists. Instead of presuming that theists were deluded in thinking that there was any order at all in nature, Atheists could now account for the relative sense of order that we perceive in nature in terms of normal statistically based processes. In this way, Atheism evolved from a policy of polite silence about a collective illusion (theism) that still left private space for non-believers, to a policy of open opposition to an unnecessary assumption (again, theism) that arguably impeded the course of science. Thus, Atheism came to be justifiable in the public discourse about order in nature, despite the continuing presumptive status of theism in the discussion.

Before considering the tenability of this turn in the history of Atheism, it is worth underscoring Darwin's own centrality to it. To be sure, Darwin never declared himself an Atheist and indeed throughout his career periodically punctuated his most general remarks about nature with references to the 'Creator.' Nevertheless, it is clear that by the time of *Origin of Species*, 'Creator' was little more than a place-holder term for how the natural history of life on Earth appeared from the standpoint of its origin. No powers—let alone any sense of direction or goal—were attributed to whatever being might have been present then.

To be sure, there have been some well-publicized, well-intentioned, yet ultimately desperate efforts to portray Darwin as a man of faith. The amply documented *Darwin's Sacred Cause* (Desmond and Moore 2009) is the most notable case in point for the key Darwin anniversary year of 2009. Given the ongoing challenges to Darwinism from creationism and intelligent design theory, it is perhaps unsurprising that *Darwin's Sacred Cause* stresses the link between Darwin's scientific doctrine of common descent and his personal belief that all the human races descend from a common ancestor, making them members of the same species. Thus, much stress is placed on Darwin's revulsion at the brutality of slavery that he saw on his youthful voyage on the *Beagle*, despite the ease with which the natural historians of his day believed in several species of 'man.' The reader is led to infer that this early revulsion represented a kind of triumph of evidence over prejudice on Darwin's part that remained throughout his career. Unfortunately, this conclusion is misdirected.

Economic issues aside, calls for the abolition of slavery in the early nineteenth century were not immediately met with widespread approval because, from a strictly naturalistic standpoint, they appeared to be based on a sentimental attachment to Christian notions of the 'brotherhood of man.' Improved communications had resulted in a rapid accumulation of evidence for the vastly different lives and dispositions of the races. Darwin was originally immune to such unvarnished empiricism or knee-jerk naturalism—depending on your view of the situation—because his mind was 'prejudiced' by a very healthy dose of Unitarianism and non-conformist Christianity on both sides of his family. However, *Darwin's Sacred Cause* wisely confines its argument to Darwin's early years, since as he grew older he tended to stress the hierarchy of the races and downplay the distinctiveness of the human condition in natural history. In other words, as Darwin lost touch with his Christian roots, his science lost touch with its humanity. Darwin began life close to believing in the natural equality of all humans and their superiority to all animals and ended life close to believing in the natural equality of all animal species and the inherent differences within each of them.

In contrast, a long line of self-avowed 'evolutionists' retained a much more robust sense of our divine presence in natural history than Darwin ever did, albeit nuanced by developments in genetics and statistics, two fields of which Darwin himself was ignorant. In this respect, the principal contributors to the Neo-Darwinian synthesis, Ronald Fisher, Sewall Wright, and Theodosius Dobzhansky, were closer in spirit to the monastic founder of genetics, Gregor Mendel, than to Darwin himself. While these geneticists followed Darwin in abandoning Lamarckian notions of the inheritance of acquired traits, the nub of their objection had more to do with Lamarck's heavy reliance on matter's spontaneously self-directing tendencies than the very idea that evolution might be provided with a direction. Whereas Mendel thought that fathoming the mathematical structure of artificial selection could help humans (as creatures *in imago dei*) to master natural selection, Darwin always held that the relationship between natural and artificial selection was merely analogical: Nature would ultimately trump human artifice. This explains Darwin's rather pessimistic attitude to research on animals to address human needs: He believed that, beyond a certain point, the level of pain necessarily inflicted on animals would not justify whatever knowledge might be turned to our benefit (Fuller 2008, chap. 2).

In a certain sense, then, Darwin is the perfect icon for new atheists. He clearly proposed a theory of evolution whose mechanisms require neither explicit divine intervention nor even divinely inspired human mediation. And of course his name is attached to the dominant and most fruitful research program in biology today. The downside of appealing to Darwin is that it is by no means clear that he would have wished to be associated with the post-World War II developments named on his behalf as 'Neo-Darwinian.' These have been really much more in Mendel's interventionist spirit. Indeed, there is a profound mismatch between Darwin's own sceptical attitude towards humanity's capacity to master the forces of nature and the great strides that have been taken to do just that (albeit with setbacks) since Darwin's day. Without downplaying the inspiration that natural selection provided for Nazi racist policies, it is worth noting that Darwin himself refused to be co-opted into providing support for the 'eugenic' social policies promoted by his cousin Francis Galton, which he regarded as unduly utopian, as if humans would ever be in a position to turn millions of years of evolutionary forces to their own ends. Darwin's own scepticism is here clearly compatible with Atheism, while the achievements to which his name has come to be attached in genetics and molecular biology comport better to the crypto-theological horizons of mere atheism.

BUT WHAT GOOD IS ATHEISM TO SCIENCE?

Could it be that the New Atheists cling so tenaciously to Darwin's legacy precisely because of its ambiguities? After all, Atheism as a freestanding worldview has always had difficulty in justifying the pursuit of science, understood as a long-term intergenerational project that aspires to a comprehensive understanding of all of reality, in relation to which 'progress' can be measured. The ease with which evolutionists accept banal non-answers to this question is breathtaking. The most popular non-answers usually involve some vague appeal to 'innate animal curiosity.' But this hardly distinguishes science from, say, gossip or sheer nosiness, let alone religion or, for that matter, attention deficit disorder. It also fails to explain why we persist in doing science even when trails grow cold or, worse, become dangerous. Most evolutionary explanations account for a trait's persistence in one of two ways: The trait either increases our chances for survival or it is the by-product of something that increases our chances for survival. But does science fit either description?

Here we need to be clear what is meant by 'science.' Of course, those aspects of science that overlap with technology might seem self-explanatory from an evolutionary standpoint; they could qualify as instances of what Dawkins (1982) calls our 'extended phenotype,' the means by which organisms transform the environment to their reproductive advantage. But even here our efforts at extending the phenotype go well beyond the call of natural selection. The measure of success in modern medical science has been the capacity to sustain the largest number of healthy humans in the widest variety of environments for the longest period, even at the cost of eliminating other species and placing the global ecology in a state of permanent emergency. We act as if no natural obstacle—not even death itself—is too great to be overcome. Thus, when medical scientists have taken Darwin to heart, they have diagnosed the urge to proliferate and prolong the lives of humans as a monotheistic residue. Indeed, they have been inclined to update the sense of death's naturalness found in the ancient Greek therapeutic philosophers, the Epicureans and the Sceptics, and all the great religions of the East. For them, death is not an affront to human supremacy but merely an instance of natural selection's maintenance of the ecosystem.

Existentialist authors used to say that death is the ultimate personal experience, to which evolutionists respond that the only thing personal about death *is* its experience, since any individual death is best understood as part of the normal process by which populations are brought into equilibrium. The 'racial hygiene' movement inspired by Darwin and ascendant in German medicine in the half-century prior to Hitler adopted just such a stance, echoes of which continue to this day in, say, scepticism towards mass vaccination and disease eradication schemes (Proctor 1988). So, while evolution might be able to explain technological advances that enable humans to sustain their populations over successive generations, it cannot easily explain, let alone justify, science's signature interest in having us know and control *everything*.

Consider physics, which at least since Newton has been taken as the gold standard of human intellectual achievement. This is a science that unabashedly aspires to adopt what the monotheistic religions recognize as God's point of view, whereby all natural phenomena—most of which are irrelevant to day-to-day human survival—are understood under a common theoretical framework that only very few of us truly grasp. Moreover, physics has been pursued not merely as an elite hobby but as the basis for practices that have put us all increasingly at risk, as epitomized by the promises and perils of nuclear energy. Thus, it comes as no surprise that the history of physics is full of monotheists—typically heterodox ones—who hid their views at least as much to avoid religious as scientific persecution. Alongside Newton, we could place Roger Boscovich, Michael Faraday, Lord Kelvin, James Clerk Maxwell, and Ludwig Boltzmann, all of whom saw the hand of God in the counterintuitive, if not downright supernatural, remote control properties associated with what we now recognize as electromagnetic fields (Knight 2004).

Although virtually all of modern science owes much to the atomistic metaphysics that underwrites Epicurean philosophy, the Epicureans themselves never practised science because of their general scepticism about the efficacy of large scale, long-term human endeavours, given the sharp break between appearance and reality suggested by their own metaphysics. Indicative of the massive worldview difference between ourselves and the ancient Greeks is the characteristic Greek response to the prospect that reality ultimately consists of atoms in motion was therapy rather mastery: they scaled down their ambitions rather than redoubled their efforts. What marks us as moderns in the Abrahamic mould is that we regard the Greeks as having been too easily seduced by fatalism. They lacked the Protestant virtue of perseverance, the most rational expression of blind faith.

As seen from Hegel's 'cunning of reason,' whereby people make history but not always as they intend it, Epicureanism has functioned as homoeopathic therapy in Western intellectual history: A little bit has been quite salutary to the pursuit of science but too much has been deleterious. Thus, it was only once Epicureanism was downsized from a secular religion to a testable theory that it became an unequivocally progressive force in human history: The strong element of chance in reality was accepted without the need to submit to its rule. The mathematical origins of probability theory lay precisely in this sense that the recognition of chance did not beget resignation but inspiration to 'beat the odds' and 'take risks.' In this respect, the massive and often fool-hardy financial investments that accompanied in the first wave of probabilistic thought in the seventeenth and eighteenth centuries— enveloping no less than Isaac Newton—were spurred by, to echo the title of Ian Hacking's (1990) classic work, the idea that chance could be 'tamed' just as God had conquered matter to bring about Creation.

Darwin's great defender Thomas Henry Huxley saw the point towards the end of his life in his famous Romanes Lecture, 'Evolution and Ethics,' in which he speculated that it was crucial to the motivation for modern science that Newton preceded Darwin, rather than vice versa, even though the substance of their theories could be understood independently of each other. Whereas Newton, fuelled by confidence in the biblical account of humans as creatures *in imago dei*, concluded that his theory had mapped the divine plan, Darwin, starting out with similar confidence, was ultimately persuaded by the evidence that humans lacked any natural privilege, not least because there was no plan beyond the actual unfolding of natural history. Both worked on their grand projects for twenty years, resulting in a reinforcement of the faith of one scientist and the removal of the faith of the other. Huxley's point was that had Darwin preceded Newton, Newton would have been bequeathed with a downscaled sense of human aspiration as just one amongst many animal species destined for extinction. He would have had no basis for believing that he could think his way out of his material moorings—to self-transcend—in order to adopt a 'view from nowhere' that would allow him to discover the fundamental principles governing the entire universe.

For Huxley, speaking in 1893, the challenge facing the twentieth century would be, notwithstanding Darwin's diminished view of our capacities, to continue to motivate Newton-sized scientific ambitions, which Huxley thought in his day were being regularly realized in advances in medicine and technology. On balance, living in the dawn of the twenty-first century, we can say that Huxley's optimism outshone Darwin's pessimism. As already noted, even the principal contributors to the Neo-Darwinian synthesis held much more robust views about humanity's privileged position vis-à-vis a divine creator than Darwin himself. In physics, the case is even more striking. The anomalies in Newtonian mechanics relating to the disposition of objects travelling close to the speed of light were not resolved by retreating from Newton's aspirations as being somehow 'unrealistic' but by adding to our intellectual armament and redoubling our efforts to achieve and understanding of them. Moreover, these additions came from Non-Euclidean geometries that had been already developed as imaginative constructions based on suspending Euclid's Parallel Postulate (i.e.,that two lines that begin parallel always stay parallel, if there is no outside interference) and imagining that space might throw some curves of its own. In short, prior to the physical evidence, our minds had anticipated the framework that would be subsequently used to expand our empirical understanding of the universe.

Indeed, several aspects of the history of twentieth-century science are difficult to explain or justify from a strictly evolutionary standpoint. While it is easy to understand how all sorts of imaginative constructions might have arisen as by-products of evolutionarily salient activities, it is harder to understand how one by-product might come to surpass another by-product that nevertheless had already managed to transform radically the terms of reference in which humans conduct their material existence. I mean here Einstein's revolutionary transformation of the Newtonian worldview. It used to be said that a mark of humanity is its relative insulation from the forces of natural selection. At first glance, the history of science as seen through successive revolutions in physics might capture that point. Unfortunately, a rather different conclusion is suggested by the environmental risks that have confronted humanity in the twentieth and now the twenty-first centuries that are clearly related to advances in the physical sciences; e.g.,air and water pollution, climate change, nuclear waste and weaponry. Humanity has not somehow transcended natural selection; rather, we have managed to organize our knowledge and ourselves in defiance of natural selection. To reap the great benefits of science, we have been willing to absorb greater risks to our long-term survival as a species (see Fuller 2006, chapters 11–14).

There is a 'no pain, no gain' strategy to all of this, but it is not Darwinian. On the contrary, a Darwinian science policy, cognizant of the vexed relations between politics and science in the twentieth century, would declare the leading tendencies in the medical and physical sciences 'counter-evolutionary' and call for a scaling back in their funding and significance before they contribute to the extinction of our own and other species. Such a policy would have a global aim of minimizing the prospects for suffering, as it raised survival rates. With this in mind, Peter Singer (1999), the great philosopher of 'animal liberation,' has called for a 'Darwinian Left.' It is too bad that the new atheists have not elevated him to iconic status. Unlike Dawkins, Hitchens, and Dennett, Singer appreciates the full measure of human self-restraint that would be demanded were we to live consistently Darwinian lives. Singer reasons roughly as follows: Our best science says that we are just one among many species that is privileged in our own eyes but in no other, since there is no transcendent set of eyes. It follows that our ethics need to be re-calibrated so that our judgements are not at the outset prejudiced in favour of our own species. In effect, the threshold of moral relevance is lowered from, say, uniquely human conditions for autonomy to that of sheer pain-avoidance, which is common to all organisms with a nervous system.

Singer (1981) famously described this revolution in ethics in terms of 'expanding the moral circle.' While the phrase made for good public relations, it was not quite accurate, since a hidden cost of maintaining equality between all species is exercising constraint within each species, so that the members of one species are not allowed to infringe unfairly on the potential of the members of other species to flourish. While one might wonder whether such an ontologically robust notion of species is not better suited to Aristotle's than Darwin's version of naturalistic ethics, the overriding point is that humans *per se* do not enjoy any moral privilege, only moral responsibility, given our superior cognitive capacity. In any case, it is clear that Darwin himself and his followers on both the left and the right have tended to presuppose a moral horizon that aims for what we nowadays call 'ecological sustainability.' A consequence of this position is that there is, to put it bluntly, a cut-off point in the population of any given species beyond which it upsets the moral order, which is to say, the natural ecology. This in turn justifies a policy of 'negative eugenics,' that is, the redistribution of resources for purposes of redressing the balance, which may include contraception, sterilization, abortion, and euthanasia.

I raise this point because as the Abrahamic scaffolding of secular humanism is removed in pursuit of a consistently Darwinian ethic like Singer's, a clear casualty will be 'moral universalism' in the sense that that phrase has come to be understood in modern ethics, namely, a normative commitment to equal liberty and dignity for all humans *simply by virtue of being human*. A good sign that this change in sentiment is already underway is the rather bald attempt by evolutionary psychology advocate Steven Pinker (2008) to blame the supposedly antiquated religious concept of dignity for the prohibition on embryonic stem cell research by George W. Bush's bioethics panel. However, this naturalistically inspired anti-universalism pre-dates Darwin. Epicurus and his followers down through the ages, not least Montaigne, Hume, and Bentham, have been inclined to take the measure of one's moral fitness by one's treatment of animals. What is striking about such thinkers is their cross-species equanimity; their benevolence towards animals is complemented by a detachment, perhaps even cynicism, towards humans. Indeed, it may well be that those who are attracted to the accounts of moral life associated with evolutionary psychology do not see much epistemological difference between making sense of people and animals. Both are equally opaque—or transparent, as the case may be—in terms of access to their beliefs and desires.

Here it is worth recalling that the classic philosophical basis for believing that we can access each other's thoughts sufficiently to pass judgement on them is that our minds are products of the same divine archetype. They are proper souls beyond simply being functioning brains. In other words, what enables us to understand God also allows us to understand each other, including humans living far away in space and time, but not animals, even ones that live by our side. Because animals lack souls, they can only be understood in terms of correlations between their behaviour and the environment. It was on this basis that Friedrich Schleiermacher founded hermeneutics as a distinct academic discipline in the early nineteenth century, which by the end of the century Wilhelm Dilthey had turned into the foundational human science (Schnädelbach 1984, 117–118). Dilthey and most of his secular followers in the twentieth century *Geisteswissenschaften* may have been atheists but they most certainly have not been Atheists. If they were Atheists a la Singer and Pinker, they would not draw such a sharp epistemic distinction between access to human and animal minds. In this respect, the ascendancy of 'the problem of other minds' as a genuine conundrum in philosophy in the twentieth century reflects a decline in the salience of the Abrahamic intuition, one that Ludwig Wittgenstein tried to reverse by arguing that our normal public use of language is itself the medium by which we read each other's minds. Though perhaps a desperate move, Wittgenstein clearly echoes the appeal to our partaking of the divine *logos* that lay behind Schleiermacher's original hermeneutical project (cf. Phillips 1994).

A fascinating if gruesome glimpse at what an explicitly Atheistic science would look like is provided in Hecht (2003a), which focuses on what can only be called a 'scientific cult' that flourished in France in the final quarter of the nineteenth century, 'The Society for Mutual Autopsy.' This collection of prominent anthropologists and medical scientists, centring on Darwin's French translator Clémence Royer and inspired by the pioneer brain surgeon Paul Broca, constituted the radical fringe of the Third Republic's systematic removal of clerical authority from the national research and teaching agenda. The Society for Mutual Autopsy might be seen as providing one comprehensive response to what you can study once you give up the idea that there is a *Geist* about which one could have a *Wissenschaft*. First, you spend a lot of time diagnosing the need for religion among otherwise seemingly intelligent people, striking the firm but patient pose evident in Dennett (2006). Next, you draw attention to all the monstrosities of nature that defy any obvious sense of intelligent design. It is less important that these creatures are accorded dignity as such than that their deviant status is invoked to refute the theologians. Finally, since you believe (following Broca) that our experiences are imprinted on our brains, friends promise to examine each other's brains posthumously to study how differences in life experiences have been reflected in different configurations of brain fissures. The Society for Mutual Autopsy lasted exactly one generation.

CONCLUSION: THE FUTILITY OF ATHEISM

Even if most scientists nowadays call themselves 'Atheists,' or even 'New Atheists,' Atheism as a positive doctrine has done precious little for science. The scientists who happily trade on their atheism justify science in one of three equally inadequate ways: First, they might point to science's practical benefits, both intended and unintended. But as two world wars in the preceding century made clear, this justification makes science a hostage to fortune, which has resulted in periodic antiscientific backlashes. Second, scientists may appeal to subjective aesthetic factors as motivating their craft. While that may suffice for the scientists themselves, it does little to justify the increasing cost (both intended and unintended) to the society supporting their activities. The sorry political fate of the Congressional legislation surrounding the Superconducting Supercollider, which would have involved building the world's largest particle accelerator underneath Texas, brought out that point with insulting clarity (Weinberg 1992). Finally, like Richard Dawkins, scientists may really be 'atheists' rather than Atheists, that is, trade on a secular version of the theological justification for science behind the fig leaf of 'humanism,' itself a doctrine that bears little scrutiny from the species egalitarian standpoint of strict Darwinism.

More generally, Atheism has not figured as a force in the history of science not because it has been suppressed but because whenever it has been expressed, it has not specifically encouraged the pursuit of science. The general metaphysical idea underlying Darwinism—that a morally indifferent nature selects from among a variety of organic possibilities—has many secular and religious precedents across the world. In each case, it has led to an ethic of equanimity and even resignation, certainly not a drive to remake the planet, if not the universe, to our own purposes. Yet, so far we have got pretty far on that drive. The longer we continue successfully, the stronger the evidence that at least human life cannot be fully explained in Darwinian terms.

Nevertheless, it is a measure of the headway that something called 'atheism' has made in the cultural mainstream that many of the revolutionary but religiously eccentric physicists of the twentieth century like Einstein, Bohr, and Schrödinger—not to mention to the twentieth century biologists mentioned in this chapter—are treated complimentarily as honorary atheists simply by virtue of not having been conventional churchgoers (e.g., Weinberg 2008). A more natural conclusion to draw from this pattern would be that cutting-edge science typically requires some personal engagement with the specifically cognitive demands of religion, resulting in what an earlier time would have called 'heretical' or 'dissenting' beliefs. By 'the specifically cognitive demands of religion,' I mean three core metaphysical ideas about the nature of reality that inform the Abrahamic faiths, on which the new atheists continue to trade; namely, that reality as a whole constitutes (1) a universe (not simply multiple realities) with (2) ontological depth (not simply the sum of direct experience), all of which is (3) potentially intelligible to the human mind, by virtue of our (divinely) privileged place in reality. This combination of ideas, while easily taken for granted in secular quarters, is hardly self-evident. From a strictly Darwinian standpoint, it is by no means clear what long-term selective advantage, if any, the pursuit of inquiry along such grandiose lines has accorded our species.

Finally, let me end by underscoring the futility of Atheism, even to Atheists. In homage to Pascal's Wager, I call it *Fuller's Wager*. Instead of examining the consequences of my belief in God if the deity does or does not exist, as Pascal did, I turn the tables and consider what follows from the deity's non-existence if I do or do not believe in God:

- If I do believe, then I will never know I was wrong (since there is no afterlife) and on the basis of that belief I may have done some good in my lifetime.
- If I do not believe, then I will not be around to enjoy that I was right (since there is no afterlife) and no one still alive will be in a position to know that I was right either.

This would appear to be a very strong pragmatic argument against Atheism, unless one doubts that theists are more likely to do good rather than harm on the basis of their belief. In any case, it shows that Atheism, while possibly falsifiable, is not verifiable.

COGNITIVE SCIENCE AND THE NEW ATHEISM

William Sims Bainbridge[1]

Consider this sentence: "I believe in God." To a first approximation, it is a combination of three elements: 1) *I*, 2) *believe in*, and 3) *God*. Traditional Atheism questions the third element, God. The new Atheism based in cognitive science questions all three elements. To be sure, most Atheists doubt that individual humans possess immortal souls or spirits, but the very notion of a unitary self is questionable from the standpoint of modern research. Belief is certainly an object of study in cognitive science, and the results of research do not closely match popular notions of faith. With respect to God, cognitive scientists can legitimately ask: If a god did exist, how would its own cognitive functions operate, and what material basis would enable them?

COGNITIVE SCIENCE

The *Stanford Encyclopedia of Philosophy* says, "Cognitive science is the interdisciplinary study of mind and intelligence, embracing philosophy, psychology, artificial intelligence, neuroscience, linguistics, and anthropology" (Thagard 2007). This is a correct definition of the Cognitive Science movement, in its early days, but it suffers from two important omissions: First, it fails to define 'mind and intelligence.' Second, it leaves out the crucial social dimension of intelligence as evidenced by its failure to mention those two highly cognitive sciences, sociology and political science.

As I see it, there were really three original factors encouraging the emergence of this new discipline. First, research and theory on human mental processes were strewn across many academic disciplines and fields of application, so multidisciplinary efforts were clearly needed. However, as just mentioned, the original scope of this new field may have been too narrow. For example, social psychology is a large and

[1] Any opinions, findings, conclusions, or recommendations expressed in this material are those of the author and do not necessarily reflect the views of the National Science Foundation.

well-recognized subdiscipline within sociology as well as psychology, and many forms of intelligence are social in nature, as illustrated by the fact that linguistics was included in the original scope. Initially, the input from psychologists was almost entirely within cognitive psychology, and the social dimensions have only more recently begun to receive much attention.

Second, the discipline of psychology suffered from excessive popularization, including the unhealthy influence of pseudoscientific therapists and educational testers within the American Psychological Association (APA) itself, so there was a need to escape the stigma of both Freud's couch and mindless IQ tests to start afresh. A parallel effort along these lines was the 1988 establishment of the Association for Psychological Science (APS, originally called the American Psychological Society) that says it is dedicated to the "advancement of scientific psychology."

Third, much of the impetus came from the emerging field of artificial intelligence (AI). On the one hand, this was a very good thing, because it meant that the definition of intelligence would be broader than just the cognitive processes of humans and animals, and research might lead to machine-based tools for augmenting human cognitive abilities. But it also had a downside because the particular brand of AI initially dominant at the origin of cognitive science conceptualized intelligence in terms of logical manipulation of strict categories, which may in fact play only a minor role in human intelligence. The classic rule-based, logical processing brand of AI denigrated among other things the competing and much 'fuzzier' neural network approach (Minsky and Papert 1969), not to mention computer vision, speech recognition, and other computational approaches to developing the raw material of perception upon which cognitive categories ultimately rest.

As cognitive science matured, individual scientists expanded its scope, and some began writing influential essays intended for a wider educated public. Both of these expansions occasionally touched upon religion, increasingly so in the past dozen years. A notable example is the popular book, *How the Mind Works* (1997) by Steven Pinker, which not only suggests that belief in God is a cognitive error, but also dismisses the psychoanalytic cult within psychology.

This is ironic, because Sigmund Freud himself wrote extensively about religion as an *illusion*, and one of his disciples called it a *shared psychosis* (Freud 1961; Roheim 1955). There are at least three hypotheses concerning why psychoanalysis was so hostile to religion. First, religion in Freud's Vienna meant Christianity, and nearly all pioneers of psychoanalysis were Jewish people who directly experienced anti-Semitism (Bakan 1958). Of course the harm caused by religion is a legitimate source of opposition to it, quite apart from whether the misbehaviour of religious people argues against the existence of their god. Second, by claiming to treat human emotional problems, psychoanalysis went into direct competition with religion, even to the extent that its claims were based on faith more than on rigorous research that actually tested the psychoanalytic theories. Third, and most important for the purposes of this essay, by seeking naturalistic explanations of human cognition and emotion, psychoanalysis directly undercut purely religious explanations of faith and religious conceptions of the self. This last point applies equally well to contemporary cognitive science (Dawkins 2006).

Many recent authors have sought to explain religion in terms of cognitive science theories about human mental processes, and we shall consider their work below. Again, by undercutting traditional conceptualizations—especially of the human mind, soul, or spirit—they change the terms of the debate without necessarily refuting the case for the existence of gods. A number of these writers have been cultural anthropologists, or others working in a similar style, which means their work tends to be interpretive rather than employing formal experiments or statistical studies. It is also the case that they have tended to define religion in terms of rather vague and general superstitions such as pre-literate people might have, rather than in terms of the elaborate religious organizations and theologies possessed by the great world civilizations.

The scientific discipline that has studied religion in modern societies most intensively is sociology, and the original scope of cognitive science left out sociology, and indeed much of social cognition in general. Therefore, this chapter will anticipate the currently progressing union of cognitive science with cognitive social science, and employ a broader definition of the field that includes social cognition, communication, and the ways that humans use information pragmatically during interaction with others.

THE SOUL

The mystery of human identity has puzzled philosophers and behavioural scientists since intellectuals first began playing these roles in society. We can recall the meeting between Alice and the caterpillar in Wonderland, written after all by a logician:

> "Who are you?" said the Caterpillar.
> Alice replied, rather shyly, "I – I hardly know, sir, just at present – at least I know who I was when I got up this morning, but I think I must have changed several times since then."
> "What do you mean by that?" said the Caterpillar, sternly. "Explain yourself!"
> "I can't explain myself, I'm afraid, sir," said Alice, "because I'm not myself, you see – being so many different sizes in a day is very confusing." (Carroll 1916, 26–27)

Alice, it must be recalled, had recently shrunk to the size of the insect, which called into question one of the standard notions of identity, that it reflects the integrity of the individual human body. Cognitive scientists have certainly not unlocked the mysteries of the mind, a feat which many of them think would be equivalent to understanding how the brain works, so they could not answer the question any more easily than poor Alice. But their research has taken them far beyond mere ignorance. For example, it seems clear that the brain is an assembly of semi-autonomous parts, structurally and functionally differentiated on many levels of scale, and its unity is, to say the least, problematic (Zeki 2003).

This fact was already apparent to leading medical doctors and psychiatrists in the middle of the nineteenth century, who had become aware of the great extent to which brain injury could alter an individual's mental abilities and personality. They immediately noticed the challenge this posed to religion, and for public relations reasons tended to downplay the issue (Bainbridge 1984). More recently, so-called split-brain research, studying people in whom the connection between the two hemispheres of the brain had been severed, revealed the local autonomy of brain structures and the problematic nature of such fundamental perceptions as time and self (Gazzaniga 1998; Turk et al. 2002; Funnell et al. 2003). Today, advanced computing technologies are steadily improving the resolution at which non-invasive techniques can map mental functions on the brain (Ou et al. 2009), and no end is in sight to discoveries about how different structures perform distinctive functions.

Humanistic philosophers and religious mystics like to talk about consciousness, often with the implication that there is some nub of perception inside the mind that constitutes the person. Yet the nearest thing to a perceptive self that cognitive researchers find is short-term memory, the metaphoric scratch pad on which we keep a list of the things we are attending to at the moment. But this is a very impoverished list, proverbially consisting of about seven items (G. Miller 1956). MIT artificial intelligence pioneer Marvin Minksy likes to describe the human mind as a society of semi-autonomous specialized agents, rather than a unified individual, and describes them as interacting on six hierarchical levels: instinctive reactions, learned reactions, deliberative thinking, reflective thinking, self-reflective thinking, and self-conscious reflection (Minsky 2006, 130).

Yale cognitive scientist Paul Bloom (2004a) explicitly says the idea that humans have souls is a delusion, resulting from the fact that the brain is not aware of its own operation. His website explains, "There is considerable evidence that adults are natural dualists—we see the world as Descartes did, as containing physical things (or bodies) and social entities (or souls). I am interested in how this common-sense dualism emerges in development, and the implications that it has for domains such as morality and religion."[2] In the *New York Times* he wrote, "The great conflict between science and religion in the last century was over evolutionary biology. In this century, it will be over psychology, and the stakes are nothing less than our souls" (Bloom 2004b).

Religions invariably seem to connect the soul with the deity, and denial of the human soul would seem to undercut the notion of a great soul, namely God. Without quite articulating this connection clearly, some cognitive scientists of religion may have found its cognitive basis the human propensity to impute agency to complex events (Atran 2002). That is, we tend to assume somebody is responsible for the things that happen. Pascal Boyer (2001, 16–17) says, "Our minds are not general explanation machines. Rather, minds consist of many different, specialized explanatory machines...more properly called inference systems." Like many other writers, Boyer says the human mind contains a very powerful module that interprets the perceptions and intentions of other intelligent beings. Some cognitive scientists think this is located in a particular brain structure, sometimes called 'mirror neurons,' and Asperger's Syndrome or Autism Spectrum Disorder may be caused by a defect in this area. Whether a localized structure or a

---

[2] For more information, see: http://www.yale.edu/psychology/FacInfo/Bloom.html

diffuse function, this 'mind reading' ability may have evolved to help proto-humans anticipate the behaviour of other humans and animals, what I like to call predators, prey, and partners. We exaggerate when we read agency into the chaotic meteorological phenomenon of a thunderstorm, imagining that Thor is making all the noise. Belief in supernatural beings, from this vantage point, represents hyperactivity of this mind-imputing function of the human brain.

Taking this line of thinking one step further, we can apply it to the soul. Evolution has given us a reasonably effective mental mechanism for modeling the behaviour of other animals and people, not accurately in a scientific sense but allowing our primitive ancestors to survive in a social environment, and this mental mechanism prejudices us toward belief in gods. But we also turn this mechanism on ourselves, understanding ourselves in terms of some functional but extremely crude metaphors of volition and identity. Consider how many words about human thoughts and feelings are little more than metaphors. A *dependent* person literally hangs on other people, whereas an *attitude* literally is a physical *posture* or *orientation*. Contemporary cognitive scientists would do well to look back at the decades-old literature in attribution theory (Heider 1958; Jones et al. 1972), especially the argument that people understand their own thoughts and feelings by observing their own behaviour and inferring principles for it as they also do with the behaviours of others. Thus, we apply our hyperactive 'mind reading' inference system both to natural processes, and to ourselves, erroneously imagining both gods and souls.

BELIEF

Perhaps because of the lack of involvement by sociologists who have studied religion in modern societies, the cognitive science analysis of religious faith is itself somewhat primitive (Barrett 2004). For example, a hyperactive mind inference module in the brain could produce animism, the 'primitive' belief that souls permeate the natural world, but it could not in itself produce faith in Jesus or obedience to the Vatican bureaucracy. Religion may exploit this inference module, but cannot entirely be reduced to it. Anthropologists have long known that pre-literate societies vary considerably in the extent to which they possess well-organized ideologies about the supernatural and the soul, and if they do want one there are several to choose from (Benedict 1934;

Ackerknecht 1943; Wallace 1959; Edgerton 1966). But many pre-literate people have very diffuse beliefs that could be described in modern terms as liberal, consisting of many discordant notions without a unifying norm requiring strict belief.

Arguably, firm belief in God is a distinctive feature of the one major monotheistic Judeo-Christian-Islamic tradition, and not of other traditions like the Hindu-Buddhist tradition. To be sure, every major tradition has some fanatic movements, but on balance most do not require the degree of faith especially common in Christianity and Islam. Some writers have suggested that this demand of faith has been essential to the success of Christianity and Islam (O'Donnell 1979). If so, then the very concept of conviction is a relic of ideological imperialism, rather than a natural feature of human cognition.

"What is truth? said jesting Pilate, and would not stay for an answer." These words of Francis Bacon refer to the confrontation between Jesus and Pontius Pilate, and the Roman's question is often rendered appropriately enough in Latin: "Quid est veritas?" An anagram of these letters is: "Est vir qui adest" translated "It is the man who stands before you." Thus Jesus himself is the truth, not any mere verbal statement about Jesus. This suggests the etymological fact that the word 'true' is not originally or solely about the verity of a formal verbal statement. The phrase 'true believer' can mean 'genuine believer' or 'faithful believer,' even when the content of the believer's beliefs is veridically false.

In totalitarian ideologies, like Christianity and Islam, *faith means loyalty* as much as it refers to a psychological feeling of cognitive satisfaction. Without loyalty to a faith, or to the Pope, Christianity could not have survived the Dark Ages intact. When European nation states arose in the early modern period, the bizarre witchcraft trials were connected with an unusual emphasis on ideological purity that presumably strengthened the political power of the centralized elites who were creating the nations (Larner 1984).

Psychoanalysis, for all its faults, was valuable for having problematized belief, suggesting that the inner feelings of a person could be considerably at variance with his or her public professions. Marxists went in a different direction, suggesting that public ideologies in capitalist societies represented false consciousness, in which common people were victims of deception about the extent to which social arrangements served their own interests. As already suggested, a fundamental debate within cognitive science, especially in its computer-oriented and artificial intelligence wing, has concerned the degree to which cognitions occur through formal manipulation of rigid categories that are equivalent to articles of belief.

The computational style of early cognitive science followed the principles of what is sometimes called *rule-based reasoning*. Cognition was like the formal manipulation of strict propositions in the derivation of mathematical theorems: Socrates is a man. All men are mortal. Therefore, Socrates is mortal. Notice that this syllogism requires us to believe in strict categories, like 'man' and 'mortal beings.' The first term of the syllogism might be rephrased today, "If Socrates is a man…" and much classical artificial intelligence consisted of coherent systems of if-then propositions. The results of logic are altered in an almost mechanical way if a concept does not belong to the operative class, for example if we define Socrates as an idea rather than a man, belonging to world-cultural heritage rather than the population of ancient Athens. In that case, we cannot conclude whether or not Socrates is mortal.

Rather quickly two related challenges to rule-based production systems arose in cognitive science. One came from neurology, what is today often called *cognitive neuroscience*, because animal neural systems and much of the human one function without the categories provided by language. The other came from the brand of artificial intelligence (or machine learning) that takes its metaphors from neurology, namely *neural networks* (Rumelhart and McClelland 1986). Neural nets encode information in terms of the connections and connection weights between a very large number of nodes, analogous to neurons connected in complex networks via dendrites, axons, and synapses. Many sophisticated neural nets do not generate uniform solutions to problems, but something even better: probabilistic tendencies to respond in a range of ways, allowing the nets to experiment with alternatives and learn when the contingencies of the environment change. That is to say that derivations are chains of probabilities, rather than deterministic logical outcomes, and strict categories may not exist. If rule-based systems are imprisoned in inflexible dogma, neural nets have free will.

An example is my own computer simulation research on the emergence of religious cognitions, modeled through network exchanges among many AI agents, each of which is a neural net (Bainbridge 1987, 1995, 2006). In its final form, the simulation postulates a community of 44,100 AI agents, each based on a neural net with nearly a hundred connection weights. I imagine that these thousands of agents represent a society with an economy, exchanging various resources that different kinds of agents generate. At the beginning of each computer run, for the given experiment, I decide how many groups of agents there will be, and which group will produce each of the resources. I then let the agents interact. At first they do so at random, but they gradually learn which kinds of other agents to go to for a particular needed resource, and the economy hums along successfully to the advantage of all the mature agents. If I change something in the middle of a run, the agents will be confused at first, but they will adapt and learn the new system. For them to adapt, they must avoid developing rigid conceptualizations of their economy, and must occasionally try different theories, even though to do so may be inefficient at a given moment.

One version of the simulation allows me to decide whether there are 2, 3, or 4 groups among the 44,100 agents, and assigns each agent to a group. These are strict categories, just like those in rule-based reasoning. The agents take turns. Suppose Agent X needs water. A subsection of its neural net consists of water memory registers for each combination. For example, one memory register represents there being two groups, and water coming from the first group. Another represents the second group among two, and still another represents the first group if there are three groups. At the start, each register contains a random number. As the agent seeks water, and either does or does not get it, the numbers in the corresponding registers increase or decrease. Needing water, Agent X consults its water neural net and selects a particular theory based on probabilities determined by the numbers in all the water-related registers. As it learns, it comes to select a good theory more and more of the time, but more than one theory may give positive results, and no theory is ever entirely ruled out. For example, if I decide there will be four groups, with water obtainable from the first group, Agent X will learn this is the preferred theory. But a pretty good theory, in terms of its empirical consequences, is the first group when there are only two groups. This theory also works pretty well, if I actually assign water to the third of four groups. Theories about three groups will do less well, simply because 2 is a factor of 4, but 3 is not. In this example, a two-group theory is less precise than a four-group theory, but not wholly false.

Religious cognition enters the picture when I make the artificial intelligence agents seek a resource that cannot in fact be obtained from other agents, for example representing eternal life. The same learning process takes place, and the computer program does not crash. Step by step, the agents learn they cannot obtain eternal life from the first of two groups, the second of two groups, the first of three groups, and so on. But they cannot effectively test some other theories that identify hypothetical agents which do not exist within the simulation. For example, suppose Agent X is seeking eternal life, and wonders if it can be obtained from the third group when there are just two groups. The neural net has a memory register for this possibility, but no agents can be assigned to this unnatural category. After many attempts, the agents will come to assume that eternal life should be sought from these categories of agents who cannot in fact exist within the simulation. These are their gods.

It may seem absurd to believe that members of a logical system containing just two categories can belong to the third of these two categories. But this is very similar to what religions do: postulate beings that have many of the characteristics of human persons, but transcend natural reality in one or two respects. Pascal Boyer (2001) and Justin Barrett (2004) say this is a distinctive feature of religious beliefs: they are *minimally counterintuitive*. They are similar to real phenomena, so they are easily remembered and discussed, but they are different enough to be memorable and remarkable. However, my AI agents would quickly abandon their gods if they could start obtaining eternal life from other agents inside their reality. They hedge their bets, occasionally still seeking this supernatural resource from natural exchange partners, and also postulating several different gods and switching between them. That is, Agent X may seek a deity in the third of two groups one time, the fourth of two groups another time, or the fourth of three groups.

More advanced versions of this simulation allow agents to communicate their beliefs. If Agent X gets water from Agent Y, the two may share information about how to obtain eternal life as well. Perhaps Agent Y has a very high probability of seeking eternal life from a god we can call Tertius, a member of the third of two groups, and Agent X lacks a strong tendency to seek it from any particular source. Agent X will be influenced by the greater conviction of Agent Y, increasing the corresponding number in the equivalent memory register. In later exchange, Agent X may pass this faith in Tertius on to Agent Z.

I can set the simulation so that at random, very high numbers are pasted into single memory registers of a few agents. This models an essentially psychiatric theory of cult formation I published years ago (Bainbridge and Stark 1979), the *psychopathology model* that messiahs develop their doctrines during episodes of acute mental illness, but regain enough sanity afterwards to share these supernatural visions with others. If the memory register happens to represent other agents inside the simulation, experience will quickly teach the agent to forget this crazy assumption. But a theory that cannot readily be disconfirmed empirically—call it a theology—can remain strong and spread from individual to individual. Several of these in a system produce competing religious sects, whose beliefs interpenetrate and naturally create many additional sects representing different combinations. Only this synergy of individual craziness and group influence produces anything like strong convictions among the agents.

This set of computer simulations grew out of conventional social cognition theory work done in collaboration with Rodney Stark (Stark and Bainbridge 1987) that sought to derive hundreds of theorems from a hundred definitions and seven axioms:

Axiom 1: Human perception and action take place through time, from the past into the future.

Axiom 2: Humans seek what they perceive to be rewards and avoid what they believe to be costs.

Axiom 3: Rewards vary in kind, value, and generality.

Axiom 4: Human action is directed by a complex but finite information-processing system (i.e.,the mind) that functions to identity problems and identify solutions to them.

Axiom 5: Some desired rewards are limited in supply, including some that simply do not exist.

Axiom 6: Most rewards sought by humans are destroyed when they are used.

Axiom 7: Individual and social attributes which determine power are unequally distributed among persons and groups in any society.

Axiom 4 introduces the human mind, which is the set of cognitive functions that directs the action of a person. It is roughly equivalent to the hardware of the brain plus the software of culture and the memory of personal experience. Alternatively, the human mind is the network of neural connections that processes information dynamically when the person makes a decision or a plan. Humans seek rewards and try to avoid costs, employing their minds to analyze their situation and identify the path to their goal. Put another way, humans solve problems by means of explanations, which are statements about why rewards may be obtained and costs incurred.

Explanations that explicitly tell a person how to obtain a reward can be called *algorithms*. This term is commonly used in computer science for programs or segments of programs that accomplish a particular task. Daniel Dennett, a prime contributor to the new cognitive science Atheism, has pointed out that evolution by natural selection is an algorithm. Stated teleologically, from the standpoint of a computer programmer, an algorithm is a step-by-step procedure for solving some problem. But Dennett defines the term without reference to purpose, so that it can include any regular mechanical process: "An algorithm is a certain sort of formal process that can be counted on—logically—to yield a certain sort of result whenever it is 'run' or instantiated" (Dennett 1995, 48).

In pursuit of desired rewards, humans exchange rewards with other humans. Indeed, this is a fundamental human algorithm: 'When in need, seek help.' In order to get help, we often have to be willing to give something in return, either now or at some time in the future.

Humans seek many kinds of rewards, some of which cannot readily be obtained by any lone individual. Rewards like food or fun get used up, and must be sought again and again. Thus, we learn to seek particular rewards through exchanges with particular other individuals or categories of people. Someone who is a frequent source of rewards, and to whom we give rewards in return, is an exchange partner. When we need a reward of a particular kind, and cannot readily provide it for ourselves, we go to a valued exchange partner, especially one who has provided similar rewards in the past.

One very important kind of instrumental reward is information about how to obtain a desired reward. This is another way of saying that algorithms can be valuable, and humans often seek them. Frequently, the best source of information is another person. Thus we have the algorithm: 'When in need of an algorithm, ask a valued exchange partner.'

Tragedy enters human life through Axiom 5, which notes that some rewards are limited in supply, and some do not exist at all. A limited supply means that not everyone can have as much of a reward as they desire. Powerful people, those with great control over the rewards they can obtain through exchanges, are able to get more than their equal share of some limited rewards, and this fact is a major dynamic of social inequality. Rewards that do not exist at all are unavailable even to powerful people. Both inequality and unavailability create frustration. However, it is impossible to know for certain that a given reward does not exist.

In the absence of a desired reward, people will often accept algorithms that explain how to get the reward in the distant future or in some other context that cannot be immediately verified. These algorithms are *compensators*, in that they compensate the individual psychologically for lack of the reward. Typically, they are promises that the reward can be obtained. Rewards vary in terms of how specific or general they are, and in terms of how readily they can be verified empirically. Religions are systems of general compensators based on supernatural assumptions that defy verification.

In addition to the psychopathology model, I identified an *entrepreneur model* and a *subculture evolution model*, both of which emphasized social cognition. While the psychopathology model said that messiahs are madmen, the entrepreneur model said that they are liars. By selling a religious idea in the absence of any real evidence about its truth, a religious entrepreneur effectively issues an IOU that rewards will be obtained by the customer, but never needs to deliver on that promise. This gives new meaning to the phrase *confidence man*, because the messiah cons people into giving credence in return for increasing their confidence that their desires can be satisfied, thus giving the messiah social status and perhaps other more concrete rewards. The subculture evolution model is a combination of the other two, suggesting that sometimes the members of a social group can begin to exchange small hopes, gradually building up a powerful edifice of delusion and white lies, perhaps a god, without any individual needing to be a total madman or a congenital liar.

God

Atheists, whether traditional or of the newer cognitive science variety, have no quarrel with people who suggest that the universe may contain many mysteries we have not yet discovered, or who wonder whether materialistic models of reality are complete. What they complain about is the confident assertion that the universe has a king, possessing will and consciousness and responsible for creating the universe from nothing. When asked my view about God, I often reply that I am a republican, unwilling to accord divine rights to any ruler, no matter how powerful or how glorious his past accomplishments. That is, I view God as a political theory advocating cosmic tyranny, as much as it is a theory about physical and spiritual nature. Thus, one may resolutely reject the idea of God, while harbouring some awareness that very ancient and powerful beings might conceivably roam the cosmos.

An early cognitive theory suggesting why we ought to believe in God is the famous wager of philosopher and mathematician Blaise Pascal (1961). Consider the alternatives: God exists or he does not. If he exists, there are clear benefits in believing in him, not the least being the possibility that he will appreciate and reward faith. If he does not exist, there is no harm believing in him. Therefore, belief is more advantageous than disbelief. Of course the fundamental flaw of this argument is the initial assumption that they are only two alternatives: the Christian (indeed, Roman Catholic) god exists, or not. Suppose we admit a third possibility, that the polytheism of the ancient Greeks, Romans, or Germans is correct. Then one must begin running from the shrine of one god to another, seeking help of different kinds from these divine specialists, with no sense that there was any overriding justice to the system. Or suppose we admit the possibility that the Zen Buddhists are correct, and all is illusion but we can learn to be comfortable with this fact, illusions though we be.

When psychology pioneer William James (1896; 1902; 1948) confronted these issues, he framed a social cognition argument in favor of Christian belief that can be summarized roughly as follows: Nobody can be blamed for believing in the dominant faith of the culture to which he belongs. This assumes people belong to coherent societies that possess consistent ideologies, and in the modern world this may not often be the case. As evidenced by his book *Varieties of Religious Experience*, James considered the psychology of religion to be a prime question for science, but perhaps his best argument for faith is implicit in his *Essays on Pragmatism* (James, 1948). From the pragmatic epistemology, truth is only the useful in the way of ideas. Thus, to say that God exists is merely to assert that belief in God benefits humans, perhaps by strengthening morality through a myth about a divine lawgiver. Of course, this is an empirical claim, and social scientific research can examine whether religious faith really has the positive consequences claimed for it (Bainbridge 2007).

What, then, about God's own beliefs? Here, the new cognitive science Atheism comes full circle. Intelligence is a result of evolution, partly individual and partly social, that provides advantages to organisms that exist in a problematic environment where rewards must be sought, and costs avoided. If God is an intelligent person, then these principles must apply to him, as well. That is, his abilities must be limited, as ours are, and his intelligence evolved from generation to generation of ancestor gods, conferring ever greater ability to manage the environment. Of course some highly secularized members of the Judeo-Christian-Islamic tradition have demythologized God to a considerable extent, draining the concept of any attributes worth debating. But for fundamentalists within these religions, God has thoughts, emotions, moods, and desires. They attribute so many human characteristics to the divine, that he must operate on very much the same cognitive principles.

Where, then, are God's neurons? Interestingly, the Christian notion of Triune God (Father, Son, and Holy Ghost) suggests that his brain may like ours be separated into semi-autonomous parts. Given that evolution requires ancestors, and verbal aspects of intelligence require a society that communicates via language, where are all the other gods that are required to make one of them intelligent? It would be entertaining to see a novel religious movement assert that God created humans precisely because he has the same hyperactive agency imputing inference system in his brain as humans do, causing him falsely to believe in our existence. Even more fun would be to hear from God himself what he believes about the greater gods above him.

Part III: Sociology and the New Atheism

ONE-DIMENSIONAL RAGE: THE SOCIAL EPISTEMOLOGY OF THE NEW ATHEISM AND FUNDAMENTALISM

William A. Stahl

> The world of everyday reality is a socially and personally
> constructed world. If one confuses that world with reality itself
> one then becomes trapped in one's own delusions, one projects
> one's wishes and fears onto others and one acts out one's own
> madness all the while believing one is a clearheaded realist
>
> – Robert Bellah (1970)

Atheism is on the march—or so one might think from the mass media. Books by prominent atheists, led by Richard Dawkins, Sam Harris and Christopher Hitchens, have been on best-seller lists for months. Yet as soon as one examines it, the so-called New Atheism appears to be a good deal less than it seems. Atheism should not be confused with secularism—it represents the extreme edge of a wide range of secular thinking and the numbers of atheists is not, nor ever has been, very large (see Bibby 2002; Cimino and Smith 2007; Kosmin and Keysar 2007). Atheism is not a social movement. Nor does the novelty, strength, or insight of the New Atheists' arguments compare favourably to those of late nineteenth- and twentieth-century atheists such as Marx, Freud, Nietzsche, Sartre, or Camus (see Haught 2008, 15–27). By comparison, the New Atheists are superficial.

What is striking about the current debate is the frequency with which the New Atheists are portrayed as mirror images of religious fundamentalists (see Bunting 2006). Critics point out that both are extreme. Both claim to have a monopoly on the truth. Both are dualistic, seeing their own positions as unambiguously good and their opponents' (and those of anyone in between) as unambiguously evil. Both engage in bumper-sticker-like polemics rather than fair-minded debate. Both are socially and politically conservative. And both groups are very, very angry.

This chapter will explore the sociology of this symmetry. Beneath superficial stylistic similarities lie deeper structural and epistemological parallels. I will argue that both the New Atheism and fundamentalism are attempts to recreate authority in the face of crises of meaning in late modernity. My argument will unfold in three steps. First, both the New Atheists and fundamentalists are absorbed in a quest for certainty. The failure of this quest leads, secondly, to a crisis of authority, which in turn, thirdly, involves both in a social and political backlash.

As representatives of the New Atheism, we will examine Dawkins, Harris, and Hitchens, the most widely-read New Atheist texts. Fundamentalism is more complex. It is a worldwide movement with 'family resemblances' in Christianity, Judaism, Islam, Hinduism, and Sikhism (see Ruthven 2004; Armstrong 2000). All are anti-modernist religious movements that arose in the twentieth century, but strictly speaking only those who are Protestant Christians can be called 'fundamentalists.' Since outside Europe and North America these other movements are strongly overdetermined by anti-colonialism and anti-Westernism, for ease of comparison we will restrict our analysis to Protestant Christian fundamentalists. In particular, we will look at Creation Science, fundamentalists opposed to teaching evolution, as the place where epistemological comparisons are most clear.

A QUEST FOR CERTAINTY

To outward appearances, the New Atheism and fundamentalism seem to be polar opposites; indeed, they claim to be each other's worst enemies. Among other things, each claims to give a different account of knowledge and the consequences of knowledge. The place this is most manifest is in how both understand religion, science, and the relationship between them.

All New Atheists agree that science is epistemologically privileged; that is, the methods of science are the ultimate means of determining the truth and falsehood of beliefs. Beyond this they differ on details. Harris's argument closely follows the positivism of August Comte: religion is seen as the outdated explanation of natural events from an ignorant, superstitious past while today science gives us a true account of nature. Although less sophisticated, Hitchens makes a similar argument. Dawkins looks to Darwin rather than Comte. All agree, though, that science has replaced religion. All agree that religious beliefs are deranged, delusional, and dangerous.

What defines Protestant Christian fundamentalism is its belief in biblical inerrancy. As Jerry Falwell (1980, 54) declared: "The Bible is absolutely infallible, without error in all matters pertaining to faith

and practice, as well as in areas such as geography, science, history, etc."
Beyond this, fundamentalists exhibit a significant range of opinions on
the relationship between science and religion. Creation Scientists, in
particular, argue that there is no *real* conflict between them because, as
Ken Ham (2003) of the creationist group Answers in Genesis says, "science, when properly understood, confirms (by being consistent with)
the interpretation based on the Bible. You will find over and over again
that the Bible is confirmed by real science." All fundamentalists agree,
however, that the kind of science advocated by Dawkins et al. leads to
moral degeneracy and disintegration of the social order.

In spite of these obvious differences, there are, nevertheless, a
number of epistemological and structural parallels between the New
Atheists and fundamentalists. Both the New Atheists and fundamentalists are obsessed with intellectual certainty. There are a number of
dimensions of this, but at root for both is a need for authority. Indeed,
as we will see, both the New Atheists and fundamentalists are caught in
what Richard Bernstein (1983, 18) called the 'Cartesian anxiety': *either*
there is some fixed foundation for our knowledge *or* we will be engulfed
by intellectual and moral chaos. This quest for certainty can be seen
most clearly in their emphasis on the propositional nature of knowledge and the normative character of belief.

Both the New Atheists and fundamentalists follow an epistemology
based on what Steve Fuller (2000, xiv-xvii) calls a *geometrical model* of
the relationship between empirical and normative dimensions of
inquiry. This is an hierarchical approach in which inferences are
deduced from first principles. The first principles give certainty of truth
(as in geometry, assuming the proper methods have been followed),
and therefore the empirical is seen as already normatively infused.
Thus for both the New Atheists and fundamentalists, religion is equated
with belief and belief means giving intellectual assent to a series of
propositions. Dawkins (2006, 50) calls this the *God Hypothesis*, the
idea that "the existence of God is a scientific hypothesis like any other"
which can be proven (or disproven) with a greater or lesser degree of
probability. All three texts make their case by progressively demolishing a series of 'arguments for God.' Fundamentalist discourse has a
similar structure. For example, Ken Ham (1999) contends that:

> Creationists and evolutionists, Christians and non-Christians all have
> the *same* evidence—the same facts. Think about it: we all have the same
> earth, the same fossil layers, the same animals and plants, the same
> stars—the facts are all the same. The difference is in the way we *interpret*

the facts. And why do we interpret facts differently? Because we start from different *presuppositions*. These are things that are assumed to be true, without being able to prove them. These then become the basis for other conclusions. *All* reasoning is based on presuppositions (also called *axioms*).

Jonathan Sarfati (1998) adds that: "Logic and reason are far from being incompatible with Biblical Christianity. Rather, they are essential. Without them it is impossible to deduce anything from the true propositions of the 66 books of Scripture, the Christian's final authority." Creation scientists usually make their case by progressively demolishing a series of 'arguments for evolution.' Thus both groups argue in tautologies, that is, their sets of propositions are true by definition and in which, as Herbert Marcuse (1964, 88) said, "the ritualized concept is made immune against contradiction."

Given this shared way of reasoning, both the New Atheists and fundamentalists claim that science and religion must occupy the same 'space,' that is, they both speak to the same reality. Both contemptuously reject the idea that science and religion are, to use Stephen Jay Gould's phrase, "non-overlapping magisteria": that each have their own proper domain that does not impinge upon the other (see Dawkins 2006, 54–61). Neither group distinguishes between belief and faith. For the New Atheists, faith is simply belief without evidence. There are no questions that the scientific method cannot, in principle, answer. (Although Hitchens and Harris concede that there may be questions for which science does *not yet* have the answer). Fundamentalists are equally strong in giving primacy to the cognitive. As James Coppedge (1973, 26) puts it: "It is important, therefore, that we have objective truth by which to check the validity of any inner experiences." They counter the New Atheists by claiming that they do indeed have objective evidence to support their beliefs. Thus Elliot Miller (1985) asserts that: "For Christianity to be true to its historic nature, it must be authoritative, because it has always understood itself to be a product of *revelation*, or acts of divine disclosure. Its legitimacy inevitably hinges on the factuality of this claim." Both groups are of people with single vision. Both see only one dimension of reality.

For both the New Atheists and fundamentalists, beliefs are authoritative, that is, they establish what is normative. Neither group recognizes the authority of community, tradition nor experience (sources of authority for other groups), or at most grants them a subordinate position to belief. Both argue that from belief flows behaviour, so that if beliefs are wrong, behaviour will be wicked. Thus for Harris (2004, 12), "Belief is a lever that, once pulled, moves almost everything else in a person's life…Your beliefs define your vision of the world; they dictate your behavior; they determine your emotional responses to other human beings." Since beliefs are essential to every other aspect of life, one must therefore have correct beliefs. Because religious beliefs are delusions, "*religion poisons everything*" in Hitchens phrase, producing nothing but bigotry and violence. This mirrors Coppedge's (1973, 25) argument: "It is important that one's philosophy of life provide a strong basis for assurance without lingering doubts on the main issues…It makes considerable difference what we believe on this subject. If our existence came about by chance, then we don't have to answer to anyone." Once one opens the door to questioning the inerrancy of scripture, no matter how apparently trivial or esoteric the issue may be, one opens the floodgates to moral chaos.

Thus, for all their outward differences, the New Atheists and fundamentalists mirror each other in their epistemology. Both are engaged in a quest for certainty, for an authoritative foundation that can ground a normative order. Both claim to find certainty through their beliefs, understood as intellectual assent to a series of propositions. Although obviously the content of their beliefs are different, there is symmetry to the structure of how they go about believing. And both groups display a 'Cartesian anxiety,' in that both see deviation from their foundational cognitive order as directly threatening to moral order as well.

Crisis of Authority

Like all quests for certainty, those of the New Atheists and fundamentalists are doomed to fail, and their failure has consequences. For both groups their own inability to establish certainty creates a crisis of authority, a crisis that mirrors the larger crisis of meaning in late modern society. Both groups respond to this dual crisis through social and political backlash. We will begin by looking at the nature of their crisis of authority, which has several dimensions. First, their structure of meaning is based on questionable assumptions, which lead away from empirical reality. Second, in part because of this, they are not able to meet their own epistemic standards. Together, these lead to the third dimension: inherent problems of incommensurability which reveal the nihilism underlying both groups.

At one point Dawkins (2006, 50–51) sets out a 'spectrum of probabilities' of responses to the God Hypothesis, ranging through seven 'milestones' from a strong theist—someone with complete certainty that God exists—to a strong atheist, someone equally certain that God does not. (Dawkins puts himself in category 6, just shy of total certainty, surely a bit of false modesty). His exercise illustrates the questionable assumptions he and the other New Atheists harbour, and which they share with fundamentalists.

The first assumption they make is that religion can be abstracted and reduced to cognitive beliefs separated from culture. Sociologically, this is a one-dimensional and impoverished understanding of religion. While doctrines and beliefs may be an important part of many religious groups (particularly in the Abrahamic traditions), they are by no means the only elements of religion in *any* group. Religion also involves experiences, rituals, traditions, and community, which for many groups are far more important than beliefs. And even cognitive elements may involve myths and stories that cannot be equated with propositional beliefs. Furthermore, to the extent that this assumption describes any group at all, it only applies to the modern world, and there, mostly to Protestantism. Before the coming of modernity it is difficult to speak of 'religion' at all. Lacking modern institutional differentiation, pre-modern religion was suffused throughout culture. People did not *have* a religion, they lived a way of life. And even within modern Christianity, the reduction of religion to belief hardly applies to Roman Catholics, Pentecostals, Orthodox, or many Anglicans or Lutherans. In other words, the New Atheists accept the fundamentalists' self-understanding and assume that it can adequately describe all religion.

Secondly, Dawkins' exercise reveals the assumption that his epistemic model applies to all religious groups, and therefore the full range of religious belief can be placed on a single continuum. In other words, there is only one way of being religious because there is only one way to know. As we have seen, both the New Atheists' and fundamentalists' epistemology is based upon a geometric model. But many, if not most, religious groups, including many mainstream Christians, use an epistemology grounded in a dialectical model. What counts as knowledge for each of these models is quite different. From the standpoint of the geometrical model, the synthetic, compromising, and quite frankly political knowledge that the dialectical model produces could hardly be considered 'knowledge' at all (see Fuller 2000). Indeed, the very existence of dialectical forms of knowledge threatens the certainty to which both these groups cling. Hence the rage directed at mainstream religion by New Atheist and fundamentalist alike. 'Moderate' religious groups are dismissed as not really being religious. To New Atheists they are weak, pitiful examples of 'empty-headed multiculturalism' that only encourage and provide cover for fanaticism (Hitchens 2007b, 33). To fundamentalists they are weak, pitiful examples of 'religious toleration' that only lead the faithful away from God (E. Miller 1985). But in arbitrarily dismissing from discussion the bulk of actual religious practice, the arguments of both New Atheists and fundamentalists become divorced from empirical reality.

In part because these assumptions lead both groups away from empirical reality, neither the New Atheists nor the fundamentalists are able to meet their own epistemic standards. While they claim foundational authority for their way of knowing, neither group actually delivers on these claims.

The New Atheists all build their case on science and therefore bind themselves to some version of the 'scientific method.' Yet, as several commentators have pointed out, their books are shockingly unscientific (see Haught 2008, xii–xv, 17–27; Hedges 2006, 45–67; McGrath and McGrath 2007, 13–15, 34–51, 95–97). Instead of systematically collecting and weighing all relevant evidence to make a judgment based on probabilities, all three of these authors sweep through history and across cultures collecting anecdotes of religious people behaving badly. Any evidence to the contrary is studiously ignored. Major theologians are dismissed in a sentence or, more usually, not mentioned at all. Two examples of this unscientific approach to evidence are particularly egregious. First, anyone who wants to argue for the inherent moral superiority of atheism has to address the rather numerous counter-examples of atheist mass murderers (Robespierre, Stalin, Mao, Pol Pot, etc). Yet all three texts simply dismiss these examples out of hand because they claim these were 'political religions' and therefore not really atheists at all (Dawkins 2006, 272–278; Harris 2004, 79; Hitchens 2007b, 244). Ironically, Dawkins himself is often accused of turning Darwinism into a 'theory of everything' and thus into an implicit religion (see Nelkin 2004; Rose and Rose 2000). Second, if your contention is that religion poisons *everything*, then a case of religious people doing good would, as Karl Popper maintained, falsify your argument. The civil rights movement would seem to provide such a case, but Dawkins (2006, 271–272) and Hitchens (2007b, 273–276) try to explain it away by claiming that Martin Luther King Jr. and the civil rights movement were *not really religious*. This is not even cherry-picking data—it is demonstrably false, as Martin Luther King (MLK), Ralph Abernathy, and others organized through the Southern Christian Leadership Conference (SCLC), while more militant organizations such as the Congress of Racial Equality (CORE) drew on religious principles of non-violence from around the world. Many of MLK's most famous speeches drew heavily on religious imagery. For the New Atheists, epistemic authority rests with science, yet when they build their own arguments they abandon the standards of science, and whether through ignorance, incompetence, or willful intention, invent or reject anything to suit their purposes.

For fundamentalists all authority rests on the inerrancy of scripture. This is usually described as *biblical literalism*, by which most mean *verbal plenary inspiration*, "the doctrine that each word of Scripture is inspired by God, and each word equally so" (E. Miller 1985). Every word of scripture is equally authoritative. So if they were consistent, the Sermon on the Mount would have no more (or less) authority than the War of the Benjaminites (Judges 19–21). But when we examine their hermeneutical practices we find that fundamentalists are no more bound by scripture than the New Atheists are bound by science. Fundamentalist hermeneutics are characterized by prooftexting and harmonization. Prooftexting means picking and choosing texts to support preconceived ideas. It is the theological equivalent of cherry-picking data. Harmonization is the doctrine that "Individual passages of Scripture must always be in harmony with Scripture as a whole" (Hanegraff 2008). In other words, because the Bible is the revealed Word of God, no contradictions, or even different theologies and traditions, are recognized within it. In practice this means that the text is subordinated to doctrine because it is doctrine which determines what 'the scripture as a whole' says. Fundamentalists have developed an elaborate midrash of interpretations to explain away any textual 'contradiction' that is not in accord with their doctrines. In the end, the 'authority of scripture' means whatever a fundamentalist preacher wants it to mean. An example will illustrate this. Jerry Falwell (1980, 12) blessed corporate capitalism (he called it "the free enterprise system") as "part of God's plan." In doing so, he simply ignored those passages in the Bible which are incompatible with capitalism, such as the Jubilee year (which demanded cancellation of all debts and redistribution of wealth—see Leviticus 25), multiple prohibitions against lending money at interest (see for example Nehemiah 5: 10–11, Ezekiel 18: 8–17, and 22: 12), and the example of the early church which held all property in common. Fundamentalists claim their arguments rest on Biblical authority, but in practice they conscript and subordinate the Bible to their theological and political agendas.

Finally, both the New Atheists and fundamentalists are stymied by the incommensurability of their discourse. Both argue that propositional truths—their beliefs—lead to certainty, and that this cognitive certainty leads to moral clarity (usually stated in the reverse—that the absence of cognitive certainty leads to moral chaos). Yet both groups see the society around them persisting in beliefs that they know to be deluded and behaviours that they know to be wicked. Thus the rage the New Atheists direct against religion mirrors the rage fundamentalists direct against secular society.

Incommensurability is an inherent problem for any epistemology grounded in the geometric model. The problem for both groups is that their quest for certainty has failed and in failing has created for each a crisis of authority. Both groups claim that their own position uniquely explains 'reality', yet the assumptions both groups make leads them into abstractions and away from empirical 'facts on the ground'—the historical and lived experiences of actual people. They are caught in what Jürgen Habermas (1990, 78–95) called a *performative contradiction*; that is, their claims to certainty (and thus authority) are undercut by the inability of either group to maintain their own epistemic standards. Thus there is nothing in either position to compel assent from anyone who is not already convinced.

They are left, then, with two incompatible and mutually antagonistic 'foundations.' Nietzsche (1961, 84) described such a situation: "One neighbour never understood another: his soul was always amazed at his neighbour's madness and wickedness. A table of values hangs over every people. Behold, it is the table of its overcomings; behold it is the voice of its will to power." Thus the New Atheism and fundamentalism present us with two totalities: closed, one-dimensional, and incommensurable systems of thought, neither capable of persuading the other nor anyone else not already party to their assumptions, and with no common standard of evaluation. Each can only be maintained by the will to power of its adherents. Beneath the rage and polemics of both groups lies nihilism.

BACKLASH

In the nineteenth century, Evangelical Protestantism was a populist movement, often in the forefront of social reform. Nineteenth-century atheism saw its aim as human liberation. In the twenty-first century the successors to these movements are socially and politically conservative, some might even say incipiently totalitarian. The final symmetry between fundamentalism and the New Atheism is their reactionary politics. There are many examples, but most dramatic is their support for Anglo-American imperialism. Both groups advocate a 'clash of civilizations' with Islam and both have enlisted in the war on terror. Both fundamentalists and New Atheists support Harris' declaration: "We are at war with Islam," although only a few of the most extreme would go along with his proclamation that "the only thing likely to ensure our survival may be a nuclear first strike of our own" (Harris 2004, 109, 129). For both, the fate of Western civilization is at stake. Their rage is backlash.

In order to understand the full dimensions of this backlash, we would have to look at the social and historical context of both the New Atheism and fundamentalism, which would require much more by way of analysis than we can do here. For this chapter, therefore, we will have to limit our discussion to a few issues arising from both groups' social epistemology.

A key question turns on their emphasis on belief. Cartesian anxiety is not unique to either fundamentalism or the New Atheists, so why does it generate such rage in these groups? As we have seen, the Cartesian anxiety exhibited by both New Atheists and fundamentalists arises from the inadequacies of their epistemological model. But it can also be understood as the outcome of a long tradition of social thought. Historically, belief has always been about social control. As Robert Bellah (1970, 221) pointed out, "The effort to maintain orthodox belief has been primarily an effort to maintain authority rather than faith. It was part of a whole hierarchical way of thinking about social control, deeply embedded in traditional society." From Plato's 'noble lies' to Rousseau's 'civil religion,' various doctrines were prescribed as necessary to maintain order among the masses. From the standpoint of those in power, the reason for this is fairly straightforward—one can never tell what is in a person's heart, but one can compel assent to a series of propositions. Belief could be used to police behaviour, with punishment awaiting those that did not believe. The coming of modernity—with its institutional differentiation, mass literacy, disembedded individualism, growing social and cultural pluralism, and continuous, rapid social and economic change—has made this approach to social control problematic. On one hand, the modern world has been characterized by a trend towards internalization of authority, a concern with authenticity that is suspicious of externally imposed constraint (Bellah 1970, 223–224; see also C. Taylor 1991). On the other hand, social and intellectual fragmentation has relativized all belief systems—none can assure authority when all are 'just beliefs.' Both fundamentalism and the New Atheism are, in different ways, attempts to recreate and impose belief as a form of external authority. Behind their rage is fear of losing control.

Thus both groups are at one and the same time an expression of a larger crisis of meaning in late modernity and a protest against it. This is well documented amongst fundamentalists. The current politically active phase of fundamentalism began in the United States in large part in reaction against the civil rights and women's movements of the 1960s and 70s, and feeds off the social breakdown and loss of community documented by Robert Putnam (2000) and others (McPherson et al. 2006; Warren 2006). These churches offer a declining middle class, trapped in the anomie of suburbia and threatened by socioeconomic change, a ready-made system of meaning, an ersatz community, and easily identifiable scapegoats for their problems. Fundamentalism is, in Chris Hedges's (2006, 37–49) words, a "culture of despair."

The New Atheists represent a similar dynamic for a different clientele. These are people steeped in the myth of progress and a utopia of a rational, secular society. Hitchens even ends his book with a call for a 'New Enlightenment.' To many Enlightenment thinkers, as with their atheist successors in the nineteenth and twentieth centuries, religion was seen as an obsolete way of thinking, doomed by the progress of science, while society was seen as progressively and irreversibly becoming more secular. But religion did not disappear and in the last few decades has returned in a bewildering variety of forms—sects, cults, New Age, fundamentalism. The New Atheists are deeply threatened by what they perceive as a society turning away from the Enlightenment values they espouse. Behind their anger is fear.

As a result, what begins as an appeal to *reason*, in the end becomes an appeal to *authority*. Both Hitchens and Dawkins refer to religion as child abuse, with all that means for intervention by the state. Dawkins (2006, 326) favorably quotes psychologist Nicholas Humphrey in saying, "children have a right not to have their minds addled by non-sense, and we as a society have a duty to protect them from it." In say-ing this they reveal the dark side of their Enlightenment values and beliefs, a willingness, in Rousseau's chilling words, "to force people to be free."

So in the end, fundamentalism and the New Atheism are mirror images of each other, sharing deep structural and epistemological par-allels. Both are attempts to recreate meaning for a world that they per-ceive as having lost is way. Both are screams of rage against those that do not conform to their one-dimensional thought. And both are expressions of a will to power that masks its own nihilism through eagerness to enforce its moral values.

THE NEW ATHEISM AND SOCIOLOGY: WHY HERE? WHY NOW? WHAT NEXT?

Stephen Bullivant

INTRODUCTION

In November 2004, the British theologian Alister McGrath published a book bearing what must, in retrospect, be deemed an ill-chosen title: *The Twilight of Atheism*. In it he argued that atheism (understood in the narrow sense of "a principled and informed decision to *reject* belief in God"), which until recently constituted "a vast and diverse empire embracing many kingdoms," has fallen into political, intellectual, and social abeyance (McGrath 2004, xi–xii). McGrath was not alone in this understanding. Also in 2004, Cardinal Poupard (2004, 12), then President of the Vatican's Pontifical Council for Culture, affirmed:

> The Church today is confronted more by indifference and practical unbelief than with atheism. Atheism is in recline throughout the world, but indifference and unbelief develop in cultural milieus marked by secularism. It is no longer a question of a public affirmation of atheism, with the exception of a few countries, but of a diffuse presence, almost omnipresent, in the culture.

That same year, Sam Harris's book *The End of Faith* became a surprise bestseller. Other, similarly-atheistic and similarly-bestselling volumes swiftly followed: Dennett's *Breaking the Spell* (2006); Dawkins' *The God Delusion* (2006); Harris's follow-up *Letter to a Christian Nation* (2007); and Hitchens' *God is Not Great* (2007), to name only the more famous. The most successful among these, Dawkins' book, first appeared in September 2006. Less than two years later, in August 2008, it had already sold over two million copies worldwide (Christine De Blase, assistant to Richard Dawkins, personal communication with author, 20 August 2008). In addition, all four authors—along with, naturally, the ideas which they so eloquently advocate—have received a great deal of popular and media attention.

This recent, unprecedented upsurge of interest in atheism has caught many people (and not only theologians and cardinals) unawares. The situation is, moreover, doubly surprising, for the new atheists have not only achieved remarkable successes in atheistic 'consciousness raising,' which is striking in itself, but they have principally done so in *both* Britain *and* the United States. As we shall see, whatever the two countries' other similarities, their socio-religious cultures are famously contrasting. Whether it is the United States or Britain (often grouped along with several other western European countries) that should be regarded as the 'exceptional' case has been keenly debated by sociologists on both sides of the Atlantic (Davie 2002, 27–53; Bruce 1996, 129–30; Greeley 2004, 197–214). In any case, the genuinely Anglo-American nature both of the authors themselves—Harris and Dennett are American; Dawkins and Hitchens are both British (although Hitchens gained U.S. citizenship in 2007)—and of their popular and media triumphs, itself requires careful explanation.

This mention of socio-religious contexts is of fundamental importance, since in this chapter the new atheism will be treated primarily as a *social*, rather than as an intellectual, phenomenon. From a sociological point of view, the most interesting aspect of the new atheism is not its ideas (however novel, cogent or well-expressed these may or may not be), but the *reception* of those ideas. A great many books and pamphlets have been published during the past two hundred years in Europe and America, lambasting religion and advocating atheism. Prior to *The End of Faith*, however, none of these have sold in great numbers. Of course, the intrinsic qualities of these new books, in terms of both style and substance, are important considerations. But these alone cannot explain their vast sales. *The God Delusion*, for example, is a brilliantly written, entertaining read. Dawkins is, furthermore, a well-respected, famous and popular writer; he could, in all likelihood, achieve respectable sales with a book on *any* subject. But the fact that his book on atheism sold fully twice as many copies in twenty-three months than *The Selfish Gene*—his first, and hitherto most successful book—managed in thirty years (Chadarevian 2007, 31), suggests that there is much more to it. This suspicion is reinforced by the realization that in other western European countries, wholly independently of their Anglo-American counterparts, homegrown atheist authors have also been enjoying conspicuous successes (Onfray [2005] 2007; Scola and Flores d'Arcais 2008). This implies that the new atheism's startling successes are explained, at least in part, in light of wider social and cultural trends in the contemporary west.

This chapter will proceed in three sections. Firstly, the general socio-religious situations of the USA and Britain will be sketched, as the backgrounds against which the new atheism is to be understood. Secondly, specific factors will be identified which may have motivated and/or sustained the new atheists and their (broadly) positive reception in society at large. Some of these will apply in both Britain and the United States; others, only to one or the other. And thirdly, drawing on the most recent statistics available, some tentative remarks will be made regarding the possible mid- to long-term effects that the new atheism may have on the British and American socio-religious climates.

A Double Surprise

Commenting on the new atheism in a recent article, the American atheist philosopher Keith M. Parsons (2008, 52) remarked:

> How odd…to find atheist books recently heading up the best-seller lists and atheists showing up on the TV to make the case for unbelief…A best-selling book is really quite a novelty. Speaking from my own personal experience, an atheist book typically sells in the dozens, and its author will die of old age before seeing a royalty check.

The new atheism's successes have, moreover, shocked even the new atheists themselves. Hitchens' comments in a 2007 article in the U.S.-based secularist magazine *Free Inquiry* (to which all the new atheists regularly contribute) are revealing in this regard. Referring to his own well-received appearance on CNN's *Lou Dobbs Tonight* in 2006, on the evening of the 'National Day of Prayer,' during which his then-new U.S. citizenship was acknowledged with the gift of a Stars and Stripes lapel-badge, Hitchens (2007e, 17) writes:

> [W]hat if I had told you a year ago that one of America's favorite mainstream middle-class broadcasters, obviously relishing the coincidence of the National Day of Prayer, would give a slice of prime time on a major network to an author who is not only an atheist but an antitheist? And would round it off (having displayed one of my less reverent paragraphs on the screen) by deliberately associating atheism with patriotism? Most secularists of my acquaintance would have said it couldn't happen.

But why this sense of astonishment? To put it simply, the United States of America is a society seemingly awash with religion and religious belief. Findings from the World Values Survey for 1999, for example, showed that a full 95.6 percent of Americans believed in God, and 82.5 percent described themselves as a 'religious person.' Outside of religious services, 55.7 percent claimed to pray every day, and 83.6 percent at least once a month or more (World Values Survey 1999). According to the 2005 Baylor Religion Survey, 47.2 percent of Americans regard themselves as 'bible-believing', and 49.2 percent attend church at least once a month (Baylor ISR 2006, 16, 4). As one might expect, there are very few American atheists. The 2001 American Religious Identification Survey suggests that only 0.4 percent of the population would describe themselves as 'atheist' (Kosmin et al. 2001, 13). Self-identification does not, of course, tell the full story: there are many reasons why people who either have no belief in God, or even actively disbelieve in him, might be unwilling to apply this label to themselves (see Bruce 2002, 193). Nevertheless, figures from the 2000 General Social Survey recorded only 3 percent agreeing with the statement 'I don't believe in God', with a further 4.1 percent subscribing to 'I don't know whether there is a God and I don't believe there is any way to find out' (Edgell et al. 2006, 214). Even among the growing numbers of Americans who are religiously unaffiliated—i.e., those who answer 'None' when asked to identify their religion—a relatively high proportion retain some form of religious belief. According to the Baylor Survey, although 'Nones' account for 10.8 percent of the general population, only 37.1 percent of these do not, even sometimes, believe in God or 'a higher power' (Baylor ISR 2006, 8, 12; cf. Hout and Fischer 2002, 178; Hunsberger and Altemeyer 2006, 15–19).

It is not only the low incidence of atheism in America that justifies Parsons' and Hitchens' surprise, however. Hitchens' mention of patriotism alludes to a crucial second factor: the suspicion with which atheism has typically been viewed in American society. A 2006 study by the University of Minnesota found that fully 39.6 percent of Americans regard 'atheists' as a group who 'not at all agree with my vision of American society.' In comparison, 'Muslims' and 'homosexuals', the next most popular choices, were selected by only 26.3 percent and 22.6 percent respectively (Edgell et al. 2006, 218). 'Atheists' also topped the 'I would disapprove if my child wanted to marry a member of this group' category, being chosen by 47.6 percent of those polled. 'Muslims' (33.5 percent) and 'African Americans' (27.2 percent), the second and third placed groups, were again outnumbered. Furthermore, a 1999 Gallup poll showed that only 49 percent of Americans would vote for a 'generally well-qualified' atheist presidential candidate, if nominated by their favoured party. This is markedly less than would vote, *mutatis mutandis*, for a Catholic (94 percent), Jew (92 percent), African

American (92 percent), or homosexual (59 percent) (Edgell et al. 2006, 215). Explanations for this striking stigmatization of atheists are not immediately forthcoming, but arguably centre on two (related) aspects of American socio-religious history and culture: the enduring legacy of Cold War rhetoric, pitting 'Christian America' against 'godless Communism'; and the oft-noted importance of *civil religion* ('Protestant-Catholic-Jew,' 'our shared Judeo-Christian heritage') for constructions of American social, cultural, moral and political identity. These are issues to which we shall return in the second section.

In Britain, atheism's new prominence and visibility is surprising for very different reasons. In the words of Steve Bruce, arguably Britain's most eminent sociologist of religion, "Self-conscious atheism and agnosticism are features of religious cultures...They are postures adopted in a world where people are keenly interested in religion" (Bruce 1996, 58). Bruce certainly has a point. Several studies have underlined the general correlation between religious vigour and outbreaks of self-conscious atheism (Campbell 1971, 124; Black 1983, 154). Vigorous is not, however, a term that is usually applied to contemporary Britain's religious situation. According to data from the 2000 European Values Survey (EVS), if asked a straight 'yes' or 'no' question, 71.8 percent of Britons admit to believing in God (Halman 2001, 86). But when presented with a greater range of options, they generally tend towards the vaguest possible affirmation of there being 'something there' (Bruce 2002, 137; Voas and Crockett 2005, 24). Equally, although 71.8 percent of the population self-identified as 'Christian' in the 2001 census, only 10 percent of these could be found in church on a typical Sunday (Brierley 2000, 27–28). The situation is well illustrated by the statistician Peter Brierley's *Pulling Out of the Nosedive: A Contemporary Picture of Churchgoing*, which was tellingly greeted as a sign of hope by church leaders. Brierley's (2006, 18) figures neither showed that church attendance was rising, nor that it was stable. Instead, for the first time in decades, the *rate of decline* was decreasing: "we are coming out of the nosedive, but no U-turn is yet in sight—we are still dropping."

Britain's strange combination of relatively high levels of (vague) theistic belief and religious self-affiliation on the one hand, and very low levels of orthodox belief and religious practice on the other—also manifest in many other European countries—has been variously described as 'believing without belonging' (Davie 1994) and 'fuzzy fidelity' (Voas 2008). However these phrases are to be understood, contemporary Britons certainly do not *appear* to inhabit 'a world where people are keenly interested in religion.' And indeed, it is precisely the *lack* of real interest in religion, one way or the other, that Bruce and others cite as proof of Britain's near-thorough secularization. That does not mean, of course, that there are no atheists in Britain. According to the 2000 EVS, for example, 5 percent of the population would describe themselves as a 'convinced atheist,' and when asked a simple 'yes' or 'no' question, 28.2 percent claim not to believe in God (Halman 2001, 81, 86). Prior to recent developments, however, there has been no indication that these respondents take their unbelief any more seriously than the rest of society takes their belief. Certainly, Britain's two main atheistic societies, the National Secular Society and the British Humanist Association, have never attracted large numbers of members, or attracted much notice. To again quote Bruce (2002, 42), "you have to care too much about religion to be irreligious." As such, the sudden rise of a militant and (in terms of media interest and book sales) highly successful British atheism, at exactly the same time as British Christianity had reached what church leaders *hope* will prove its lowest ebb, evidently requires a great deal of explanation.

Finally, it is worth underlining the contrast between Britain and the United States regarding atheism's social acceptability. While the word 'atheist' may still cause disquiet in certain British circles, unbelief itself carries few negative associations. If anything, Britons reserve more suspicion for the seemingly *too* religious than for those who are not religious at all (Levitt 1996, 107–108). Atheism is, moreover, no obvious impediment to gaining political office. This is amply attested by the 110-strong Parliamentary Humanist Group, comprising members of both Houses, and the fact that Nick Clegg, the leader of the Liberal Democrats (Britain's third largest political party), has publicly admitted to not believing in God. According to an October 2008 poll commissioned by the Christian think-tank *Theos*, when asked 'if all their other qualities were acceptable to you, would you vote for a political leader, such as a prime minister or a president, who was an atheist?' 75 percent of respondents answered 'yes.' This is the same percentage as would vote for a homosexual, and 3 percent more than would vote for a Muslim. Admittedly, this is significantly less than the 91 percent who would vote for a Christian. It is worth noting, however, that the term 'Christian' admits of a vague cultural sense—which is how most of the 2001 census' 71.8 percent of 'Christians,' a clear majority of whom do not attend church or believe in a personal God, presumably understood it. The term 'atheist', on the other hand, arguably implies a level of interest in, or conviction regarding, religious matters that 'Christian' generally avoids. Certainly, it is noteworthy that Tony Blair consciously avoided speaking of his own Christian faith while Prime Minister. As he put it in a 2007 interview, drawing an obvious contrast to American politics: "You talk about it in our system and, frankly, people do think you're a nutter" (BBC 2007).

Explaining the New Atheism

Thus far, explanations of the new atheism phenomenon have generally focused on the personal motivations of the new atheist authors themselves. These have typically identified two overriding factors: the impact of Islamist terrorism, and the growing influence of Creationism and/or Intelligent Design theory (R. Stewart 2008, 6–7). The importance of both of these is undeniable, and they duly recur time and again throughout the new atheists' writings. It is no coincidence that Sam Harris began writing *The End of Faith* the day after 9/11. Nor is it a coincidence that Dawkins and Dennett are both established Darwinist theorists and educators. According to Dawkins (2007c, 230), for example: "A fierce religious war is systematically being waged against the values of scientific truth, and the frontline trenches—by the enemy's choice—are in the field of biological education and specifically Darwinism."

A more interesting question, however, is not what has motivated the new atheists themselves, but what might account for their startling and unprecedented popular and media reception? Or to put it another way, what has contributed to the 'social nerve' that the new atheists have so evidently 'touched'? The same two factors mentioned above loom large here also. Both Britain and the United States have, of course, suffered greatly from terrorist attacks, and the spectre of future ones continues to haunt. The Intelligent Design movement continues to gain political and educational momentum in America. Despite a recent handful of well-publicized skirmishes concerning 'faith schools', however, it seems inconceivable that it could make significant inroads in Britain or the rest of Western Europe. Although these are, therefore, undeniably major factors in the popular and media interest in atheism, it is however unlikely that they are the only ones. In what follows, a number of other potential factors will be briefly delineated and explained. As will become clear, some of these are relevant to both Britain and America; others only to one or the other.

It is worth remembering that *The God Delusion* is *not*, in fact, the most successful book in recent years with an anti-religious theme. By a very large margin, that distinction belongs to Dan Brown's 2003 novel *The Da Vinci Code*. While *The God Delusion* sold over two million copies worldwide in its first two years, *The Da Vinci Code* had sold over forty million copies in its first three (Times 2006). The comparison may seem (and to a certain extent is) a strange one. After all, *The Da Vinci Code* is a work of fiction—an entertaining, fast-paced, page-turning thriller—and not much more besides. But this only raises the question why it has been so phenomenally successful. Central to the book's plot is the idea that Christ was not the son of God, and that through a combination of suppression and self-deception the (Catholic) Church succeeded in keeping this secret. The Church, represented by members of the lay ecclesial movement Opus Dei, will go to any length, including theft and murder, to safeguard the wealth and power it has accrued through perpetuating this lie. Needless to say, Dawkins avoids such flights of fancy (although like Brown, his grasp of ecclesiastical history is by no means impeccable).

Nevertheless, it is not too improbable to suppose that behind the vast sales of both books there lies a diffused, societal cynicism concerning organized religion (the Catholic Church being, of course, a paradigmatic example). This cynicism is, for example, both fuelled by, and expressed in the popular fascination regarding, church sex scandals—pedophile Catholic priests (and subsequent cover-ups), and the Ted Haggard drugs and male prostitution scandal, being obvious examples (Gau 2005, 23–24). Also relevant here is the widespread distrust, common to both Europe and America, in all authorities and institutions (Dogan 2002), religious ones included. According to the EVS, for example, 45.9 percent of Britons have 'not very much' confidence in 'the church,' while 19.7 percent have 'none at all' (Halman 2001, 184–199). This culture of (fairly low-level) cynicism and mistrust towards religious organizations might easily result in a general receptivity to witnessing it being entertainingly ridiculed and attacked. Certainly, this would go a long way to explaining, in conjunction with the novel's intrinsic merits and a number of other factors, *The Da Vinci Code*'s successes. And if *The Da Vinci Code*'s, then why not also *The God Delusion*'s?

In the previous section, I noted the puzzling fact of the new atheism's impact in secularized, religiously indifferent Britain. This situation might, however, be partially explicable in light of a phenomenon first identified by José Casanova in his influential 1994 study *Public Religions in the Modern World*. His central contention was that although the secularization of modernized societies is a fact, this has not inexorably led, as some theorists had supposed, to the privatization of religion. On the contrary, he notes:

> Religion in the 1980s 'went public' in a dual sense. It entered the 'public sphere' and gained, thereby, 'publicity.' Various 'publics'—the mass media, social scientists, professional politicians, and the 'public at large'—suddenly began to pay attention to religion. The unexpected public interest derived from the fact that religion, leaving its assigned place in the private sphere, had thrust itself into the public arena of moral and political contestation. (Casanova 1994, 3)

Despite having lost many of their members and much of their (direct) influence, modern religions have not only retained, but have in some cases greatly intensified, their public presence and profile. For example, Casanova (1994, 161) cites the emergence of the New Christian Right: "A well-organized, vociferous minority, whose unexpected mobilization caught everybody by surprise but whose very loosely defined potential constituency never reached 20 percent of the population, had miraculously become, in the minds of many, a threatening majority."

Arguably, something broadly similar is at work in contemporary Europe. Certainly, sociologists have begun to speak more and more of the 'new visibility of religion' (Hoelzl and Ward 2008). In Britain, where only a small minority of the population is actively religious, religiously themed stories frequently make the newspaper front pages. This reflects *both* a willingness of religious leaders and groups to enter public debate, *and* a persisting interest in religious matters on the part of the media and the public at large. The latter was also reflected, for example, in the unprecedented attention given to the death and funeral of Pope John Paul II, and the subsequent election of Benedict XVI, in April 2005 (Davie 2006, 106). Entries for religious studies courses, both at school and university level, have also been increasing for a number of years (Reisz 2008). And as several scholars have indicated, evidence for this growing interest in religion predates 9/11 (Hoelzl and Ward 2008, 1–2). This new visibility of (and interest in) religion also helps us to understand the new visibility of (and interest in) atheism in two ways.

First, it goes some way to explaining how, notwithstanding statistics for church attendance and religious belief, early twenty-first century Britain might still be construed as a 'world where people are keenly interested in religion'—albeit in a 'detached' and limited manner compatible with secularization. Second, it contributes to the feeling of panicked *urgency*, explicit in the writings of Dawkins and others, and arguably implicit in the high levels of interest and sales that their books have generated. For example, judging by literature distributed by the National Secular Society, of which both Dawkins and Hitchens are Honorary Associates, one might think that Britain was on the brink of an imminent theocratic take-over: at the time of writing, a banner advertisement on the front page of its website proclaims, 'Join the National Secular Society... and protect YOUR freedom!' Needless to say, to the nation's handful of regular churchgoers—not to mention their increasingly ignored church leaders—such suggestions appear risible. This disconnect between appearance and reality, however, makes considerable sense of the new atheists' unexpected impact.

The previous paragraph primarily relates to the British situation, and perhaps solves the puzzle of why strong avowals of atheism should suddenly resonate in so irreligious a society. The specifically American puzzle is, however, rather different: Why, in so religious a society, have strong avowals of atheism not *previously* been more popular? In addition to the ones already mentioned, two factors are important here. Recall the findings from the above-cited Minnesota study: 'atheists' are the least trusted social grouping in American society. What is more, these conclusions are well supported by other statistics and anecdotal evidence (Hunsberger and Altemeyer 2006, 55; Dawkins 2006, 44–45; R. Stewart 2008, 1–2). The realization of this fact motivates a major theme for several of the New Atheists, the need for 'consciousness-raising,' 'Atheist Pride,' and the 'coming out of closet atheists' (Dawkins 2006, 4; Dennett 2006, 245). This terminology intentionally echoes that used in previous notably successful campaigns of feminists and gay rights activists. As Colin Koproske (2006, 49) put it, responding to the Minnesota study:

> Just as tolerance for Muslims, Jews, immigrants, and gays tends to be positively correlated with exposure to diversity, acceptance of and sympathy toward an atheistic worldview will rely on Americans' exposure to atheists and their opinions...when we hear people say that they've never met an atheist, or even that they're surprised anyone could hold such an extreme view, we're seeing firsthand the effects of our silence.

The consciousness of being a marginalized and misunderstood minority in American society would thus account for the new atheists' vocal declarations of unbelief, as well as the particular attention all of them give to the alleged superiority of atheistic morality. By the same token, it would also explain the enthusiasm with which they appear to have been received by America's non-believing minority. Significantly, the new atheists' books are not as *negative* as is often supposed, or their titles might imply. They in fact contain much of an emphatically constructive, life-affirming nature. Undoubtedly for many in American society harbouring religious doubts, being assured that one can indeed 'be an atheist who is happy, balanced, moral, and intellectually fulfilled' (Dawkins 2006, 1) would be immensely empowering.

The Minnesota study does not, however, reflect any radically new situation; atheists have long been mistrusted in American society. A 1966 study found, for example, that 61 percent of Americans thought that 'an acknowledged atheist should not be permitted to teach in a public high school,' and 35 percent thought that 'an acknowledged atheist's book ought to be removed from a public library.' According to a mid-1980s Gallup poll, only 24 percent of American Catholics, and 23 percent of American Protestants, would feel 'friendly and at ease' in the company of an atheist (Stark and Bainbridge 1985, 63, 93). One might, therefore, have expected American atheists to 'come out' much sooner. This raises the obvious question: why now, but not before?

Cold War rhetoric was mentioned in the previous section as a plausible reason for lingering current suspicion towards atheists. And indeed, perhaps until very recently, the mental image of an atheist for most Americans would almost certainly have been Madalyn Murray O'Hair, the litigious founder of American Atheists, Inc. O'Hair, who famously had prayers banned from public schools, was a self-confessed socialist, and even tried defecting with her family to the Soviet Union (who refused her). (Compare this with the British 'public atheists'— Bertrand Russell, A. J. Ayer, Antony Flew—all Oxbridge intellectuals, and thus broadly respectable 'Establishment' figures). In light of this, the identification of atheism with un-Americanness was an easy one to make, and overwhelming social pressures would militate against open avowals of personal unbelief.

But the Cold War ended nearly two decades ago, and while lingering suspicions still remain, 'coming out' as an atheist is thus no longer a socially inconceivable option. Furthermore, America's new enemy, Islamist terrorism, is obviously *not* atheistic. In fact, the 2001 attacks on the World Trade Center have enabled the emergence of a novel (but hitherto overlooked) phenomenon: American *patriotic* atheism. Harris makes plain his belief that it is religious faith *in general*, and not a minority interpretation of Islam, that caused the atrocity—and thus, that global atheism would have prevented it and countless others. Both Harris and Hitchens have defended American military involvement in Iraq and Afghanistan. What is more, Hitchens (2005) has written in defense of Guantanamo Bay, while Harris (2004, 192–199) openly supports the use of torture in the interrogation of terrorism suspects, at least in certain situations. In both print and broadcast media, therefore, two *atheists* are outspoken and loyal defenders of America's most controversial defence and foreign policies. Such linking of atheism with American patriotism, highlighted by Hitchens in the passage quoted earlier, is a significant development. It also invites comparisons—although not ones that the new atheists might choose to emphasize—with the gradual acceptance of Catholics in American society during the Cold War. The staunch anti-Communism of the American hierarchy, led by New York's Cardinal Spellman, greatly helped assuage suspicions regarding the un-American nature of Catholicism, and made possible the eventual election of a Catholic president in John F. Kennedy (Casanova 1994, 183). Although it seems unlikely to result in an atheist president in the foreseeable future, the novel situation of a self-consciously patriotic American atheism has nonetheless, in combination with some or all of the others mentioned above, made possible the sudden, unexpected rise of the new atheism.

WHAT HAPPENS NEXT?

Is the new atheism merely a media-hyped flash in the pan, soon to be forgotten? Or will it have a profound and lasting effect on the social and religious landscapes of Britain, America, and beyond? Might it be the first fruits of a great, atheistic awakening in the western world? Or perhaps the death-throes of an ideology in its twilight years? At the present time, of course, it is impossible to tell. Less than five years since the publication of *The End of Faith*, any predictions regarding the mid- to long-term impact of the new atheism can only be of the most cautious sort. Even its immediate impact is very difficult to quantify just yet. Due to the complex and time-consuming nature of large-scale data collection, comprehensive statistical information may not appear for some time. But as long as this is kept in mind, it may nevertheless be worthwhile to conclude this essay by offering a small number of tentative speculations. In part, these will be based on some admittedly limited statistics which are already available. These seem to offer *clues* as to the possible effects of the new atheism—clues that may well, in the fullness of time, turn out to have been red herrings. For the most part, however, the following predictions rest on personal (and arguably tendentious) judgments and interpretations. If nothing else, it will be interesting to see quite how wrong they will turn out to be.

As a preliminary to this, it is worth clarifying that throughout this article mention of the new atheists' 'popularity' and 'success' has been intended in the easily quantifiable, and thus fairly superficial, sense of book sales and media coverage. Naturally, these do not necessarily imply success in terms of the new atheists' stated goals. Needless to say, two million copies of *The God Delusion* sold certainly does not entail two million copies read; and still less, two million people convinced and converted to Dawkinsian atheistic humanism. And certainly, in addition to overwhelming anecdotal evidence, statistics already suggest that a significant proportion of the book's readers, as one would expect, are religious believers interested to know what all the fuss is about, and who are not swayed by the book's claims (Bullivant 2008b, 366–367).

That said, it seems certain that the vast sales and interest generated by the new atheists will indeed produce a notable increase in the numbers of Britons and Americans who, for example, do not believe in the existence God, regard themselves as religious 'nones,' and/or self-identify as 'atheists.' Undoubtedly these effects will be most marked in Britain, where a large proportion of the population already exhibits only weak, residual levels of religious belief and practice, typically accompanied by indifference, apathy, and a vague agnosticism (Voas and Crockett 2005). And indeed, *The God Delusion* at least, explicitly and implicitly, is largely directed towards such people (R. Stewart 2008, 7). As Dawkins (2006, 1) writes on the very first page of the preface:

> I suspect—well, I am sure—that there are lots of people out there who have been brought up in some religion or other, are unhappy in it, don't believe it, or are worried about the evils that are done in its name; people who feel vague yearnings to leave their parents' religion and wish they could, but just don't realize that leaving is an option. If you are one of them, this book is for you.

And later in the book (2006, 46), a subsection bears the title 'The Poverty of Agnosticism.' Thus far, a handful of statistics appear to bear out this supposition. According to the European Social Survey, the number of Britons who identified themselves as belonging to a religion decreased from 50.7 percent in 2004 to 48.6 percent in 2006 (in addition to *The God Delusion*'s publication in September, Dawkins' much-discussed two-part documentary *The Root of All Evil?* was broadcast that January). In the same period, the percentage describing themselves as 'not at all religious' increased from 11.3 percent to 17.3 percent. Furthermore, the British Humanist Association's membership has increased by an impressive 103.5 percent in four years, from 3713 members in January 2004 to 7556 in January 2008 (Bob Churchill, BHA Membership Manager, personal communication with author, 11 December 2008). In roughly the same period, the number of humanist ceremonies (funerals, weddings, baby namings) performed by BHA-accredited celebrants increased by 27.9 percent from 5734 in 2004 to 7334 in 2007 (Tana Wollen, BHA Head of Ceremonies, personal communication with author, 12 November 2008).

From the United States also, statistics show a recent sharp increase in the (albeit still small) numbers of college freshman who are religious 'nones,' and who never attend religious services (Downey 2007). Although it would be difficult to prove that such increases are causally related to the new atheism, this assumption seems a reasonable one. At the very least, there is strong evidence for at least some people becoming atheists on the strength of reading *The God Delusion* (see, for example, the 'Converts' Corner' at RichardDawkins.net). In Britain at least, this phenomenon seems to be most evident among former (self-described) 'agnostics' (Bullivant 2008b, 366).

These predictions that the new atheism will produce greater numbers of self-ascribing atheists and non-believers, that this effect will be less marked in the United States than in Britain, but that also (as discussed in the previous section) the social stigma attached to atheism in the United States will decrease noticeably, are arguably not much more than common sense. They are, I suppose, exactly what one might expect. Consider, therefore, some rather more counterintuitive British statistics. Again according to the European Social Survey, the percentage of Britons describing themselves as 'very religious' *also* increased, from 4 percent in 2004 to 4.6 percent in 2006. The British Social Attitudes Survey shows that, among those who regard themselves as belonging to a religion, the number who attends religious services (at least) once a week increased from 11.81 percent in 2004 to 14.19 percent in 2006—the highest figure for over a decade. Recent figures from the Catholic Church in England and Wales, furthermore, show notable increases in the number of vocations to the priesthood: 24 in 2003, 27 in 2004, 31 in 2005, 44 in 2006, 44 in 2007 (Judith Eydman, National Office for Vocation, personal communication with author, 7 January 2009).

Admittedly, these statistics are even less clear-cut than the ones presented in the previous paragraph. *Prima facie*, however, British religion is undergoing a (however slight) resurgence. Paradoxically, I would argue that this too is an unintended effect of the new atheism. As mentioned previously, Britain's socio-religious culture has for a number of decades been characterized by a diffused indifference. Suddenly however, whether or not one holds religious beliefs, the content and significance of those beliefs is being presented in television and radio programs, newspapers, and bestselling books as a question of crucial importance. For some, this will be the catalyst for them deciding that they are not, in fact, religious people. For others, it will prompt a more thorough consideration of the religious beliefs that they do indeed hold, and hence perhaps a create (re)new(ed) commitment to their religious tradition. This effect can be seen, for example, in the proliferation of books either critiquing, or otherwise responding to, the new atheism (and especially Dawkins) from a religious perspective. The profusion of these books suggests that they are selling in good numbers (relative to the usual sales of the religious book market, at least). But who is buying them all? Aside from a few sold to curious atheists, the vast majority are presumably bought by religious believers who, although they may feel challenged by the new atheists, believe (or hope) that their arguments are not insuperable. For a significant number of these believers, then, *The God Delusion* (or whichever book) may eventually lead to the strengthening, rather than the abandoning, of religious faith and practice.

Considering all of these (highly speculative) predictions together, therefore, it seems reasonable to think that, in Britain at least, the new atheism will result in *both* more non-believers and self-ascribing atheists, *and* more committed, practicing religious (and predominantly Christian) believers. That said, however, the former increase should outweigh the latter by a considerable margin. The latter effect is, however, likely to be noticeable only in Britain (and in similarly secu-larized European countries), rather than in the already religiously robust United States. Here, then, one might expect to see a moderate, but by no means overwhelming, increase in those claiming non-belief and non-religion, accompanied by a significant increase in the social acceptability of being an atheist.

THE NEW ATHEISM AND THE SECULARIZATION THESIS

Michael Ian Borer

INTRODUCTION

Many post-Enlightenment social theorists predicted the demise of religion in modern Western society. Theorists of many persuasions, ranging from Karl Marx to Sigmund Freud, expected religion to fade away as, first, the natural sciences and then the social sciences, propelled by instrumental rationality and reason, came to dominate ways of thinking in contemporary, industrialized society. Others, who interpreted religion in more functional terms, foresaw the disappearance of religion in its familiar forms, replaced by 'socially constructed' worldviews based on non-supernaturalistic and non-transcendental foundations. In fact, Auguste Comte, known for coining the term 'sociology,' sought to invent a new religion, 'The Religion of Humanity,' founded upon the rational and scientific foundations of the new science of sociology in order to fill the void. Emile Durkheim redirected the location of the sacred to society itself, while envisioning the beginnings of a new functional equivalent to religion emerging from the ideals and values of the French Revolution. Max Weber saw social life becoming dominated by bureaucracies that would, in the end, leave people 'disenchanted' in a world devoid of spirit. Taken together, these ideas comprise the once almost universally accepted and now hotly debated and doubted *secularization thesis*.

In this chapter, I examine the debates surrounding the rise and decline of the secularization thesis and discuss the ways that the emergence of the New Atheists provides evidence that both supports and contradicts the secularization thesis. Placing the New Atheists within the ongoing debate about secularization sheds light on this new 'movement' and will ultimately show that the New Atheists are not necessarily products of secularization but are, instead, purveyors of it. The typically belligerent, impassioned, and overly hostile tropes of the New Atheism's Four Horsemen—Richard Dawkins, Daniel Dennett, Sam Harris, and Christopher Hitchens—show that religion has retained an extraordinary amount of power in the modern world. If we lived in a secular world, their writings would be trite and unnecessary. That is, there would be no need for such writings or such a movement if most people were not religious in some way or another. There would be no need for their ferocious attacks on religion if there were no opposition. As their collective vigilance and vehemence shows, that opposition is strong, and because it is so strong, the New Atheists, armed with their sceptical faith in science, fight back even harder.

A History of the Secularization Thesis

Over the past one hundred and fifty years, the secularization thesis has, like religion itself, undergone a number of transformations in both form and content (see Swatos and Christiano 1999). For the purposes of this discussion, we can delineate three separate phases in which the secularization thesis has sequentially been supported, modified, and opposed. It should be noted that, like any history of ideas, this delineation is only one way of contextualizing theories about secularization. Indeed others have offered more detailed versions than the one offered here, delving deeply into the unsettled and often unsettling waters of the secularization thesis (see Dobbelaere 1981; Tschannen 1991; Chaves 1994; Goldstein 2009). The periodization presented here, however, offers the reader an introduction of sorts that will help contextualize the current influx of the New Atheist polemics.

After showing the career of the secularization thesis, we will be able to see how the New Atheists' writings are, in many ways, a throwback to the First Phase of the theory's development. This throwback creates an obstacle to understanding what is new about the New Atheism. Furthermore, we will see how the New Atheists have repackaged older ideas with new terminology and with an ardent devotion to their beliefs. Their collective and individual impassioned writings differ from any of the social scientists writing about religion and secularization with regard to their intentions and motivations. Instead of presenting their work as scholarship that seeks to understand the state and role of religion in contemporary society, their writings are treatises on the way the people *should* relate to, and ultimately dismiss, religion.

The First Phase: Secularization Theory and the Modern World

The first phase encompasses the original laying out of the foundations of secularization as a process by which the presence of traditional religion would decrease, perhaps even to the level of full extinction. The writings of the early founders of sociology mentioned above (Comte, Durkheim, Weber) and their relative contemporaries (Marx, Freud, Toennies) mark the first phase with a distinct air of boldness and conceit. Rodney Stark and William Sims Bainbridge make clear in their book entitled *The Future of Religion* (1985)—a less than subtle poke at Freud's well known work on the evolutionary/developmental disappearance of religion entitled *The Future of an Illusion*—that secularization was accepted as a given for most Western intellectuals.

> The most illustrious figures in sociology, anthropology, and psychology have unanimously expressed confidence that their children, or surely their grandchildren, would live to see the dawn of a new era in which, to paraphrase Freud, the infantile illusions of religion would be outgrown. (Stark and Bainbridge1985, 1)

Perhaps constructed more as an ideological prophecy than as a scientific prediction, the first phase of the secularization thesis was intricately connected to the grand social changes that were taking place while these theorists opined about the future of religion.

Early social scientists were acutely aware of the tremendous transformation that was taking place in the world (especially in Europe) from the Enlightenment forward. Collectively, their goal was to explain what was happening and why. Much of their theorizing can be incorporated under what came to be known as a theory of modernization whereby the world was rapidly growing in complexity and sophistication. Anthony Giddens, a seminal contemporary scholar of modernization theory, characterizes the modern world as 'a post-traditional order' (1991, 2; also see Giddens, 1994). According to Giddens, modernity's main features include: industrialism based upon machine production, capitalism based upon commodity production and the commodification of labor power, a massive increase in organizational power (i.e., bureaucracy), increased use of instrumental reason determined by efficiency or cost-benefit analysis, the control of the means of violence and the industrialization of war (weapons of mass destruction), and the development of the 'nation-state' (the basic referent for what we call 'society') (1990, 15; 1991, 5). For Giddens these factors help to generate the characteristic sense of dynamism in modern social institutions, in the sense that the modern world is a 'runaway world.'

Giddens asserts that there have been two images of modernity that have dominated sociological discourse: the first, taken from

Weber, is that of the 'iron cage,' the bureaucratization of the life-world (*Lebenswelt*); the second, taken from Marx, is that of modernity as an impeding monster that, while irrational in the form of capitalism, can be tamed in the form of utopian socialism. Alongside these, Giddens proposes his own image, that of the "juggernaut—a runaway engine of enormous power which, collectively as human beings, we can drive to some extent but which also threatens to rush out of control and which could rend itself asunder" (1990, 137–139). This juggernaut rolls over anything in its way, including traditional ideas that are based on pre-scientific beliefs about the world and our place in it. More to the point, religion is trampled beneath the wheels of modernity's science- and technology-fueled juggernaut.

Modernization changed the basic fabric of social organization. As such, secularization was thought to be, from early on, intimately connected to the social changes taking place in the modern world. As the process of modernization was occurring, so to was secularization, at least in the way it is explained by Bryan Wilson: "as the process by which religious institutions, actions, and consciousness lose their social significance" (1982, 150). By 'social,' Wilson means society at large rather than on an individual basis, though he concedes that with the decline of religion's importance in society as the primary organizing instrument and source of meaning, men and women may "gain psychological or individual independence of it" (1982, 151). The First Phase of secularization theory, then, is marked by an overall belief that the social forces behind the onset of modernity would eventually, unrelentingly and unrepentantly, lead to a religionless society.

THE SECOND PHASE: SECULARIZATION AND PLURALISM

Beginning in the 1950s, becoming *au courant* in 1960s, and maintaining vitality into the 1980s, the secularization theory was simultaneously invigorated and challenged. New sociological findings and theories emerged to contend with the social changes of the post-World War II era. Will Herberg's seminal text *Protestant-Catholic-Jew* (1955) became a touchstone for many who sought to connect secularization to other social and cultural processes. Herberg acknowledged that American Protestants, Catholics, and Jews were all Bible-based Abrahamic faiths that inherently had some things in common. More importantly, for Herberg, was the fact that each religion was presumed to possess the same 'spiritual values' of 'the American Way of Life,' by which he meant a soft-hearted faith in democracy (political, economic, and religious) combined with a more robust faith in idealism, activism, and moral conviction. Their original, conventional religious beliefs had morphed into the dominant secular values of the nation. As such, religion had leveled out across a common plane, decreasing the power of any religious authority and thwarting the possibility of a lone religious monopoly outside of a somewhat ambiguous 'exceptional' Americanism.

The issue that lies at the base of Herberg's discussion is pluralism. The issue of secularization and pluralism has been discussed in most detail by Peter Berger. Berger emerged in the 1960s as one of the most prominent and outspoken proponents of the secularization thesis, defining secularization as "the process by which sectors in society and culture are removed from the domination of religious institutions and symbols" (1967, 101). This process is a consequence of living with and near others who hold different beliefs about the ways the world works, where it comes from, and what we're supposed to do while we're here. For Berger, a pluralistic society will inevitably become secularized because the presence and availability of alternative worldviews prevents any one religion from dominating the beliefs and values of society. In effect, exposure to alternative worldviews tears an individual's, a community's, and a society's 'sacred canopy'. In a social setting where an individual can choose one religion or another, the 'plausibility structure' of each religion will become more flimsy. That is, when religion is presented as a choice in a pluralistic society, then all religious worldviews will lose their plausibility as being the True religion. As such, religion, as an institution that provides meaning and order, will lose its authority and individuals will likely search elsewhere for answers, and for community.

It would be a mistake, however, to assume that the secularization thesis was not without its early detractors. Providing a useful survey of the collective idea of secularization and showing how the concepts had been used in a number of very different ways—though with some overlap and consensus but also used in contradictory ways—Larry Shiner was the first to advocate abandoning the secularization thesis (1967). After giving a history of the thesis, beginning with its Latin roots and its use in the negotiations of the seventeenth-century Peace of Westphalia, Shiner distinguishes six meanings or uses of secularization and discusses problems with each. First, secularization refers to the decline of religion whereby previously accepted religious symbols, doctrines, and institutions, have lost their prestige and significance, ultimately culminating in a society without religion. Shiner notes that there are two problems associated with secularization as 'decline' of religiosity: where and when was the supposedly religious age, and how can we measure such a decline (1967, 210)?

The second use of secularization refers to greater conformity with *this* world in which attention is turned away from the supernatural and toward the exigencies of this life and its problems. Religious concerns and groups become indistinguishable from social concerns and non-religious groups. Shiner has problems with creating a false dichotomy between this world and other world concerns due to theological con-notations. Such a dichotomy masks more than it explains in criticizing Herberg for using such distinctions to support a secularized 'common faith' (Shiner 1967, 211).

Third, secularization has been applied to explain the separation of society from religion. Here, religion withdraws to its own separate sphere and becomes a matter for private life, thus acquiring a wholly inward character and ceasing to influence any aspect of social life out-side of religion itself. Following Talcott Parsons, Shiner argues that 'dif-ferentiation,' which is a key aspect of modernization, is a better way to understand the separation of religion from other social spheres and institutions (1967, 214). This is consistent with the notion of 'laiciza-tion,' whereby "religion becomes just one institutional sphere among others, enjoying no necessary primary status" (Chaves 1994, 757). Fourth, religious beliefs and institutions may mutate into non-religious forms, as beliefs, behaviours, and institutions that were once thought to be grounded in divine power become purely human phenomena. Shiner sees problems with this 'transposition thesis:' it is methodologi-cally difficult to identify and measure because of the uncertainty of the origins of almost any belief or idea (1967, 215).

The fifth meaning relates to the desacralization or 'disenchantment' of the world, which was first given its theoretical wings by Weber (1946, 139). The world loses its sacred character as humans and nature become the object of rational-causal explanation and manipulation in which the supernatural is extricated. Shiner writes that "The inherent prob-lem with the desacralization view is its assumption that religion is inextricably bound up with an understanding of the world as perme-ated by sacred powers" (1967, 216). He then uses examples from Judaism and Christianity that show how even religious doctrines give power to humans over the world rather than to supernatural entities, beings, or forces. Finally, the sixth use of secularization might simply mean the movement from a 'sacred' to a 'secular' society in the sense of an abandonment of any commitment to traditional values and practices, the acceptance of change, and the founding of all decisions and actions on a rational and pragmatic basis. This view goes well beyond understanding religion's place in society and is more about general views of social change.

Clearly the secularization thesis has taken on many forms and many issues related to the role, use, and practice of religion in the modern world. Though Shiner's critical analysis was on the margins at the time, along with David Martin's views of secularization (1969), it opened up a number of avenues for scholars to challenge and critique the secularization thesis.

The Third Phase: Religious Economies and the Death of the Secularization Thesis

Like any '-ation' word, secularization implies movement, transformation, and change. Understanding secularization as a process leads inherently to questions of where or how it started and where or how the modern world is different from the past. Is there any reason for us to assume that religion in modernity is unique? As Shiner noted, there has been, and still is, much dispute over whether or not contemporary society is less religious than the past. The 'Age of Faith' may be as much a myth as the 'Secular Age.' Mary Douglas addressed this issue, condemning 'uncritical nostalgia' for religious adherence in the past:

> Let us note at once that there is no good evidence that a high level of spirituality has generally been reached by the mass of mankind in the past times, and none at all that their emotional and intellectual lives were necessarily well integrated by religion. Some people have been religious in a commercial way, buying and selling occult powers. Sometimes they withdrew into the desert. Sometimes they focused all their religious energy on celebration of the social calendar, sometimes on obtaining states of trance. Given all this variety of religious life in our past, when we also recall that charlatanism, skepticism, and forsaken churches are also part of our heritage, we dare to question the whole modernization argument. (Douglas 1982, 29)

Douglas's statement is important because she is attempting to dispel the falsehood of past piety that has plagued some interpretations of contemporary religiosity, namely, those interpretations that support the secularization thesis. She wants to move the agenda away from debating whether or not religious beliefs have decreased, toward more pertinent empirical issues. Such issues, which include questions about how and why some religions grow (especially during a time of supposed secularization) and others decline, were picked up by a collection of scholars with the pronounced intention to devise the Third Phase of the secularization thesis.

A loose band of scholars who are often labeled collectively as the 'new paradigm' or 'religious economies/rational choice' theorists, have taken on Douglas's task by looking at the ebb and flow of the religious marketplace. These scholars take the opposite view of Berger, who argued that when religions begin acting like competitive agencies in a pluralistic society, each religion will lose its sanctity as a plausible option and will be forced to compete with potentially more plausible secular alternatives (1967, 138). Adopting a 'new paradigm' for understanding the religion marketplace (Warner 1993), William Bainbridge (1985), Lawrence Iannaconne (1992; 1995), Roger Finke (1992; 1997; 2000), and Rodney Stark (1985; 1992; 1999; 2000) start with the basic assumption that religious organizations' competition for believers is open to analysis through the application of concepts and models traditionally used to explain the economic sphere (Iannnaconne 1995). In this sense, religion is taken to address subjective demands that arise from universal psychological dynamics, such as the need for meaning and the desire for rewards (Stark and Bainbridge 1985, 5–14; Stark and Finke 2000, 85, 91).

Religions are in the business of supplying populations with chances to seek compensation for their faith. The greater rewards are granted by the most 'costly faiths' which are by and large the more conservative, fundamentalist, 'fire-and-brimstone' organizations (Finke and Stark 1992, 235). Even though there are certainly problems with the 'supply-side' religious economy approach (Bruce 1993, Demerath 1995), it has added a new layer of complexity to the way religious organizations function in society and to the way we should interpret the secularization thesis. If religions that demand a lot from people are on the rise, then it seems that much of the secularization thesis should be turned on its head.

The emergence of the New Atheists within an environment saturated with 'costly' conservative religiosity adds another layer of complexity, however. New Atheism is a 'costly faith,' less because of its beliefs and more because of its outsider social status. Because they have tried to show that New Atheism offers important rewards (e.g., a 'truer,' more empirical version of reality), the Four Horsemen's secularism is further evidence that secularization has not occurred, as New Atheism competes with other 'firms' in the religious marketplace.

THE NEW ATHEISTS' PASSIONATE FAITH IN SCIENTIFIC AUTHORITY

As the secularization thesis has undergone its various transformations due to changes in both the social and academic worlds, it has taken on a life of its own. This was certainly the case in the First Phase and into the Second Phase as well. In the early 1970s, Robert Bellah had criticized the secularization thesis on the basis that the theory of progressive secularization functions to some extent as a myth, creating an emotionally coherent picture of reality. In this sense, it is itself a religious doctrine rather than a scientific one (1971). As the theory had started to go out of fashion, though never fully departing from the writings of social scientists interested in the ways religions have grown and shrunk in the modern era, Jeffrey Hadden followed Bellah's declaration that the secularization thesis was more a belief than a piece of scientific knowledge. In his presidential address delivered at the annual meeting of the Southern Sociological Society in 1996 (which was later published in *Social Forces*), Hadden argued that the original secularization thesis was a product of its time, a time of immense social change, a time when many traditional ways of living were being replaced by new forms of social organization, behaviour, and belonging (1987, 589).

Secularization was so greatly accepted during the First Phase that it became a piece of taken-for-granted social science folklore that following generations took as a given to the extent it had become untouchable, or, in a word, sacred. According to Hadden:

> Sociology emerged in Europe and America during a period of social upheaval that left intellectuals personally disillusioned with religion. The overwhelming influence of Darwinian thought during that period quickly shaped a theoretical perspective that postulated the imminent demise of religion. Our heritage, bequeathed by the founding generations, is scarcely a theory at all but, rather, a doctrine of secularization. It has not required careful scrutiny because it is self-evident. We have sacralized our commitment to secularization (1987, 594).

Many sociologists, regardless of whether or not they still find elements of the secularization thesis viable, have taken up Hadden's call to desacralize the theory. The New Atheists, however, have reverted back to the First Phase, perhaps unaware or uninterested in contemporary sociological theories of religion. In effect, by promoting their own brand of secularism, they have re-sacralized the secularization thesis.

In order to better understand the New Atheists' relationship to the secularization thesis, I will first discuss and highlight the dynamics of their scientistic/naturalistic fundamentalism and then show how their passionate treatises (somewhat ironically) provide evidence to refute many of the precepts of the original First Phase secularization thesis. Some elements of the New Atheists' vehemently heated style of confrontation and coercion can be understood by using Christian Smith's 'subcultural identity theory' (1998). According to Smith, the worldview of a movement or population will likely be strengthened and reinforced by purposely maintaining a tension with society. In oddly similar ways to the Evangelical Christians that Smith studied, the New Atheists have assumed a marginalized position in Western society, acting out against what they see as the audacious confluence of religion and society. Their writings can be read, in part, as propaganda to support their subcultural anti-theological and anti-religious position. As such, like Evangelicals, the New Atheists present themselves as an 'embattled' minority at least in part to help their claims thrive.

What the New Atheists share is a belief that religion should not simply be tolerated but should be countered and criticized by rationality and scientific investigation. The entire notion of faith, as opposed to knowing, is condemned by the New Atheists as infantile and fantastic. Harris defines faith as "belief without evidence" (2004, 59–73, 85), Hitchens sees faith as a practice that "poisons everything" (2007b), and Dawkins writes that "Faith can be very, very dangerous. ... Suicide bombers do what they do because they really believe what they were taught in their religious schools: that duty to God exceeds all other priorities" (2006, 9). Religious faith stands in direct opposition to the New Atheists *faith* in Science (with a capital S). For them, Science beholds the ultimate authority that can tell us what religion is really about and for, and naturalistic Science can provide better answers than supernaturalistic religion to every important question people ask. Dawkins goes as far as to assert that Science is even equipped to determine whether or not God exists. In *The God Delusion* (2006), Dawkins admits that the existence of God cannot be proven scientifically, but religious experience and belief in the existence of a God can be explained scientifically. He argues, however, that the existence of a God would appear to be extremely unlikely when weighing all of the available evidence, claiming that the "factual premise of religion—the God Hypothesis—is untenable. God almost certainly does not exist" (2006, 158). Though the use of 'almost' by Dawkins can be used against claims of atheistic fundamentalism, we nevertheless can see here the plea for, and perhaps valorization of, evidence as the most important ingredient in the production of knowledge.

In many ways, the New Atheists *faith* in Science and rationality mimics the First Phase of the secularization thesis, though in a far less systematic way and with a far more antagonistic motivation. Even though Dawkins and Dennett enlist new findings and terminology from evolutionary biology and neuroscience, their basic arguments are very similar to those made by early social scientists as well as those writing in the other two phases of the secularization thesis. Hitchens' declaration that "religion is man-made" (2007b, 10) is a poor simulacrum of Berger's lengthy and compelling discussion of "religion as a social product" (1967, 10). Regardless of their collective recapitulation of old themes, theories, and ideas, however, the New Atheists do offer something different. What is new here is not their devout belief in Science. In fact, Hitchens calls for a renewed Enlightenment based on "pursuit of unfettered scientific inquiry" (2007b, 283). Such claims have led critics to decry the New Atheism as a rebranded form of atheistic fundamentalism (see McGrath and McGrath 2007). These assertions have been rejected and denied by the most vocal New Atheist propagators (Dawkins 2006, 155; Dennett 2006, 311). Though some critics in the Third Phase of the secularization thesis have elevated the role of science as a key force behind secularization (Stark and Finke 2000, 61), science has no direct causal effect on religious beliefs (Bruce 2002, 27). Science can, however, provide the foundations for an alternative, non-religious worldview. Adopting and adapting this worldview is at the heart of the New Atheists' writings. Indeed, for them, Science is not simply another worldview among others; it is *the* worldview, the one that breaks the spell of our historically conditioned 'need' to believe in God.

What is new about the New Atheists is their collective combative attempt to publicize their worldview, one that is very much based on Science as well as on observations of historical and contemporary religiously motivated atrocities (see Hitchens 2007b, chap. 2). In order to make their worldview and themselves more known and identifiable, the New Atheists have adopted the political techniques of the minority outsider, ironically paralleling the tactics and patterns that Smith (1998) discusses in his study of American Evangelicals. In order to highlight their differences from society at large, some New Atheists have championed the use of 'brights' as a more attuned replacement for outmoded labels like 'atheist,' 'agnostic,' or 'secularist.' Dawkins argues that adopting the name 'brights' as a replacement for older designations would be an exercise in 'consciousness-raising' (Dawkins 2003) and would establish and maintain a definitional boundary between the New Atheist and both older secularist philosophies and religious worldviews. He even likens this purposeful labeling to the identity politics of homosexuals.

> A triumph of consciousness-raising has been the homosexual hijacking of the word gay. I used to mourn the loss of gay in (what I still think of as) its true sense. But on the bright side (wait for it), gay has inspired a new imitator, which is the climax of this article. Gay is succinct, uplifting, positive: an "up" word, whereas homosexual is a down word, and queer, faggot, and pooftah are insults. Those of us who subscribe to no religion; those of us whose view of the universe is natural rather than supernatural; those of us who rejoice in the real and scorn the false comfort of the unreal, we need a word of our own, a word like gay. (Dawkins 2003, 13)

This type of linguistic play is a strategy utilized to distinguish between the religious and the anti-religious. Applying the term 'brights' to followers who have adopted New Atheistic belief implies, somewhat paradoxically, their minority status and their elitism. Even though Dennett denies that referring to himself and his cohort as 'brights' denotes superiority (2006, 21, 51), like Dawkins, he wants to adopt the term to set boundaries and to imply that the worldview of 'brights' has historically been, er, kept in the dark.

CONCLUSION

In his extensive history of 'unbelief' in the United States and across the majority of Western society, James Turner notes that unbelievers in the nineteenth century redirected the 'normal' impulses once directed toward God along new paths.

> In fact, agnostics discovered a variety of springs of reassurance and objects to revere. Science, art, and nature each provided consolation, comfort and a kind of holiness. Personal background or mental bent inclined some unbelievers to lean toward one, others to another. But these ideals were not jealous gods, indeed they mixed fairly easily; and

agnostics drew satisfaction promiscuously from whichever one or ones offered most help in given circumstances… Unbelievers did not devise a new god. They found a way of living without God. (Turner 1985, 249)

Though the New Atheists share many things with Turner's unbelievers, there is one key distinction. Science *is* the New Atheists' new god, and Charles Darwin is their patron saint.

Science stands at the forefront of their ideas and is the tool they use to combat religious believers. As Sam Harris writes in his *Letter to a Christian Nation*:

> The core of science is not controlled experiment or mathematical modeling; it is intellectual honesty. It is time we acknowledge a basic feature of human discourse: when considering the truth of a proposition, one is either engaged in an honest appraisal of the evidence and logical arguments, or one isn't. Religion is the one area of our lives where people imagine that some other standard of intellectual integrity applies. (2008, 64–65)

Harris not only reveres and valorizes Science, but also, quite intentionally, ridicules religion as an illegitimate form of knowledge. Again, we see the New Atheists argument against faith as a lesser, insufficient way of knowing about the world. For the New Atheists, Science has swept away the mysteries of life that religion merely imagines, or imagines to answer. As Bryan Wilson put it, for believers in scientism, "The unexplained is no longer the 'mystery,' it is only the 'as yet unsolved problem'" (1976, 268).

Though social scientists have been debating the secularization thesis for well over a century, there still remains little consensus about its merits and efficacy. The New Atheists provide an interesting case. On the one hand, they seem to support the secularization thesis, showing how religious authority has decreased to a point where Science can step in and fill the void. We can see how rationality trumps religious belief and how scientific knowledge towers over religious faith. But, then again, how widespread are such phenomena? On the other hand, when we see the New Atheists as an 'embattled' minority, intensely fighting against the religiously devout and faithful, we can see just how much people have held on to their religions as the primary source of meaning and order. If the secularization thesis had panned out the way the early writers in the First Phase had predicted, the New Atheists would not have to fight so hard to make their case. If we actually lived in a 'Secular Age,' then, like God, the New Atheists would cease to exist.

THE NEW ATHEISM AND THE EMPOWERMENT
OF AMERICAN FREETHINKERS

Richard Cimino and Christopher Smith

I may naively have thought that the book had a good chance of convert-
ing devout religious people to atheism. I'm not sure that's realistic; what
does seem to be happening—and Christopher Hitchens and Sam Harris
report the same thing—is an enormous upsurge in people who are
already sort of atheists, or people who at least aren't very religious…hav-
ing their consciousness raised to the point that they realize 'actually I am
an atheist and apparently a lot of other people are too, and I never realized it' – Richard Dawkins commenting on the popularity of The God
Delusion.[1]

It has long been recognized that American society is more religious
than most European societies. As such, it is important to consider what
space is available for atheism and other forms of irreligion. In this
chapter we will address how the 'new atheism' has created new space
for 'freethinkers', though such an opening carries its own tensions and
ambiguities about the future of secularism in the United States.

If religion acts as a norm and a 'natural' standard by which all devia-
tions are judged abnormal and deviant, perhaps we might be justified
in asking if "American civil religion has served as a functional equivalent to an established national church" (Mennell 2007, 291). We don't
think it would be overstating the case to say that the space for atheism
in America has been largely limited historically. This is not to say that
atheism has not had space; but the space has been and continues to
be cramped, particularly as many atheist leaders' and activists' long-
held dream of a progressively secular American society has failed to
materialize.

Atheists have lacked "the ready-made structures of history, narrative, and tradition that would enable the easy passage" from the periph-
ery to the centre (Thoburn 2003, 19). 'Coming out', then, has not been
simply a matter of expressing oneself as an atheist along a well-worn

---

[1] This quote, which is slightly modified by the authors for ease of reading, is from
the December 7, 2007 Point of Inquiry podcast "Science and the New Atheism"
(Dawkins 2007e).

legitimate route. It has involved emerging from invisibility to claim a personal and social identity that has carried a fair degree of stigma. We believe this stigma is likely weakening, since even before the emergence of the new atheism, there has been a growth of organizations and activism galvanizing freethinkers to make a place for themselves in American society (Cimino and Smith 2007).[2]

That the appearance of the new atheism signals a further weakening of the 'atheist taboo' in American society is especially evident to atheists. The phenomenon of the new atheism is hailed as a harbinger of advancing secularism. However, as we will seek to argue in this chapter, the situation is far more complex than one of secularism versus religion. The new atheist books and the responses, debates, and criticisms they have generated creates a new space where atheists are empowered and mobilized through their interaction and contention with each other and with their antagonists.

A Sociology of the New Atheism

Media in the form of books, magazines, websites, blogs, and online forums plays an important role in the social phenomenon of new atheism. In highlighting the role of media, we will be focusing on both the content and the medium. An analysis of articles devoted to new atheism in two magazines, coupled with responses from a sample of self-identified atheists on new atheism, will allow us to see how 'freethinkers' (a term we use throughout this chapter to include self-designated atheists and secular humanists) themselves are interpreting and evaluating the new atheism. The medium is understood here as "a type of setting or environment that has relatively fixed characteristics that influence communication in a particular manner—regardless of the choice of content elements and regardless of the particular manipulation of production variables" (Meyrowitz 2000, 432–433). Examining both the content and medium surrounding how the new atheism is received will allow us to examine questions concerning how the media are reshaping relationships among atheists themselves as well as altering the symbolic boundaries between atheists and theists.

---

[2] In spite of the 2003 national survey studied by Edgell et al. (2006) that shows stigma against atheists and atheism is still very much alive and well in America.

We believe that content analysis and medium theory both offer insightful approaches for studying atheism. Far from being incompatible, these two approaches can actually strengthen each other. Rather than setting the content as messages to one side and the medium as a context to the other, we believe that a more productive approach is "to have the assumptions, methodologies, and the object of analysis of each approach work itself, so to speak, into the analysis of the other" (Carpignano 1999, 178).

In focusing on how the new atheist phenomenon has been received and appropriated by those involved in atheist and secular humanist organizations, we first analyze and discuss articles on the new atheism, which have appeared in two of the most prominent freethought publications, *Free Inquiry* and the *American Atheist,* between January of 2006 and March of 2008. Secondly, we analyze and discuss responses to a questionnaire (containing both open and closed questions) we created on the phenomenon of the new atheism, as well as ethnographic interviews we conducted among 37 atheists and secular humanists from an earlier study (Cimino and Smith 2007). The 15 respondents for the questionnaire were found by way of a volunteer sample drawn from the websites and listserves of organized freethought groups. The only criteria for selecting such respondents were that they self-identify as atheist. Readers should note that we use 'involved' here as a very loose category to capture those ranging from lone activists who engage in atheist protests, to those who are active members of atheist and secular humanist societies, to more marginal participants who subscribe to freethought publications.

Organized Freethinkers and the New Atheism

The majority of articles in both *Free Inquiry* and the *American Atheist* viewed the 'new atheism' as a positive phenomenon demonstrating the relevance and persuasiveness of the freethought message to American society. Yet there was also a minority of articles in both publications that criticized the style and substance of the new atheism, although for different reasons.

Free Inquiry followed and commented on the publishing of the new atheist books most frequently, which is not unusual considering the amount of space the magazine devotes to promoting the positive identity of secular humanism and debating the public image and strategies of freethinkers in general. In fact, all of the new atheist authors had been frequent contributors to *Free Inquiry* before their best-selling books were published. Harris and Hitchens are still regular columnists while Dawkins and Dennett are both regularly cited and contribute feature articles, usually on religion, atheism, and science. Dawkins by far has been the most active in the secular humanist movement, speaking and writing on both internal (i.e., using the designation 'brights' for consciousness-raising by freethinkers) and external (criticizing and debating theism and religion) concerns.

Dennett's 2006 book *Breaking the Spell* received two reviews in the same issue of *Free Inquiry*, one negative and the other more positive— a pattern that would foreshadow the ambivalence secular humanists and atheists have had about the new atheist writings. The first review (Sosis 2007) criticized Dennett's negative portrayal of religious people, adding that the book would set back the study of religion and lead to more distrust among believers toward scholars. The reviewer, an anthropologist, charged that in his attempt to disprove the premise of religion, Dennett undersells the evidence that shows a positive correlation between health and religion. The second review (Hoffmann 2007) argued that while Dennett had it right about the illusions of religion, he conceded too much to the religious side. In 2006, the book did win a book award by *Free Inquiry*, citing Dennett's treatment of religion as a natural phenomenon "whose psychological and cultural dimensions should be evaluated using the same tools of scientific scrutiny we would apply to any other area of human endeavor" (Free Inquiry 2006, 9). In fact, *Free Inquiry* and other freethought publications categorized Dennett's more scholarly work as part of the new atheist literature only after it had been portrayed as such by the media and other critics.

Atheists and secular humanists treated the new atheism as a new phenomenon only after Dawkins' book *The God Delusion* had become a best-seller and had been linked by the media with Harris's, Dennett's, and (later) Hitchens' books as the touchstones of the new atheism. Since the material in these books was part and parcel of the articles that *Free Inquiry* had run since its inception, the new atheist literature was treated by the magazine mainly as a way of popularizing the freethought message, but also as a means of legitimizing atheism and secular humanism in American society. The tension between, on the one hand, spreading secularism and attempting to expose the fallacies of belief, and, on the other, seeking acceptance in a largely religious society is evident in the treatment of the new atheism by secular humanists (and in secular humanist activity in general).

On the whole, however, *Free Inquiry* appeared to be an enthusiastic booster of the new atheists early on. Starting in 2007, the new atheists' books were grouped together as a single phenomenon and were seen to represent a new stage of secularist assertiveness. Norm Allen, the director of African Americans for Humanism, wrote that the new atheists are following in the path of the abolitionists and other 'radicals' throughout American history who have sought to "accelerate the agenda of moderates." Allen adds that moderates who believe in dialogue with theists should not stand in the way of 'radicals' such as Dawkins and Harris "who are taking atheism and naturalism to the masses in a way that's seldom been seen in this century" (Allen 2007, 52). In the same issue, Christopher Hitchens defended the new atheists (of whom he is one) against charges that they are espousing a new fundamentalism in their attacks on religion. Hitchens wrote that such a 'time-wasting tactic' devised by religious fundamentalists may appeal to 'moderates' who want to appear even-handed, but it is a diversion from the argument against fundamentalism and theism.

Among the strongest affirmations of the new atheism in *Free Inquiry* was an editorial wherein Paul Kurtz (2007c, 5) noted that the magazine was 'gratified' that several of its writers and their views were finding a wider audience, though he criticized the media's use of the term 'evangelical atheism' to describe the phenomenon. Kurtz adamantly refused to concede to the media criticism that the new atheist authors were unfairly attacking religion and religious people, adding that Dawkins, Dennett, and Harris were paying the price for "breaking the long-standing American taboo of not critically examining religion and calling into question the existence of God." He added that the "war against secularism by the religious right is unremitting; why should the non-religious, nonaffiliated, secular minority of the country remain silent?"

The media was once more reprimanded for its treatment of the new atheism in a reprint of an article originally published in the politically leftist magazine *The Nation* (Politt 2008). Writer and activist Katha Pollit criticized the political left media for its lukewarm reception of the new atheist books. She asked leftists to own up to their atheist/agnostic identity rather than seeking to build bridges to religious liberals and Democrats. There was also an attempt to broaden the canon of new atheist literature to include new authors with similar critiques of theism. Thus French atheist philosopher Michel Onfray's 2007 book *Atheist Manifesto* is hailed as "[holding] back nothing in its condemnation of both religion and religiosity. [Like the new atheist authors], Onfray is correct when he claims the necessity for atheists to go after religion with full intellectual fury. Holding back and making nice is not an option when the opposition refuses to do the same" (Layton 2007, 65; for a review of a similar book see also Flynn 2007).

Alongside the sympathetic treatment of the new atheism was wariness about the consequences of attacking religion with 'full intellectual fury.' In a later editorial Kurtz himself sounded a cautionary note about the limits of evangelical atheism. He restated his long-time concern that secular humanists should not be known as 'nabobs of negativity,' defined by the beliefs they oppose rather than for their positive system of ethics and philosophy. As in his previous writings, Kurtz called for secular groups to create their own metaphors and symbols to meet the existential and aesthetic needs usually supplied by religion.

Interestingly enough, a British contributor in a symposium on the future of secularism in 'post-Christian' Europe wrote the most critical article on the new atheism. Philosopher Julian Baggini (2007, 42–43) wrote that the 'shock-and-awe tactics' of Dawkins and Dennett are 'bound to fail,' producing a polarization that could radicalize believers even more. Baggini argues that, "Secularists have also misjudged the mood of the people they have purportedly liberated. People who once lived under the yoke of oppressive religion now have the freedom to believe, read, and do what they want. So why have the ungrateful bastards not become full-fledged atheists? The answer from some quarters seems to be that not all have got the message, so what they need is some reeducation in the folly of religion and the joys of science." He added that the new atheist tactic of blaming religion for most of the world's ills "just isn't credible. Images of murderous inquisitors just don't square with the English impression of tea with kindly vicars and genteel carol services at Christmas. In summary, we are wrong to respond to the rise of religion by squaring off for the big fight. To protect secularism we need to win the hearts and the minds of the moderate majority" (Baggini 2007, 43).

OLD ATHEISM MEETS THE NEW ATHEISM

One might expect that self-proclaimed atheists would be far more supportive of the new atheism than secular humanists who tend to see atheism as only part of their identity. An analysis of the *American Atheist*, however, suggests a similar level of support but more ambivalence than found in *Free Inquiry*. There was less frequent citation of new atheist books in the *American Atheist*, most likely due to the fact that its authors had not been part of the network of activists and writers that make up its parent organization, American Atheists.

The more activist thrust of American Atheists and its magazine tended to colour the coverage of the new atheism in a political direction. In an editorial (2008) American Atheists president Ellen Johnson wrote that the popularity of the new atheist books (and her own appearances on national television) were helping to educate and mobilize non-religious voters to the polls to press for their own rights (E. Johnson 2008). Another article cited the use of new atheist books in activism and recruitment for the cause. The writer doubted that religious people would be exposed to such arguments, even if they were authored by 'big names atheists,' since they would not read such books in the first place; he called for ordinary atheists to 'come out of the closet' and directly confront religious truth claims in their local media (Bice 2007).

Other articles defended the new atheists from charges of extremism, viewing them as a useful arsenal in the battle against religion. A strongly positive review of Hitchens' *God is Not Great* states that each of the new atheist books can serve specific purposes: "I like to visualize a pair of 'good-cop; bad-cop' teams of interlocutors going forth to do battle with believers of all stripes. I would send Christopher Hitchens along with 'good cop' Daniel Dennett to do battle with the theologians and apologists" (Guardia 2008, 30). At the same time, each of these articles criticizes the new atheists on a number of points. One article criticizes them for targeting and debunking the Judeo-Christian God while ignoring the gods of other religions. Similarly, a feature article by Indian rationalist author Meera Nanda (2008, 22) takes Harris to task for his espousal of Eastern spirituality, even as he attacks the monotheistic religions, especially Islam. Nanda charges that Harris "loads spiritual practices with metaphysical baggage, all the while claiming to stand up for reason and evidence. By the end of the book, I could not help thinking of him as a Trojan horse for the New Age...It is hard to believe that the author of this stuff is the most celebrated rationalist of our troubled times." The uneasiness and questions about Harris's 'secular spirituality' was also evident in *Free Inquiry* (see Hoffmann 2006).

A cover story entitled 'Is Dawkins Deluded?' was more critical of the atheist leader than most articles found in *Free Inquiry*. Writer Massimo Pigliucci (2008), while agreeing with Dawkins more than the bold headline might indicate, argued that the *God Delusion*'s equating child abuse with early religious education was 'downright pernicious'—a charge that could be turned against Unitarians and even some non-theist groups while ignoring the critical thinking encouraged in some religious traditions. Pigliucci especially criticized Dawkins for claiming that science could disprove the God hypothesis, arguing that only philosophy could play such a role.

SELF-IDENTIFIED ATHEISTS AND THE NEW ATHEISM

The way in which the new atheism is seen as affirming a secularist identity is clearly on display in the responses from atheists and secular humanists to our questionnaire on the phenomenon. Almost all of the respondents had read at least one of the books or had seen Bill Maher's film, *Religulous*. All of the respondents except for one agreed that the new atheist books had given them "a greater sense of acceptance or support in society." The fact that the books were best-sellers obviously encouraged in the respondents a feeling of being in the mainstream. The sense of acceptance they felt was also related to the belief that the new atheism was helping to dispel forms of belief that were especially intolerant toward atheists. One respondent wrote that he was 'glad' about the new acceptance, adding, "I think many people are tired of the bullying by the Religious Right." One person felt that this sense of greater security might be short-lived. As one respondent wrote: "I expect a stronger pushback if [these books] become more popular (I am in Oklahoma!)" The only respondent who did not feel such a sense of acceptance wrote that "Individuals who base their life on... mythology are unable to confront reality. Actually, for such individuals with immature minds, the more vocal and public we are, the more threatened they feel, and act."

Interestingly, even though the media have portrayed these books and the movie as divisive and negative toward religious believers, the majority of respondents tended to believe that the theists who read them would have a more positive view of atheists and atheism. Some respondents did wonder how many religious people would actually read the books, but there seemed to be little concern that they would be offensive.

In fact, the contentious and critical nature of the new atheism was one of its major draws, regardless of whether theists, society or the media approved of it. As one respondent commented: "We have been too nice to the religious for decades and it has gotten us nowhere…a plain no-non-sensical statement of our views is long overdue. Dawkins, Hitchens are my heroes where this is concerned." While the media were praised for introducing new atheist views, respondents also noted that atheism still faces media discrimination and oversight. One respondent wrote, "Atheism has always been cast in the lowest regard by the media and most everyone in America. I tend to be more outspoken now [after the new atheist books] than ever before. I now refuse to just nod my head to religious conversations and say nothing to irritate those conversing. I really don't care what anyone else thinks regarding my lack of religious belief. Actually, I am rather proud." More in the minority were those who were concerned about the perception that the new atheism was too negative toward religion and religious people. In response to a question about the media's charge that the new atheists were being too 'nasty,' one person answered, "I think such 'nasty attitudes' are self-defeating. 'Achieving' atheism is a matter that requires much thought, with as little extraneous noise as possible."

Although the respondents were drawn from the listserves and forums associated with atheist and secular humanist groups, somewhat less than half were regular participants in such organizations. This pattern confirms the weak ties that make up the freethought community in the United States. Yet almost all of the respondents who were involved in organized atheist or secular humanist groups agreed that they had witnessed more people joining these groups since the publication and release of the new atheist books and movie. Most reported that their group had not formally studied or discussed the books, but they believed that the books and movie created both an atmosphere that encouraged non-theists to be more outspoken about their views and more involved in group activity with like-minded freethinkers.

A central premise informing this article is that the substantial transformations in our contemporary mediascape are creating a new space for atheists to come out, speak out, and 'meet up' in a still largely religious society. The responses to the questionnaires seem to go some way towards confirming this. In point of fact, only two respondents—one answering bluntly, "No; I'm a print person," and the other asserting, "I need no further "informing!"—said that the internet "didn't inform their atheism." The rest answered affirmatively.

These positive responses varied in substance. Some highlighted the ease with which the internet could be used to obtain information. One said that the internet helped him "learn about authors he hadn't heard about before" and another allowed that the internet was his "main source of info about atheism." Others highlighted the joy they get from watching "great thinkers, authors, philosophers, [and] scientists discuss atheism on YouTube and other websites." Still others highlighted how "blogs, forums, and other user-created media online (such as YouTube)" have allowed them a space to both "explore and express" their views. From the perspective of media theory, one of the more interesting responses was the following: "Yes, [the internet does 'inform' my atheism], I *participate* in a Facebook group and subscribe to several email lists to *keep in touch* with local events. It [also] helps me to be able to talk to some people from around *the world* in the least liked 'group' of all" (emphasis added).

This response is interesting for a few reasons. It exposes the 'global village' effect, which brings those spaces and people previously unreachable within reach. It also shows an appreciation for the profound changes the experience of commonality is undergoing.

THE NEW ATHEISM IN A MEDIATED CULTURE

The new atheist books—and the enormous amount of secondary literature that interest in them has generated in the form of articles, blogs, forums, podcasts, webcasts, conferences, lectures, news stories, debates, deconversion narratives, blasphemy challenges, bus ads, and even (rebuttal) sermons—have succeeded in familiarizing much of the world with atheism. Prior to this, public interest in atheism was largely confined to academic and theological circles; it is no longer the case, which is one reason why the new atheism has scratched a nerve among theists. Not only has there been a series of evangelical books responding to the new atheism, but also large numbers of laity and clergy have read these atheist books (Garrison 2008; Mohler 2008; Aikman 2008; Marshall 2007).

To some extent, it is the mere accessibility of the information and the visibility of atheism that threatens the norm of religiosity: atheism is *here* and not over *there*. This is one way to understand the new atheist claim that atheism is becoming less private, and it also helps us understand why atheists may be feeling a greater sense of acceptance in a society that is still largely religious. Atheism is becoming a legitimate option. In a 1952 address to the Freedom Foundation, U.S. President Eisenhower stated that "Our government makes no sense unless it is founded in a deeply felt *religious* faith—and I don't care what it is." By contrast, in his inauguration speech earlier this year, President Obama stated that "We are a nation of Christians and Muslims, Jews and Hindus—and *non-believers*."

In saying that it is "the *mere* accessibility of the information and the visibility of atheism that threatens the norm of religiosity," we by no means wish to imply that the specific content of the books is unimportant for explaining the phenomenon of new atheism. From a particular perspective—whether it be theological, philosophical, or cognitive scientific—discussing, debating, and critiquing the actual content of the new atheist books might be necessary and lead to significant insights. We only wish, playing the role of devil's advocate, to ask if this designation of newness—that in popular parlance is often coupled with pejorative associations, such as 'nasty,' 'aggressive,' 'outspoken,' and even 'fundamentalist'—is more a product of a forced pluralism at the level of information than anything particularly new, subversive, or 'deviant' about the information in the new atheists' texts themselves.

Certainly it is the case that having best-selling books by openly avowed atheists for the first time in Western history *is* something new. And clearly these authors are saying something new compared to atheist authors of the past. The reading of these books, however, cannot simply be reduced to the experience of intellectually consuming a product; it involves belonging to a world. One only has to switch on the nightly news or buy a daily newspaper to know that this world is constituted more and more by an increased interdependence and communication well beyond the confines of any particular geographical location. (One thinks of the current *global* economic crisis, for example.) This is a world where "the membranes around spatially segregated arenas [have] become more *informationally* permeable, through television and other electronic media, [and where] the current trend is toward integration of all groups into a relatively common experiential sphere—with a new recognition of the special needs and idiosyncrasies of *individuals*" (Meyrowitz 1993, 43; emphasis added).

In Meyrowitz's view, there is an intimate relationship between access to social situations and informational-systems, and tension between individuals and groups in a given society. The merging of once-isolated social situations and distinct information-systems is one of the principal motives responsible for increasing "one's awareness of physical, social, and legal segregation" (Meyrowitz 1993, 43). Drawing on George Herbert Mead's theory of the 'generalized other,' Meyrowitz (1985, 131–132) highlights how media extend the boundaries of experience so that those who we perceive as significant others or as part of our generalized other are no longer only the people with whom we experience face-to-face communication:

> This 'mediated generalized other' includes standards, values and beliefs from outside traditional group spheres, and it thereby presents people with a new perspective from which to view their actions and identities. The new mediated generalized other bypasses face-to-face encounters in family and community and is shared by millions of others.

Just as prior to the highly publicized conservative upsurge in the 1980s many atheists in the United States may not have been *as* conscious of the evangelical element as they are now; before the introduction of television many individuals and groups may not have known the extent to which they weren't like others. As many people's grandparents say, 'we were poor, but we never knew it.' To be ignorant of the extent of one's deprivation (due to geographical and cultural isolation) compared to others more fortunate is no longer possible. Today people are shown the extent of their poverty nightly in the *comfort* and *privacy* of their own homes.

This notion that situational and informational integration heightens the perception of segregation is consistent with what we found in our earlier study (Cimino and Smith 2007), where most participants in secular and atheist groups made the transition from being an inactive or 'nominal' secular individual to becoming involved in secular humanist groups and activism through *contact* with individuals and a growing concern about issues associated with the religious right. As one New York educator and former leftist activist we interviewed put it,

> I didn't know much about the religious right until I had to work with them. I started *seeing* what they were about and became very frightened at the rhetoric. I realized the Board of Education in New York is permeated with born-again Christians. The rhetoric was borderline fascist, with attacks on single mothers. I was harassed on the job when [they found out I was an atheist]. It was openly racist and it was coming from black and Hispanic people. But the left wasn't serious about the born-again threat. The threat to the first amendment was a non-issue for them. *I always knew I was an atheist but never saw the need to talk about it until I saw how [these] people were threatening freedom.*

It is also consistent with what we found in the responses to our questionnaire. For example, one respondent stated that he "started donating more money to Humanist organizations after seeing clips of the film 'Jesus Camp' and the CNN TV series 'God's Warriors.'" Another said that she is now "much more aware of religious biases on American TV and movies, and [that she] tries to read and watch more products from the non-religious perspective." Another, recalling seeing only three examples of "atheists on TV: the atheists in *South Park*'s 'Go God Go' episodes, the main character on *House*, and Reginald Finley in an episode of *Wife Swap*," concluded that mainstream television "make[s] atheists seem unsociable or hostile." This last point—that the mainstream media is always portraying humanists/atheists in a negative light—was echoed throughout the articles and questionnaires, as well as in our earlier interviews.

The formation of an 'atheist consciousness,' then, can be seen as a consequence of atheists' heightened awareness of the increasing distance between their strongly held views and the views of the 'majority'— which ironically is a product of diminishing distance due to the larger, more inclusive access to the same experiential sphere. In this case, the initially limited conflict of an atheist harassed at work after 'coming out' is generalized on the basis of the expansion of communicative networks until it becomes a common matter, turning private matters into public issues. Consciousness-raising from this perspective "would not be limited to a set of assumptions derived from life experiences that are used to confront, challenge, or resist, from the outside, the dominant ideology" of theism. Consciousness-raising "could also be conceived as a product of an electronically defined common place that, by virtue of being electronically reproduced, can be considered a public space" (Carpignano et al. 1993, 115–116).

Consciousness-raising, then, has to be understood against the backdrop of a relatively common experiential sphere that allows for "a greater sense of personal involvement with those who would otherwise be strangers—or *enemies*" (Meyrowitz 1994, 58; emphasis added). As a diffuse population, this sense of involvement allows atheists a greater sense of acceptance (being in the company of like-minded strangers) while also intensifying their sense of exclusion from the dominant discourse and the political institutions that ensure the reproduction of religion (which could potentially lead to 'freethinkers' forming stronger coalitions and communities with each other). This interval between atheists' raised expectations—which is apparent in their frequent citing of the gay rights movement, as in the example to follow—and the actual institutional opportunities available for non-theists to enter sectors of power (beyond academia), perhaps, goes some way towards understanding the issue of atheists' being considered 'outspoken' and 'on the offensive.' On the one hand, this claim is clearly nothing more than a consequence of atheists' greater visibility and of theists feeling vulnerable. On the other hand, this is a sincere expression of atheists' raised expectations due, at least in part, to the popularity of the new atheism.

If one were to look only at the content of the new atheists' books and the articles in *Free Inquiry* and *American Atheist*—to say nothing of the vast array of blog posts, forum entries, podcasts, and videos on the Internet debating atheism and new atheism, secularism humanism and atheism, new humanism and new atheism—one might suggest that one effect of the new atheism is to weaken atheism. The content is very contentious, divisive, and one-sided. Still, despite complaints about the new atheism being mean-spirited, aggressive, and even counter-productive, the possibility remains that what "is conceived as a confrontational device becomes an opening for the empowerment of an alternative discursive practice. These discourses don't have to conform to civility nor to the dictates of the general interest. They can be expressed for what they are: particular, regional, one-sided, and for that reason politically alive" (Carpignano et al. 1993, 116).

The experience of space introduced by electronic media plays a decisive role here. First, the mediated experience of being-in-common— where the critical distance of a perspectivistic relationship to strangers and enemies gives way to a personal involvement and objective closeness—makes it difficult to continue to conceive of commonality solely on the basis of rational deliberation and exchange. As Meyrowitz (1994, 58) asserts: "While written and printed words emphasize ideas, most electronic media emphasize feeling, appearance, [and] mood ... The major questions are no longer 'Is it true?' 'Is it false?' Instead we more often ask, 'How does it look?' 'How does it feel?'" Second, the experience of space introduced by television and digital technology make problematic the strict, ontological distinction between private and public spheres. While, in principle, print has always played a public role in mediating between the common good and private interests, or public life and private concerns, the Internet is radically transforming this by encouraging new relationships, connections, sentiments, affections, and a fluidity between the private and public that works to short-circuit the separation between deliberation and public opinion traditionally maintained by the press. This is because the new digital media, not unlike the medium of television, are inherently concerned with mobilizing audiences.

With blogging, YouTube, or Facebook, for example, it no longer makes sense to speak of a private audience, or a passive spectator as opposed to an active, public participant; online, "people are provoked into performing in public, as themselves, unscripted and unrehearsed, as writers of their own texts and producers of their own public pronouncements and utterances...these discursive practices represent an unprecedented intrusion of civil society into the discursive apparatus of the media" (Carpignano 1999, 187). Focusing on television, Carpignano and Meyrowitz both connect this blurring to the rise of social movements, particularly those for civil and gay rights and for gender equality. They also link this visibility and penetration by civil society to a process of disenchantment: in "making visible the circuits of exposure that create public figures [television and the Internet reveal] the mechanism of publicity, the making of representations... Public figures are such to the extent that they inhabit the mediatic space, but this is the same space the audiences inhabit. This not only accounts for the demystification, irony, and game playing with which public figures are dealt with or to which they are subjected, but it might ultimately explain the crisis of legitimacy of institutions of representations, from political institutions to the institutions of media themselves" (Carpignano 1999, 187).

This situation poses simultaneous advantages and disadvantages for atheism. Favourably, this new visibility leads to a feeling of greater acceptance and an opportunity for participation. Unfavourably, the dissolving of the public and the private boundary that accompanies such visibility severely threatens the atheist agenda of keeping religion out of the public sphere. In addition, the retreat from the public use of reason and a dive into emotional and sensory involvement would seem to pose a serious challenge to any notion of consensus-formation that rests wholly on the authority of a stronger argument (a la Habermas). It is increasingly difficult to fall back on customary sources of authority and interpretations, given the greater range of cultures, interests, and experiences online. While considerably more criticism and debate may be elicited, criticism and debate as traditionally understood are undermined—an interesting, if unsettling, situation for freethinkers weaned on Enlightenment rationalism.

THE NEW ATHEISM AND THE FUTURE OF AMERICAN FREETHOUGHT

The new atheism functions as a tool for the advancement and legitimation of atheist ideology, as well as consciousness-raising among freethinkers who have hitherto felt marginalized in American society. The tension between debunking religious belief and pressing for equal treatment in a religious and pluralistic society runs through much of the discourse of American freethinkers. This tension is especially heightened for secular humanists who emphasize a positive system of ethics. Secular humanists and atheists have employed strategies such as engaging in identity politics and mimicking evangelical styles of apologetic debate (viewing conservative Protestants as their main antagonists and sparring partners), fighting culture wars, and organizing outreach to win adherents. This is especially the case as persistent religious belief and its increasingly public role has challenged the older triumphant vision of building a secular America. It could be argued that the new atheism employs a distinctly evangelical approach. This can be seen when Dawkins encourages newly minted atheists to tell their accounts of 'deconversion,' mirroring evangelicals 'giving their testimonies' of being born again.

The dilemma remains that while the freethinkers believe that they are treated as second-class citizens, their classic repertoire of ridiculing and attacking religious belief increases their conflict with society. In the case of the new atheism, the 'missionary impulse' to roll back the 'ignorance' and 'unenlightenment' of religion has been revived among freethinkers to an extent that outweighs the concern about equal rights. Even secular humanists, who have attempted to build ties to liberal religious groups on social issues, threw caution to the wind in supporting the new atheist attacks against all religion. For the most part, they viewed the public reception of new atheist books as a unique opportunity to present a 'united front' of secularism in the United States, regardless of what 'moderates' thought of the strategy. This is not to say that there are not some differing impulses at work. Ironically, it is in part because of the increased visibility, the success of the books, and participants' and activists' intensity, that some within the movement now find themselves, at least mildly, on the defensive. Paul Kurtz, for example, has used the opportunity to reiterate the distinction between secular humanism and new atheism, stating that "for the secular humanist, it is not so much the stridency of these books that is at issue, as it is what's missing from these books."[3] Kurtz believes that what is missing from this *par destruens* driven by a hatred for religion is a *pars construens* that affirms ethical values, humanistic virtues, and democratic principles.[4] A similar sentiment was conveyed by one of our questionnaire respondents: "I do think that advocating an anti position is a disadvantage. I prefer that we speak of what we value in positive terms: reason, scientific inquiry, separation of church and state. I do not want to be seen as a nihilist."

We should be cautious, though, about drawing the conclusion that the books are having a negative impact. A social movement open to internal antagonism is a movement that is active, not fractured. Moreover, this could be advantageous pragmatically and strategically. As one respondent noted, "I wish people would stop fostering the perception that secularists are [seriously at] odds with each other over semantics and approaches…Sure, secularists have different approaches to furthering the same causes, but the different approaches seem to be effective under different circumstances. It seems that Epstein and 'the new atheists' appreciate each other's work despite any disagreements."

The secularist movement does indeed appear to be an anomaly in terms of its openness, individuality, and room for dissent within its own ranks, when compared with other more sectarian social movements throughout history, and certainly when compared with excessively hierarchical institutions such as the modern university or the Catholic Church. One reason for this anomaly is the fact that much of the secularist movement is made up of unaffiliated *individuals*. Another reason for this is the dispersed and weak tie nature of the movement. As Christopher Hitchens (quoted in Cipolla 2007) says:

> We're not a unified group. But we're of one mind on this: The only thing that counts is free inquiry, science, research, the testing of evidence, the uses of reason, irony, humor, and literature, things of this kind. Just because we hold these convictions rather strongly does not mean this attitude can be classified as fundamentalist.

---

[3] This quote is from the press release for Kurtz's paper, "What Is Secular Humanism?" retrieved from, http://www.secularhumanism.org/index.php?section=press&page=pr_pos_paper on March 30, 2009.
[4] See the September 14, 2007 POI podcast with Kurtz: http://www.pointofinquiry.org/paul_kurtz_the_new_atheism_and_secular_humanism/

Certainly the new atheists are viewed as leaders of a sort among many secularists; the texts they have written are viewed as important documents for 'advancing the cause' (be it through raising consciousness or deconversion). However, there is no collective manifesto that unites all secularists, nor any intellectual vanguard that claims to speak on behalf of all secularists today. Moreover, the common commitment in the secularist movement is a minimal 'no' to theism. This is both a strength and limitation of the current secularist movement.

New atheism has become a visible element of an increasingly complex society. And while new atheism has opened up a space for freethinkers, this is the same space occupied by their antagonists. This agonistic place/space—where a plurality of publics, or publics-within-publics, increasingly form against a backdrop of common options and information and are "superimposed more and more obviously and effectively on economic, aesthetic and political divisions" (Tarde 1969, 284)—is not only a *place* grounded in the medium of talk and *acting in concert*, but is also a *space* constituted by media events, technologies and *action at a distance*. Is the new atheism a social movement? A journalistic creation? A commercial phenomenon? It is only in taking a broader view and not privileging one medium or metaphor (of war for example) over another that allows one to grasp new atheism as a total social fact: individual and collective, psychological and social, cognitive and perceptual, economic and cultural. Relinquishing institutional and normative determinism demands that we attempt to grasp the entire unfolding of atheism in all its variety and turn our attention towards the actions and events from which such values, norms, and social institutions ultimately arise. Perhaps, taking the role of the atheist, only one question remains: will the future society be as propitious to an atheist revolution as it was for some books on atheism?

Part IV: Philosophy, Ethics, and
the New Atheism

ETHICS, OUT-GROUP ALTRUISM, AND THE NEW ATHEISM

Gregory R. Peterson

Historically, atheism and immorality have often been equated. In *A Letter Concerning Toleration*, John Locke (2003, 246) argued at length for state toleration of religious diversity, but excluded atheists on the grounds that "Promises, covenants, and oaths, which are the bonds of human society, can have no hold on the atheist." Presumably, since the atheist believes that there is no God to enforce the moral law, the atheist has no external compulsion requiring the keeping of one's word if it proves inconvenient. With no other no motivation than self-interest, the atheist will not be committed to higher values of commitment and sacrifice in a way that is recognized by the religious.

It is a shared theme of the new atheism that this argument is not only wrong, but that it should be turned on its head. The new atheists almost uniformly claim that it is modern atheists who hold the moral high ground, and that it is the practitioners of the world's religions that are immoral, both in historical practice and in fundamental commitment. An important feature of this critique is the supposed differential between atheism and theism on one value in particular: out-group altruism. While atheism is understood to be compatible with and even to support out-group altruism, the theistic religious traditions presumably do not. If true, this could be a very powerful critique of theistic worldviews. One traditional line of argument for theism is that belief in God undergirds our moral perspective and action, and that a serious consideration of moral duty provides grounds for belief in God (Kant 1993 and C.S. Lewis 1952 provide two well-known but very different approaches). Not only would the new atheist critique undermine this class of arguments, it would provide reasons to not believe in theism.

The truth, however, seems closer to Locke's view than the new atheists. While we may disagree with Locke today in his equating atheism with immorality and in his proposed intolerance of atheists, it is not at all clear that atheism as described by the new atheists truly supports out-group altruism, while it seems fairly clear that at least one of the major theistic traditions of Western civilization, Christianity, does.

Further, it is not altogether clear that the new atheists are consistent in their own advocacy of out-group altruism, and while it may be inappropriate to make too much of their sparse and individual ethical recommendations in what are essentially polemical works, the statements that they do make suggest a rather different perspective.

SOME PRELIMINARIES

For the argument to proceed, some preliminary remarks are in order. Although there are a number of authors with books that might be aptly put under the label of the new atheism, I will be focusing solely on four authors: Richard Dawkins (2006), Daniel Dennett (2006), Sam Harris (2004), and Owen Flanagan (2007). The reason for including the first three is obvious: they are the most prominent advocates of the new atheism and their works have had the most impact at the popular level. The inclusion of Flanagan is less obvious, but important. As will be seen, the treatment of normative ethics by the new atheists is rather sketchy, and Flanagan's recent book provides in many ways a best-case proposal for a normative account of ethics grounded in the general worldview that the new atheists appear to share. If Flanagan's approach does not richly support out-group altruism, then the prospect of the new atheism doing so generally seems dire.

The argument for the support of out-group morality within a theistic context will be similarly limited, arguing that the Christian tradition properly understood does in fact promote out-group altruism, contrary to the critiques put forth by the new atheists. Admittedly, the history of Christians in practice, as is the history of practitioners of any tradition that has been around long enough, has had its share of moral failures, as the new atheists keenly point out. Although this history is to some degree relevant, it is not the primary point: either a tradition provides rational support for out-group altruism or it does not. There are further issues of connecting principles with practice, some of which will be discussed below, but that is not the focus here, as empirical diversity in Christian communities allows one to find an example of nearly any variation in belief or practice. There are no doubt communities that do in fact believe that a proper understanding of Christian faith and tradition does not support out-group altruism. All that can be said about such communities in this context is that they seem to be profoundly mistaken in their understanding of their own faith tradition.

Finally, it is necessary to clarify what is meant by 'out-group altruism.' Generally, an out-group can be defined in terms of any group with which an individual does not currently identify. Altruism may be defined variably as the helping of others at cost to oneself—the biological definition—or as helping others with no benefit or expectation of return, a definition which is also widely used. Human history is replete with out-group hostility exemplified by war, national rivalry, racism, and class conflict. At the same time, out-group altruism is also evident, though arguably more rare. Obvious cases could be found in the effort to eradicate poverty and injustice in distant places, or within the abolitionist movement in the United States or among Holocaust rescuers during World War II. From the perspective of some religious traditions, missionary activity may be seen as altruistically motivated in principle. Even simple acts such as leaving a tip at a restaurant to which one does not plan to return may be understood as an essentially altruistic act, even if a rather trivial one.

The new atheists seem to assume that the affirmation of out-group altruism is a widely accepted value in modern Western nations. At some level, they are probably correct, although the claim is not as obvious as it might at first seem. It is certainly true that a good many individuals in Western societies display out-group altruism to varying degrees, as might be evidenced by their support for disaster relief, support for foreign aid for the purpose of helping the poor, activism in support of human rights issues in foreign countries, advocacy on behalf of out-groups within their own nations, and so on. Although these actions certainly seem altruistic, they may be otherwise in individual cases. Foreign aid may be promoted with an eye towards national self-interest, and individuals may donate to charities, not because of sincere concern for others, but out of a desire to look good. Thus, actions which appear altruistic on the surface are not always so; an altruistic action may be performed for non-altruistic motives. The distinction between altruistic action and altruistic motive is an important one, and can sometimes create considerable confusion (Sober and Wilson 1998). In addition, although many do have altruistic motives and engage in altruistic actions, many do not, choosing not to support the kind of actions listed and sometimes doing so precisely on what they perceive to be moral grounds. In this vein, it should be noted that the support for out-group altruism in moral philosophy is similarly complex. Out-group altruism is clearly endorsed in the utilitarian tradition, which is disinclined to see distinctions based on family relations or national borders as having primary significance. Peter Singer exemplifies the modern utilitarian's commitment to a high level of out-group altruism, being a consistent and vocal proponent of international assistance to the less advantaged, and an advocate for considerable financial sacrifice on the part of those living in the developed world. The endorsement of out-group altruism is more complicated, however, in more standardly deontological or rights-based frameworks, in which it is common to make a distinction between obligatory and supererogatory acts and to distinguish between principles of non-maleficence and beneficence, with the former carrying the greater weight. On such accounts, the ethical life certainly commands us to do no harm, but the command to actively do good, especially to those not near at hand, is often seen to be considerably weaker (for one such account, see John Arthur 2007). The denial of the importance of out-group altruism is sometimes placed on other grounds as well (Rand 1989).

OUT-GROUP ALTRUISM AND THE NEW ATHEIST CRITIQUE OF RELIGIOUS ETHICS

Although the work of the new atheists tends to focus on the question of the rationality of religion, there is also substantial discussion of the relation of religion to ethics. Indeed, Harris, Dennett, and Dawkins each devote at least a chapter to the relation of religion and morality, and comments about the relation appear elsewhere in their works. Part of the reason for this is a sense of outrage—apparent particularly in Harris—over the relation of religion to violence, especially as it is manifested in religiously motivated terrorism. Further, since it is often claimed by religious believers that atheists are immoral and that morality can only be properly grounded by belief in God, the new atheists are eager to show that not only is this not true, but that religious morality itself is, in important respects, defective. Thus, Harris criticizes the role of religion in making illegal 'victimless crimes' such as prostitution, while Dawkins faults the doctrine of original sin as being intrinsically immoral, and Dennett makes the claim (without irony) that religious belief leads to a dangerous sense of moral certitude that lends itself to abuse in the hands of fanatics (Harris 2004, 159; Dawkins 2006, 250–252, Dennett 2006, 294–297).

It is not possible here to address the entire range of arguments given, some of which are more substantive than others, and some of which rely on misinterpretation or crude characterizations of the authors' religious opponents. Several arguments rely on not very serious considerations of interpretation and the role that scripture plays in religious communities. Thus, Dawkins relishes in re-telling accounts of the misbehaviour of the biblical patriarchs, seemingly unaware that, however the biblical patriarchs are understood, they are generally not understood as moral exemplars *simplicitir* in contemporary religious communities, nor are they regarded as such in the context of scripture itself. Sometimes there is a simple misquotation, as when Dennett cites Acts 3: 23 as evidence that the New Testament commands death to apostates, when the passage in question is itself a quotation of Deuteronomy in a sermon by the Apostle Peter, and it is doubtful that the reference to a death penalty in the original passage is the point of Peter's use of the quotation (Dennett 2006, 289).

At other times, poor argumentation is the primary culprit. Both Dennett and Harris blame religious moderates for 'providing cover' for religious extremists, and argue that religious moderates are responsible for the actions of the extremists for whom they provide cover. Dennett uses the analogy of a backyard swimming pool as a legal nuisance: it is up to the owner to make sure others don't come to harm in it, and it is similarly up to religious moderates to make sure that religious extremists don't cause trouble (Dennett 2006, 298). It is difficult to believe that Harris and Dennett are serious about making such a claim. It is certainly the case that religious moderates (for lack of a better term), because of their familiarity with the tradition, are well placed to engage in monitoring extremism, and, apparently unbeknownst to Dennett and Harris, many 'religious moderates' do engage in such activity. If taken seriously, however, their claim would have to hold for the activities of other extremists. Should environmental 'moderates' be held responsible for acts of environmental vandalism and violence? Must peaceful protesters of economic injustice be held responsible for their more intemperate counterparts? I doubt that Harris and Dennett would apply their standard to these cases.

A prime feature of the new atheist argument seeking to disconnect religion and morality, however, deals specifically with out-group altruism; Western theistic religions are targeted for their alleged rejection of out-group altruism and for their advocacy of out-group hostility. Part of the argument relies on the citation of specific scriptural texts that are said to support out-group hostility and, in particular, violence and even genocide. These are admittedly not hard to find in the Old

Testament, but Dawkins claims to find similar out-group indifference
or hostility in the New Testament; his sole source for this view being an
article by John Hartung in *Skeptic* magazine. But the argument is but-
tressed by historical examples of religiously tinged malfeasance—the
crusades being an obvious reference—and contemporary links between
religion, violence, and terror, including the attacks of September 11
and the intemperate American response to them.

Presumably, the dual consideration of scripture and empirical reference is intended to provide a complete argument: the analysis of scriptural passages is intended to show that theistic religions do not support
out-group altruism in principle; the referencing of empirical moral
failures is intended to demonstrate that theists do not engage in
out-group altruism in practice, but often enough exhibit out-group
hostility instead. The conclusion the authors draw is that theism, and
specifically Christianity, promotes an inferior morality and immoral
behaviour. This implies that out-group altruism is indeed a positive
moral value and that it can be held consistently with the presuppositions of the new atheism. If this were not the case, the argument would
carry considerably less weight, and the conclusion might well be that
out-group altruism is unsupportable whatever metaphysical view one
takes. It is not clear, however, that the worldview espoused by the new
atheists has any real connection to out-group altruism, and while there
is nothing inconsistent about being a new atheist and an out-group
altruist, there is no necessary link either.

LINKING OUT-GROUP ALTRUISM AND THE NEW ATHEISM

The word 'new' in the label 'new atheism' is misleading in important
respects. The new atheism draws on long-standing currents of anti-
religious sentiment and, in particular, articulates a worldview sometimes referred to as materialism, physicalism, or, to use the now
commonly preferred term, philosophical naturalism, which holds that
the only things that exist are those entities that are currently described
by contemporary science or which can be understood to be some emer-
gent property thereof. Philosophical naturalism generally acknowledges that there are scientific discoveries yet to be made, but holds that
any future discoveries will not significantly upset our current understanding of the kinds of beings that exist. In particular, philosophical
naturalists are clear in their belief that science has shown some very

specific kinds of beings *not* to exist, those that we conventionally call 'supernatural.' Souls, ghosts, God, or gods are all on the list of disallowed entities. While science may discover new kinds of matter and even allow for the existence of an infinite number of unseen and unobservable universes, the philosophical naturalist asserts that science excludes the divine. Correspondingly, human beings are themselves purely natural, with the soul replaced by the mind, understood as emerging from the activity of the brain in interaction with its environment. Philosophical naturalists disagree on how best to understand the relation between mind and brain, but they share the conviction that however this relation is understood, it is a purely natural one (for similar descriptions of philosophical naturalism, see Flanagan 2007; Goetz and Taliaferro 2008).

Both Daniel Dennett and Richard Dawkins are philosophical naturalists, and are among the view's chief popularizers. Indeed, Dennett's influential book *Darwin's Dangerous Idea* provides a kind of systematic atheology for philosophical naturalism, giving an account of cosmic origins, human origins, ethics, and purpose, much as theologians do within a religious context. In what follows, I shall assume that Harris is also a philosophical naturalist, although categorizing him as such is problematic, as Harris surprisingly proclaims his openness to paranormal phenomena and life after death (cf. Harris 2004, 41, 208). Since Harris does not elaborate on these points, and since most of his arguments seem to presume the kind of philosophical naturalism that Dawkins and Dennett share, I will assume that Harris also shares this view until there is some further clarification.

For the philosophical naturalist, an initial problem is that of moral scepticism: if there is no divine lawgiver or sacred order from which moral values are derived, then it is not clear to what extent moral values have any grounding at all. Friedrich Nietzsche provided a classic analysis of this issue in his reflections on the death of God, and it has been a theme repeated in different ways in twentieth-century philosophy (Nietzsche 1999). It is noteworthy that the new atheists are not moral sceptics—they seem to believe that there genuinely is something called morality, and that dedicated philosophical naturalists can have it. The question is, how?

Given the epistemic priority that the new atheists give to the sciences, it is not surprising that Harris, Dawkins, and Dennett all turn to the sciences in one form or another for an answer, calling upon evolutionary theory, empirical work in psychology and neuroscience, or both (for relevant aspects of Dennett's account of evolution and morality, see Dennett 1995, 2003). Although evolutionary theory provides grounds for the naturalness of much of human co-operative, and therefore, moral behaviour, it is not clear that out-group altruism is consistent with evolutionary theory. Categories of kin altruism and reciprocal altruism are now well-recognized: evolutionary theory is consistent with and supports heritable traits that promote, within limits, care for and even sacrifice on behalf of near kin. Reciprocal altruism, by contrast, explains some non-kin co-operation—it can make sense to help someone if it can be expected that the favour will be returned at a later time. Both kin altruism and reciprocal altruism are well-recognized principles, and both appear in Dawkins' signature work *The Selfish Gene* written more than thirty years ago. Both, however, are quite limited, and so subsequent efforts have endeavoured to explain how evolutionary theory can give rise to the extensive forms of co-operative behaviour in which human beings engage. Reputation theory provides one form of enhancement: if I willingly co-operate with others, I will build a reputation of being co-operative and agreeable, and so will be sought after by potential partners in the future. Reputation theory is an extension of reciprocal altruism, but has the advantage that the repayment does not need to be made by the one to whom aid was initially offered. On the other hand, reputation theory provides no motivation for co-operation when there is no likelihood that such actions will enhance one's reputation. With respect to out-group altruism, reputation theory would suggest that it makes sense to engage in such acts only if there is reason to believe that they would become public to those likely to be able to reciprocate in the future (Alexander 1987).

Richer support for co-operation can occur if principles of group selection can operate. Revived in particular by Elliott Sober and David Sloan Wilson, group selection supports altruism towards fellow group members as long as groups are tightly defined and migration between groups is limited (Sober and Wilson 1998). Group selection may be enhanced considerably if groups incorporate punishment of 'cheaters,' those who take advantage of the generosity of the group without themselves contributing (Boyd et al. 2003). But, although group selection combined with altruistic punishment extends the reach of evolutionarily supported theories of altruism, they are still limited to in-group as opposed to out-group forms of co-operation. Sober and Wilson are especially clear on this point, noting that group-selectionist accounts of co-operation have a concomitant dark side, being perfectly consistent with out-group hostility. Indeed, it is not difficult to see human history as the result of a group-selectionist biology, enabling us to form strong within-group ties of co-operation but leaving us prone to extremes of out-group competition.

Beyond this limit, evolutionary biology does not seem able to go, except to speculate that evolution has a 'long leash,' and that while out-group altruism does confer survival value, it is not harmful enough in a species like ours to be selected out of our behavioural repertoire (E. Wilson 1978). Therefore, evolutionary theory actually requires that the origin and development of the idea of out-group altruism is the result of cultural transmission rather than based on evolutionary accounts of behaviour. The acknowledgment that moral precepts derive from culture rather than biology is sometimes dressed up in the language of memes, a move that rhetorically suggests that one is not talking about culture but about biology still. This is the move that Dawkins makes, and the language of memes comes from him (see Dawkins 1989). Of course, the need for meme theory arises because biological explanation has reached its limits, and in the case of out-group altruism, that is precisely the point.

Even though evolutionary biology seems limited in its ability to explain out-group altruism, this does not mean that there are no other ways of biologically explaining human moral behaviour, and the past decade has seen a new wave of theorizing about morality from the perspective of psychology, economics, and neuroscience. In this new science of moral cognition, there appear to be two primary goals: the first is to show that there are universal moral norms that can be said to be biologically grounded, and the second is that the exercise of these moral norms can be correlated with and perhaps explained by distinct patterns of brain activity. Some of this research comes from the field of behavioural economics, which has demonstrated that actual performance in the playing of economic games deviates from narrow self-interest. A standard example is that of the ultimatum game, which is played between two individuals, one of whom is given a sum of money and the opportunity to split it with a second player, who has the opportunity to either accept or reject the money. If the second player rejects the offer, however, neither receives any of the money. From the standpoint of rational choice theory, the first player should offer the second player the smallest sum possible, and the second player should accept it, since there is no second round to the game and to reject the offer would leave both with nothing. Contrary to this expectation, the first player typically offers more than the minimum, and the second player usually rejects offers below 20 percent of the total, which are considered to be unfair (see Hauser 2006 for a summary).

Using a different approach, biologist Marc Hauser has used moral dilemmas to tease out moral intuitions, particularly with respect to disagreements between utilitarianism and deontology (Hauser 2006). Using data from a website on which individuals can volunteer from across the globe to respond to the moral dilemmas, Hauser concludes that responses are largely the same independent of cultural effect, including that of religion. For Hauser, this along with other data supports the view that human beings have an innate moral sense or module, and so our moral nature is as natural as our ability to learn language.

The ultimatum game and Hauser's dilemma research reflect the general character of the field, which is ongoing and includes debates concerning the respective roles of reason and emotion, as well as brain activity correlates and the causal role of neurotransmitters (cf. Greene 2001, Zak et al. 2007). For the new atheists, these studies are conceptually important, for they appear to bolster the claim that moral discrimination and behaviour is simply part of our biological nature and that our moral impulses are independent of religion. Thus, Dawkins makes much of Hauser's moral dilemma studies, and Harris expresses considerable confidence that we will soon have a science of morality that will explain to us what is in fact right and wrong (Dawkins 2006, 222–226; Harris 2004, 170–203). It is problematic to assert, however, that these studies show that we have a natural, in-born moral nature that simply matches our modern standards of ethics in Western society. While Hauser himself is prone to push the case for the naturalness of our moral judgments, he also acknowledges that there is a significant cultural component as well. Willingness to co-operate in another economic game, the public goods game, varies considerably across cultures, as does willingness to punish and accept punishment (Herrmann 2008).

Indeed, what the data seems to show is that our moral nature is quite mixed, containing within it the seeds of goodness as we usually understand the term, but also the seeds of more self-centred and destructive behaviour as well. Although most of us may share the intuition that in some circumstances it is permissible to sacrifice one to save five, we have differing intuitions about who matters morally and how they should be treated, a point driven home by Stanley Milgram's classic experiments. Milgram's experiments, in which most subjects proved willing to shock an apparently innocent test subject, indicate our willingness under some circumstances to inflict pain on others (Milgram 1963). Further, the empirical data to date concerning the relation of religion and ethics is more complicated than the new atheists seem inclined to admit (cf. Norenzayan and Shariff 2008). These observations indicate the limits, at least so far, of the current scientific literature on moral behaviour. By themselves, behavioural studies do not address nature/nurture relations, assuming that such relations can in fact be disentangled. Nor do they show how widely-held moral values came to be. Although atheists may give the same response as religious individuals to trolley-type moral dilemmas, most atheists grow up in societies strongly influenced by religious values. Left out is the important question of the influence of developmental history and influence, even when no longer consciously recalled in the adult. And, while biology may tell us how human beings are likely to behave in a given situation, it does not tell us how human beings *should* behave. This is perhaps a good thing, for human history, which is a broader source of empirical evidence about human behaviour than scientific experimentation, suggests that we are neither angels nor demons, but are quite capable, on occasion, of playing the role of both.

Owen Flanagan's Eudaimonics as a Best Case

If out-group altruism cannot be straightforwardly derived from evolutionary theory, and if empirical research does not demonstrate that humans have innate preferences for out-group altruism, where may the new atheist draw support for valuing out-group compassion? Owen Flanagan—whose work is highly relevant to the new atheists' agenda, as he shares with them their broad commitment to philosophical naturalism and to the kind of scientifically-informed approach that the new atheists endorse—has recently made an effort to support an expansive account of ethics that includes strong support for out-group altruism. In some respects, Flanagan's account may be seen as the best case possible for the new atheist, as it reveals the extent to which out-group altruism may be endorsed within the confines of a naturalistic framework—but it shows the limits as well.

Like Harris, Flanagan envisions a science of ethics, although one more broadly conceived than what Harris seems to propose. Flanagan envisions a 'eudaimonics,' a science of the good life, informed thoroughly by contemporary developments in the biological, psychological, and social sciences. As the term eudaimonics implies, Flanagan understands ethics to concerned with the good life, which involves addressing what Flanagan calls the "really hard problem": finding meaning within the context of philosophical naturalism. Although, Flanagan labels this a really hard problem, it is also clear that he views it as one that is eminently solvable, drawing on a range of studies, from data collected from Buddhist meditators to research on happiness and positive psychology, as well as the research that new atheists cite on evolutionary models of co-operation and on moral cognition.

Flanagan acknowledges that our nature is morally mixed, and he draws inspiration from the Chinese philosopher, Mencius, who speaks of the sprouts of goodness that must be nurtured in order to thrive. Further, Flanagan speaks optimistically about our Platonic nature in the sense that human beings naturally grasp at the categories of the good, the true, and the beautiful, categories, he says, that we now realize exist purely in the realm of the natural. The pursuit of happiness, then, is not the pursuit of ephemeral moments of pleasure, but something closer to what Buddhist meditators achieve after years of effort. Further, the good life includes the 'Aristotelian Principle' of seeking to maximize our capabilities and our willingness to engage in a 'wide reflective equilibrium' to resolve moral disputes and dilemmas, ideas that Flanagan borrows from John Rawls (1971). In the final chapter, Flanagan outlines his support for universal altruism, including out-group altruism, which he sees based on the rational understanding that if I desire to flourish, I must acknowledge that others have a right to flourish as well.

As appealing as this last claim is, it is not at all clear that it is entailed within the confines of philosophical naturalism, and acknowledgment that others have a right to flourish is not the same thing as out-group altruism. At best, it embodies the principle of non-maleficence—'do no harm'—not beneficence. Why, indeed, should I go out of my way to help others when there is no benefit to myself? One may certainly choose to do so, but it is difficult to maintain that there is any sort of necessity to this moral choice from within the context of philosophical naturalism. Indeed, from the perspective of philosophical naturalism, there is no such thing as moral necessity at all, only preferences that most of us share because of our common biological and cultural inheritance. In the framework of philosophical naturalism, morality is spelled with a lower-case 'm,' and is described as a working out of our drives in the context of a complex, social world.

Although the loss of the supernatural can lead one to a sense of despair—the feeling of being cast adrift into a cold, hostile universe—there is no requirement for one to feel this way. From the perspective of philosophical naturalism there are, ultimately speaking, no requirements at all. One may choose the option of despair, but not much is gained by such a choice, and wallowing in despair is distinctly unpleasant. As Aristotle observed, we all desire to be happy, and happiness is attained in part by living in community with others who engage in mutually supportive, reciprocal relations and which includes group-level altruism. In exploring the possibilities of this path, much of what Flanagan says is of interest and commendable from multiple moral perspectives.

It is not clear, however, that out-group altruism, or universal compassion, plays any significant role in the good life as so elucidated. Certainly, one is free to engage in out-group altruism if one is so inclined, and for some this may in fact bring considerable happiness and satisfaction. That all human beings have this impulse, or that all human beings have it equally, however, is far less plausible. It may be the sort of thing, as Flanagan suggests, that can be cultivated; but why cultivate it, if one can be happy without it? Must affluent Westerners seek to end poverty across the globe in order to achieve the good life in the sense that Flanagan describes? This seems doubtful.

Nevertheless, out-group altruism may be argued to make particular sense in the twenty-first century, partly on prudential grounds. As society becomes increasingly interconnected and globalized, the way our ancestors made distinctions between in-group and out-group altruism becomes less and less relevant. Not only can we reach across the world to affect others, others can also affect us, and doing good to others can have practical, reciprocal benefits. Further, modern media makes avoiding the suffering of others harder to avoid, at least when it takes place on a large scale, and so our involuntary sympathetic reactions, honed to react to far smaller group interactions in our evolutionary past, impel us to action, if only to assuage our guilt. Thus, out-group compassion may be a positive and productive value given our unique and complex social relations made possible by modern technology and progress. A good argument can be made to support this view, but it is a far cry from a universal endorsement of out-group altruism. Out-group altruism is a contingent moral value, dependent on time, place, and social circumstances, with a favourable conjunction only occurring now, having not been present for most of human history.

It is important to note here that I am not claiming that philosophical naturalism entails immorality. Rather, I contend that philosophical naturalism's morality includes only a contingent place for out-group altruism. It is differently moral from ethical theories that do entail out-group altruism. This leads us back to the new atheist critique of religious ethics. The new atheists claim that religious moralities are faulty in part because they are said to reject out-group altruism. But this critique falls apart because the worldview shared by the new atheists, that of philosophical naturalism, does not itself entail such a value. If out-group altruism is not a value to be prescribed, the failure to endorse out-group altruism cannot be considered a vice. The situation, however, seems to be far different even from this, for while the new atheism fails to make a compelling case for out-group altruism, such a case can arguably be found in at least some of the world's major religious traditions. If out-group altruism is to be held as a positive moral value, one that is more than contingently affirmed, then it is the worldview of the philosophical naturalist that appears to be deficient.

CHRISTIANITY AND COMPASSION FOR THE OTHER

A strong case can be made that compassion for the other, including out-group compassion, is a value shared widely across the world's religious traditions. Although I will be speaking specifically about the Christian tradition, I believe that similar arguments can be made from the perspective of other religious traditions with respect to out-group altruism: the major religious traditions share an awareness of the transcendent that moves human motives beyond the merely prudential.

From the perspective of the new atheist, it is not at all clear that a Christian understanding of morality has much to commend it, due in part to the upalatability of many scriptural passages to modern moral scruples, the history of moral malfeasance by Christian communities, and the content of some forms of Christian morality today. The unfortunate reality is that many Christians are not very sophisticated in their moral thinking or interpretive practice, at least no more so than the general populace. As previously indicated I cannot claim to represent all modes of interpretation and practice found in existing Christian communities, rather I will argue for what may be understood as an optimal case of Christian support for out-group altruism. Although the specifics that follow may be particular to this account, the general outline is widely shared by Christians, scholars, ministers, and laypersons alike.

Christianity begins with the encounter with Christ, both as a historical figure who lived some two thousand years ago, and as a real presence today. The Christian claim is that in Jesus we see God, and so we are willing to embrace the risky and somewhat unclear language that God had become incarnate in Jesus. As such, Jesus' life and action are revelatory, pointing to God's identity and providing, through his life and teaching, a model and point of reflection for living a truly good life. Among these actions and teachings are those that point to care for the radically other in society, as embodied in the Sermon on the Mount, the Parable of the Good Samaritan, the healing of the centurion's daughter, and numerous other passages, including the Great Commission that concludes the Gospel of Matthew, although its command to make disciples of all nations tends to be understood in a primarily confessional sense. But if the language of discipleship is taken seriously, it implies something much more: a following after the pattern that Jesus has set.

I begin with this observation to counter a profound misunderstanding on the part of the new atheists; that Christianity simply consists of reading biblical texts much like one would simplistically read a contemporary code of law, woodenly applying isolated biblical texts shorn of context to contemporary moral issues. Their misunderstanding is understandable, as it is widely shared by many on the religious right who have in recent years wielded considerable political power, sometimes to terrible effect. But any thorough engagement with the tradition and with theological reflection quickly suggests this approach is problematic in multiple ways. The theological starting point of the Christian faith is not a book, but a person and an understanding of that person's significance. Consequently, it is the understanding of Christ that informs the reading of the Old Testament, and not the other way around. Indeed, the Old Testament is so-named for a reason, and one of the earliest disputes in Christian history was precisely about how to understand the significance and relevance of the Old Testament. Even the documents of the New Testament need to be interpreted with this understanding in mind. Scripture is better understood as a resource than a law book; it is something to turn to for inspiration, reflection, and sometimes-difficult moral wrestling, not as a list of directives to be slavishly obeyed.

A concern for the other, the outsider, can be found in the life and teachings of Jesus, but it can also be connected to the broader Christian worldview. By the Christian account, the world is itself created, and the creation is affirmed as good. There is a telos, a structure to creation that is affirmed, however hidden it may sometimes seem. For the Christian to speak of good lives, then, is to speak of lives in the context of this larger understanding. Accordingly, the goal of life is not an Epicurean pursuit of personal pleasure, but a life engaged in service and commitment to the other. Such a life need not preclude happiness in the ordinary sense, and one may expect such a life to result in the realization of deeper forms of happiness and well-being such as Flanagan commends. But such a life may also call upon us to suffer on behalf of the other. The cross itself is a symbol of this suffering, a recognition that God co-suffers with us while calling on us to engage the suffering of the world.

Rather than being a foreign element reluctantly grafted onto it, the concern for the other, including the radically other, is at the heart of the Christian understanding of the moral life, embodied in God's own creative and redeeming actions. Indeed, a central problem for much of Christian theology has been its repeated inability to meet such ethical demands, thus the extensive reflection on categories of guilt and grace, from Paul to Augustine and Aquinas, and from Luther and Calvin to the present. This concern for the other, inclusive of out-group altruism, is something that can be shared by the new atheist informed by philosophical naturalism, but there is nothing about the new atheism as a philosophy that compels such a move. It is optional, much as it is optional whether one chooses to be a dentist rather than a lawyer. That the new atheist authors do proclaim this value does not say as much about the new atheism as it does about the religiously informed cultural milieu that they inhabit.

Concluding Thoughts on Toleration and the Content of Ethics

It is remarkable that, more than three centuries later, Locke's arguments concerning toleration remain relevant. Locke's context was quite different than our own, written in the wake of the wars of the Reformation and amid ongoing political and religious unrest in seventeenth century England. Locke argued against persecution on grounds of religious belief, but also required that religious communities be of such character as to not violate basic principles of law and civil order. The idea of toleration, embodied in principles of freedom of speech and freedom of religion, have been staples of western democratic understandings of civil rights and moral expectations, and as time has gone on, our understanding and appreciation of the principle of toleration has been deepened and broadened to include groups not previously understood to be deserving of such respect.

That the new atheists directly challenge this principle of toleration is troubling, although it is no doubt due in part to the rise in influence of intolerant forms of religious practice in the past decade. Nevertheless, the new atheists envision nothing less than the abolition of religious belief. The only thing that is unclear is the means and the extent to which this intolerance is to be carried out.

Although Harris's volume *The End of Faith* contains a number of vitriolic passages describing the evils of religion, it is not altogether clear what he recommends as the solution to what he sees as the blight of religious ignorance. Presumably, proper education is the very least that is called for, and it may be surmised that Harris would like to see that those who are beguiled by religion be informed of the error of their ways. It is instructive, however that some of Harris's political commitments suggests a stronger approach, for in the latter chapters of his book he endorses U.S. support of despotic governments as a means of controlling potentially violent fundamentalist movements, and he also supports torture of terror suspects on the grounds that it is equivalent to the suffering and collateral damage that occurs even in a just war (cf. Harris 2004, 132, 194–196). Although Harris's concern in these passages is directed towards extremists, his willingness to characterize all religious individuals as extremists makes such statements troubling. They also rob the new atheism of whatever moral high ground it may have; an ethic that readily supports torture and tyrants undermines its own moral sensibility.

Dawkins' recommendations for religion are more direct, as he seriously and unapologetically has put forward the argument that religion constitutes a form of child abuse. No parent, Dawkins argues, has the right to indoctrinate his or her children with religious beliefs. Further, appeals to the value of cultural diversity and acceptance of differences do not have standing, claims Dawkins; when it comes to issues of raising children, the potential for longstanding harm is too great (Dawkins 2006, 311–344). These arguments are also put forward by Dennett, who articulates along with Dawkins a demand for cultural education that exposes children to all traditions, allowing them freedom of choice (Dennett 2006, 321–339).

Certainly, a program that encourages greater cultural literacy, including literacy about the world's religious traditions has much to commend it, and the specific cases of religious upbringing that Dawkins cites in defence of his position are deeply troubling. The willingness to use these cases to tar all instances of religious upbringing as instances of child abuse, however, is equally troubling. Since all three authors proclaim religious 'moderates' to be complicit in the activities of extremists, there would seem to be no middle ground; if one is religious and brings up their children to be similarly religious, one is a child abuser. Given this charge, surely more is warranted than a good public education. In an earlier work, Dennett recommends that religions be put in cages and those deemed threatening quarantined (Dennett 1995, 515–519). Perhaps Dennett is not serious about this, or perhaps Dennett is just talking about religiously motivated terrorists engaged in conspiracy to break the law. Child abuse is a serious charge. Should not child abusers be put in prison, or at least be separated from their children?

Even if the new atheists do not intend such a conclusion, their rhetoric makes more charitable interpretations difficult. I also doubt that the new atheists are calling for an end to freedom of speech and conscience, but then what they are recommending? The wisdom of the Enlightenment rightly discovered that tolerance is at least a political virtue. Is it also a moral virtue? Should one put up with views one thinks are obviously wrong, and at what point should tolerance be withdrawn?

It is instructive that in their arguments supporting intolerance of religious belief, there is little mention of toleration of political belief. If raising a child Christian or Muslim would be child abuse, so too would be raising a child to be a Nazi, a Leninist or a monarchist, a racist or sexist, or perhaps even a Republican or Libertarian. Pushed too far, the political absurdity of these arguments becomes clear, even if the moral question remains: how tolerant must I be of my neighbour who harbours political views I find unpalatable? I certainly am not inclined to be tolerant of a neighbor who holds (for instance) neo-Nazi commitments, nor would I approve of how they raise their children.

I may even forbid my own children to associate with their children to protect them from such harmful ideas and ways of life.

At the same time, we may ask a different question, how best can I love my neighbour? The new atheist solution seems to be to vilify my neighbor as publicly as possible, threaten to remove their children, and then forcibly educate them with opposing ideas. Perhaps this would work, but it could hardly be called love. Love, it would seem, requires engagement and encounter, without being weak or unprincipled. To the extent that toleration is a moral virtue, and not just a political one, it would seem to entail such engagement. True concern for the other involves engagement and even sacrifice, even when that engagement and sacrifice is not reciprocated or deserved. That the new atheists fail to recognize this suggests the limits to which they embrace the ethic they claim to espouse. If the new atheists pursued such a course, and it turned out that they were correct that religious commitment is unfounded and best replaced by a philosophical naturalism, then they might well expect that religion would indeed wither away in the face of reason. But they also might discover that religious commitment is different from the caricature they have drawn, and that rational reflection on those things which are ultimate, lead down different paths than the ones they have trod.

DISPARATE DESTINATIONS, PARALLEL PATHS: AN ANALYSIS OF CONTEMPORARY ATHEIST AND CHRISTIAN PARENTING LITERATURE

Jeff Nall

INTRODUCTION

According to available research, Americans hold atheists suspect more than any other group, including Muslims, and homosexuals. Americans tend to identify atheists as 'other,' associating them with immorality and selfish indulgence. Moreover, since common wisdom holds that religion is a source for morality, many believe that children are better served by being raised in a religious environment. Atheists whose voices have become increasingly present in popular culture, however, are challenging this perception, both indirectly and directly. The following work draws particular attention to the recent birth of atheist parenting literature, which implicitly challenges the broader American public's many assumptions. Moreover, in a kind of reversal, the literature explicitly critiques religious approaches to parenting, a minority of which (Richard Dawkins, for example) expresses concern that religious indoctrination harms children. In particular, this work tests the prevailing wisdom about the differences between atheist and Christian approaches to parenting. Unsurprisingly, I find that Christians aim to develop their children into faithful followers of God, while atheists aim to develop their children into rational free-thinkers who disdain dogmatism. The significant discovery, however, is that while the overarching aim of these parenting approaches is fundamentally different, the moral qualities which both seek to instill in their children are virtually identical. In short, both Christian and atheist parenting approaches are enthusiastically committed to instilling in their children a deep appreciation of honesty, consideration of others, and honest living. Finally, this chapter also shows that emerging leaders within the atheist movement generally are highly critical of the ridicule and abuse of religion exerted by the new atheists specifically.

JUSTIFICATION FOR CHOICES OF TEXT

One may question the criteria for selecting material for a work of this kind. My choices are based on both the popular impact and represent-ative nature of the works and authors. The rationale for choosing the texts used to represent atheist parenting is two fold. First, the texts are the first and only known non-religious parenting books to have been widely published. The source I principally use to represent atheist parenting, *Parenting Beyond Belief: On Raising Ethical, Caring Kids Without Religion*, has achieved significant sales success. As of January 13 2009, it ranks 16,153 out of several million at Books on Amazon. com, including eleventh in the category of 'Parent Participation,' fourth in 'Morals & Responsibility' (a subdivision of the 'Parenting & Families') category, and third in 'Reference' (also a subdivision of 'Parenting & Families'). Secondly, I utilize sections from Richard Dawkins and Christopher Hitchens, which exemplify new atheist attitudes on the subject of parenting.

To analyze Christian parenting approaches, I use two key Christian texts that reflect a popular view of Christian parenting in the United States. It should be stated, however, that these texts largely reflect a conservative Christian viewpoint and do not reflect the views of the nation's growing liberal Christian population. I have chosen George Barna's *Revolutionary Parenting: What the Research Shows Really Works* as a representative work for two key reasons. First, Barna is one of the most prominent Christian leaders in the United States. He has written thirty-nine books addressing Christian issues ranging from church life, spiritual growth, various trends, and children. Barna is also the founder of The Barna Group, a well-known market research firm which focuses on studying American religious belief and behaviour. The book also has a high sales rating on Amazon.com. (As of January 13, 2009, *Revolutionary Parenting* ranked number 21,462 in Books on Amazon). Secondly, the work offers advice based on the views and approaches of committed Christian parents. As such, it is perhaps one of the most representative texts on Christian parenting practices. My choice of *Parenting by The Book* (2007) by John Rosemond is based on the work's bestselling status; it ranks 13,868 in books on Amazon.com. The work also ranks high in two of Amazon's sub-categories within the cat-egory of books: second in 'Psychology & Christianity,' and seventy-first in 'Child Development.' The author of the work is equally popular, hav-ing written a total of eleven best-selling parenting books and having appeared on numerous television programs including *20/20*, *Good Morning America*, *The View*, Bill Maher's *Politically Incorrect*, and *The Today Show*.

ATHEISTS AS OTHER

Atheists are perhaps the most disliked minority in the United States. According to Penny Edgell in the Public Agenda poll (2006), in a presidential election, Americans are more likely to vote for a homosexual or Muslim than an atheist. Moreover, parents cite atheists among the least likely groups they would wish their children to marry (Edgell et al. 2006, 212). Whereas, while an increase in acceptance for racial and religious minorities has been on the rise in the United States, atheists have not benefited from this increase in tolerance (212). In fact, when asked whether atheists agreed with their vision of American society, a total of 78.6 percent of respondents answered either 'somewhat' or 'not at all.' Almost 40 percent answered 'not at all' (218). What is equally striking is that, among those who reject atheists, approximately 17 percent of non-religious respondents say that "atheists do not at all share their vision of America, while about one in ten indicate that they would not approve of their child marrying an atheist" (218). A number of presumptions are bound up in these statistics, influencing most Americans' attitudes about atheists. Foremost, many tend to have trouble believing atheism can be congruent with family values. Since most Americans reflexively associate morality with religion, they tend to mistrust atheists, who fail to subscribe to any religious system and by extension do not belong to a well-defined community (213). Moreover, because they connect morality with religion, Americans naturally tend to believe it is detrimental to the character development of children to raise them without religion; 74 percent agreed that 'it is a bad idea for families to raise children without any religion.'

When asked to identify the most important meaning of being religious, 53 percent of respondents said, "making sure that one's behavior and day-to-day actions match one's faith." The authors of the Public Agenda poll conclude that, for many Americans, to be religious "means to be a moral human being." This is likely the reason that about 50 percent of Americans said they would not vote for an openly atheistic presidential candidate. Such "widespread political rejection of atheists and others who profess no religion" indicates a significant exception to the notion of increased social tolerance over the last three decades. Others reviewing changes from 1937 to 2000, however, believe that current attitudes are part of the constant pattern of intolerance for atheists. While acceptance of Catholics, Jews, African Americans, and homosexuals has significantly risen over the years, acceptance of atheists has increased minimally (215).

In particular, the poll's respondents tended to associate atheism with either "illegality, such as drug use and prostitution—that is, with immoral people who threaten respectable community from the lower end of the status hierarchy," or "rampant materialists and cultural elitists that threaten common values from above—the ostentatiously wealthy who make a lifestyle out of consumption or the cultural elites who think they know better than everyone else." The net representation of atheists is one of self-interested individualists who are "not concerned with the common good" (226–227).

According to the 2001 American Religious Identification Survey (ARIS), 14 percent, or more than 30 million Americans, do not subscribe to any particular religion (Keysar 2001). While some atheist groups have mistakenly taken this to mean that 30 million Americans are implicitly atheists,[1] further inspection of the study proves otherwise. Of those who responded to the question, "what is your religion?" by saying "no religion," 45 percent strongly agreed that God exists. In fact, 36 percent of "nones" actually considered themselves religious or somewhat religious. Only 21 percent of "nones" disagreed or somewhat disagreed with the statement that God exists (about 3 percent of the population). 9 percent somewhat disagreed and 12 percent strongly disagreed (Keysar 2003, 32). Polls tend to support the conclusion that avowed atheists make-up about 2 to 3 percent of the United States population. The 2005 Associated Press/Ipsos poll found only 2 percent of Americans "don't believe in God" and a 2005 Pew Research Center poll found that 3 percent of Americans "don't believe in either" God or universal spirit/higher power. While slightly confusing the generalized boundaries designed to interpret our surroundings, one might also consider the interesting but little-discussed phenomenon of 'Christian atheists.' In October 2003, the Harris poll found that even some Christians do not believe in God. The Harris poll reported that 8 percent of

---

[1] After the release of the 2001 ARIS, American Atheists reported that the "ARIS count now shows that the non-believer population has grown to 29.4 million, roughly 14.1 percent of the American community" (American Atheists, 2005).

Catholics and 2 percent of Protestants in the United States 'believe there is no God.' In total these 'Christian-atheists' make-up nearly 3 percent of the entire nation. An additional 13 percent of Catholics and 6 percent of Protestants are 'not sure whether or not there is a God.' That makes what we could call 'Christian-agnostics' of another 6 percent of the nation. Since they first identify themselves as "Christian, these Christian-atheists may be in addition to the 2 to 3 percent of the standard atheist community. In any case, while atheists comprise a small percentage of the overall U.S. population, at six million or more they constitute a significant block of like-minded people.

CHRISTIAN PARENTING LITERATURE

Published in 2007, George Barna's *Revolutionary Parenting: What the Research Shows Really Works* states his desire to assist parents in producing a particular kind of young adult, which he calls a 'spiritual champion.' George Barna began his research into parenting by reviewing the wealth of existing popular parenting literature. Barna (2007, xii) found that authors asserted that good parenting encompasses five dimensions: personal attributes, imperative parental practices, parenting philosophy and perspectives, child-rearing skills, and tangible outcomes. Barna, however, found the hundreds of works he reviewed to be insufficiently thorough. "Virtually every book is based upon personal observations, experiences, or assumptions," he wrote. "Very little of the content is based on objective, projectable research." Moreover, parenting books rarely recognize "the fact that the child is a special gift and that raising children is a responsibility assigned to parents by God." Parenting books fail to "acknowledge that God has designed every human being as a unique individual, eliminating the possibility of effective one-size-fits-all parenting strategies" (Barna 2007, xiii).

Operating from the presumption that children are gifts to their parents from God, Barna (2007, xiv–xv) writes that parents should conduct what he calls 'revolutionary parenting.' Revolutionary parents are first and foremost Revolutionary Christians, defined as Christians "for whom God is their priority in life, and everything they do stems from their perception that they live only to love, obey, and serve God" (Barna 2007, 102). In the same passage, Barna also defines several of these kinds of Christians: (1) evangelical Christians—"many of whom are Revolutionary in their perspective, and all of whom engage in spreading the gospel of Christ and adopting an orthodox view of Scriptures." (2) Non-evangelical, born-again Christians who "have confessed their sinfulness to God and sought His forgiveness through Christ, but whose interpretations of the Bible and commitment to thoroughly practice its admonitions are spotty." (3) Notional Christians — "those who think of themselves as Christian but are not deeply spiritual and do not have a life-changing relationship with Jesus Christ. Their commitment is more to being religious than it is to being transformed by Christ and living differently because of that faith." (4) Revolutionary Christians; they stand out in this crowd as those most capable of producing truly godly children. These kinds of Christians have what it takes to be Revolutionary parents, aiming to "raise children who make their faith in God, and relationship with Him, their highest priority in life, and proceed to live as intentional and devoted servants of God." Only revolutionary parenting can produce a spiritual champion, which is one who embraces Jesus Christ as Savior and Lord, and accepts the Bible as truth and as the guide for life, seeking to live in obedience to its principles and searching for ways to continually deepen his or her relationship with God (Barna 2007, xvi).

The basis for Barna's parenting suggestions comes from The Barna Group's research into the parenting styles of those who have produced spiritual champions. He used interviews with young adults who had been identified as leading 'transformed lives' as well as interviews with their parents to develop a scheme for quality parenting (2007, xix–xx). Barna works from the presumption that there is a crisis in American parenting, beginning with the way in which we judge whether or not children are doing well. Barna (2007, 6–7) writes that we would be missing the point if we determined the state of parenting by focusing on "the decline in educational performance"; "the percentages of teens and adolescents having sexual intercourse, smoking, drinking, using drugs, or being victimized by violent crime"; the "13 million children who live in poverty, or the 18 million who are being raised by a single parent"; "the 12 million children who are overweight, or the millions of children (particularly girls) who wrestle with anorexia and bulimia, or the 8 million children who receive sub par health care because they have no health insurance." The fundamental criterion missing to truly determine the wellness of our youth, writes Barna, is God's notion of what they should be. The point parents miss is that "God is the absolute judge of how well our children are doing, that His standards examine the character and faith of our young people, and His ways are often not facilitated by many of the activities we promote or endure, regardless of our ignorance or good intentions." Barna's (2007, 7) guide operates from the presumption that God "create[d] us to love, serve, and obey Him," and therefore parents should strive to produce children who fulfill that calling.

To be a Revolutionary Parent one must first become what Barna (2007, 16) describes as a good coach. Parents can become good coaches by impacting their children's lives "proportional to the depth of the relationship you have fostered with them." Quantity as well as quality, contends Barna, is of supreme importance. He writes that his "research underscores the silliness of the 'quality time' argument; there is no substitute for investing substantial time in your relationship with your children" (2007, 19). Revolutionary Parents are those who act as the constant coach, directing the child toward right paths, "wholeheartedly embrac[ing] the outcomes you are pushing the child to achieve"; continually addressing "the developmental needs of the child at the time when such feedback will have the greatest impact" (Barna 2007, 20). Parents should take "the lead in driving the dialogue and must be lovingly candid," create a parent led dialogue rather than a monologue that dominates rather than influences; and work toward achieving the goal of "raising a God-honoring human being" (Barna 2007, 20–21).

Above all, Barna believes the responsibility for a child's positive development lies with the parents. Among his most important findings, Barna (2007, xii) writes that parents "have the most dramatic personal influence on a child." He places very little importance on the value of outside agents in helping the child's growth. Above all, it is the responsibility of parents to produce spiritual champions, not the church, schools, government, or friends. Operating with a greater sense of duty and personal responsibility for their children's development, Revolutionary Parents are far more active in their children's lives than most parents. Revolutionary Parents and their children engage in somewhere between 90 and 120 minutes of direct dialogue compared to "the typical American family," which "registers less than fifteen minutes of direct parent-child conversation each day" (Barna 2007, 33–34). Revolutionary Parents utilize this additional daily talk time to explain why seeking their own spiritual growth is important. These parents also begin talking to their children at an early age and follow through with specific parenting objectives. Along the way they analyze their progress, adjusting their approach as they go along.

One of the most salient characteristics of the parenting model suggested by Barna is its focus on teaching not so much how to think freely, but rather providing children with the appropriate frame with which to think. Of course the specific frame Barna wishes children to utilize in examining and understanding the world is evangelical Christianity. In order to ensure children do indeed have a Christian frame, Barna writes that it is of paramount importance that parents begin influencing their children as soon as possible: "Many studies confirm that children begin absorbing values and beliefs as soon as they can understand language." Revolutionary Parents take this opportunity to begin influencing their children's thinking at an early age (Barna 2007, 38). "Transformational parenting entails adopting a leadership position when it comes to fostering a child's faith; leaving the job to the religious professionals is an inappropriate transfer of authority and power to people and organizations that God never intended" (Barna 2007, 96). Revolutionary Parents are devoted to God and incorporate their devotion into every facet of their lives. Not all the Revolutionary Parents he talked to possessed what Barna (2007, 105) calls a "biblical worldview," and many did not believe that "absolute moral truth exists." The Parents tended to encourage examination, but limited questioning to areas "within reason." But, in general, Revolutionary Parents recognized the importance of enforcing rules such as curfew and bedtime, and punished violations by grounding children. They also played an active, although often subtle, role in influencing their children's choice of friends.

Character is at the heart of Barna's model for parenting. He writes that his research found 100 percent of the Revolutionary Parent groups surveyed "agreed that the most important focus of their children's training was the development of godly character" (2007, 46). Specifically, Revolutionary Parents emphasized honesty over intellect, being a Godly servant over being a 'superstar,' and treating people fairly over athletic and academic accomplishment. Critical character traits one should look for in a child's development include: honesty, kindness, gentleness, reliability, encouragement, mercy, discipline, compassion, patience, self-control, consistency, humility, maturity, trustworthiness, love, joy, loyalty, perseverance, justice, stability, and sincerity. To instill these values in their children Revolutionary Parents generally laid out the following chief rules for their children: (1) be honest and reliable; (2) be honorable, specifically, never cheat or steal; (3) be respectful, even to those you do not agree with or like; (4) be helpful when possible; (5) refrain from using profanity or speaking angrily; (6) judge behaviour "insofar as it personally affects you or family members," not people's motives; (7) take up health habits such as physical exercise;

(8) actively pursue "your faith, in whatever form that journey takes"; (9) strive to succeed in school; (10) contribute to the family unit by carrying out household chores; (11) notify at least one parent of your whereabouts, and request parental approval before going out; and (12) "accept the penalties for inappropriate behavior" (Barna 2007, 65–66).

Discipline is critical to the process of instilling the prescribed values in children. Revolutionary Parents made sure that their children were well aware of and understood the rules. Moreover, rules were consistently applied without malice or parental inconsistency. The methods that Revolutionary Parents used to discipline their children varied. They had what Barna calls an 'unexpectedly broad' approach to discipline: "One couple said they recommend using a leather strap on children to enforce discipline. Another parent said neither she nor her husband had ever spanked their children or even raised their voices to them" (Barna 2007, 75). While refusing to wholeheartedly endorse it, Barna (2007, 135) makes clear that his approach does make room for parents who use spanking as a means for discipline: "There is no excuse for physical abuse or harshness, but the Scriptures do state that they won't die if you spank them. Physical discipline may well save them from death."

To choose revolutionary parenting is to choose a counter-cultural existence. This parenting model "creates the greatest emotional tension in the parenting marketplace of ideas and practices" (Barna 2007, xiv–xv). Barna makes it clear that a spiritual champion will face difficulty in society: "Spiritual champions live in ways that are noticeably different from the norm—even when compared to the average churchgoer." More specifically, spiritual champions believe in moral absolutes and acknowledge "the continual spiritual war between God and Satan" (Barna 2007, xvi). Barna envisions that the ideal child would develop keen discernment, carefully screening the media they ingest. Barna (2007, xvii) also projects that the ideal child would set out daily to "strive to change the world in small but life-impacting ways, whether it is done through feeding the hungry, counseling the bereaved, encouraging the confused, protecting the environment, or other means."

John Rosemond, a family psychologist and professional speaker and writer on parenting, writes that as American culture changes, parents will face new challenges. He points specifically to the change that occurred in the 60s and 70s: "By 1970, a cynicism and general disrespect had developed toward all forms of traditional authority, of which there are five: political, military, institutional, church, and family"

(Rosemond 2007, 20) He contends that what was assaulted was noth-ing less than "the very Judeo-Christian principles upon which Western civilization was built." The attack on the traditional family came from psychologists and other mental health professionals allying them-selves "with neofeminists to characterize the traditional family as the primary institution through which the so-called patriarchy exerted its domination of women and manipulation of children." He writes that feminists "equated traditional marriage with slavery and pro-moted 'open' marriages in which neither party was obligated to be faithful. Feminists and the increasingly female-dominated mental health elite joined with the media to demonize men as natural aggres-sors" (2007, 21).

The so-called assault on traditional marriage and family is of funda-mental importance to Rosemond's thoughts on parenting. He contends that quality parenting begins with a solid foundation between husband and wife. Children derive a sense of security when the parents have a strong marriage. "It follows that nothing makes a child feel more secure than feeling his or her parents' marriage is rock solid." In order for husband and wife to become quality parents, they must invest in their relationship. Rosemond (2007, 121) suggests, for instance, that parents vacation without children and refuse to share the marital bed with children, even as infants, to strengthen marriage. "The family that does 'everything' together is not a family operating according to God's instructions."

In terms of developing children's character in accordance with bibli-cal precepts, Rosemond insists that parents must lead by example. For starters, parents should not tolerate 'contrarian' behaviour from their children, even at the early age of three. Children who exhibit behav-iour such as contradicting parents about how nice the weather is or whether or not the grass is green should be forced to sit in time-out until they admit that the parent was correct: "I've heard of three-year-olds who sat for several hours before finally admitting that the grass was green. Such is the power of a child's rebellious spirit!" Contrarian behaviour, writes Rosemond (2007, 135), is a child's attempt to assert authority over the parent. Behaviourally, children as young as three who laugh or cry when it 'is not appropriate' should be taken aside and 'read the proverbial riot act.' Rosemond (2007, 136) writes: "A three-year-old who does not know that a certain impulsive reaction is inap-propriate should be taught, as forcefully as necessary, that the reaction is inappropriate."

Rosemond echoes Barna's assertion that parental influence is something that cannot be underestimated. Citing Deuteronomy, he writes that God demands that parents should be the most significant influence in their children's lives. In reality, however, most parents allow outside influences such as teachers, coaches, television, music and the internet to dominate. Parents should take direct action in making sure that their influence is number one in the child's life, even if that means systematically forcing children to reorder competing influences.

In terms of character, Rosemond criticizes most parents for failing to give parenting adequate attention. Instead of "training up an adult of character," he writes that parents are too often focused on "training up an adult of prestige, power, and position" (2007, 149). Parents are too focused on nearsighted goals, without being focused on producing character in children. Self-esteem, he argues, is also an area of concern. Rosemond writes: "I cannot emphasize enough that according to both the Bible and good research, possessing high self-esteem and being a person of character are incompatible." Instead, parents should go back to America's supposed earlier model in which "high self-confidence" is "tempered by realistic self-assessment" (2007, 142). More humility, in short, is what is needed: "The opposite of high self-esteem is humility, modesty, and 'meekness' (strength under control)." "Jesus was the only individual who has ever lived who had no self-esteem." As an example, Rosemond (2007, 143) writes that the Amish see opinionated outbursts of self-esteem as prideful.

According to Rosemond (2007, 205), "Postmodern Psychological Parenting and traditional biblical child rearing have nothing in common. They are, in fact, antithetical." One of the key areas in which this statement is made manifest is discipline. Rosemond (2007, 192) contends that "talking, reasoning, and explaining," is not discipline at all. He argues that behaviour modification is not discipline. Behaviour modification cannot work on human children because, according to Rosemond (2007, 200), they possess "two attributes that an animal does not possess: free will and a rebellious nature." He writes: "In the 1970s, I was the first parenting pundit to assert that a family should be operated as a benevolent dictatorship" (2007, 190). In terms of how children who misbehave should be disciplined, Rosemond explains that spankings, while not a be-all and end-all, do have their place. He dismisses anti-spanking arguments as misleading and unscientific. His contention is that spankings seem most effective for children who are between the ages of two and six.

ATHEIST PARENTING LITERATURE

In his *Raising Freethinkers: A Practical Guide for Parenting Beyond Belief,* Dale McGowan (2009, vii) writes that we are amid "the *birth* of a nonreligious parenting movement." McGowan initiated both *Raising Freethinkers* and *Parenting Beyond Belief: On Raising Ethical, Caring Kids Without Religion* (2007), the philosophical predecessor to the practical guide. In the foreword to *Parenting Beyond Belief,* Michael Shermer (2007, vii) responds to the presumption that atheist parents are ill-equipped to produce moral children: "It is almost a given in our society that kids should be raised with religion, because if they aren't, they will grow up to be juvenile delinquents, right?" This assumption is "bigoted" and "breathtakingly inane," insists Shermer. While the objectives of Christian and atheist parenting approaches are dramatically different, much of the advice proffered by the two previously studied Christian authors is found in the atheist approach to parenting as well.

Dale McGowan identifies seven virtues that atheist parents should be particularly concerned with instilling in their children; the first being humility. McGowan (2007a, 126–127) does not disdain having a high self-esteem as Rosemond urges; however he does chide "arrogance" which he describes as "extreme self-importance mixed with a dose of contempt for others." In this respect, we see a similarity between the seemingly disparate points of view. First, Rosemond's criticism of high self-esteem is hyperbolic. He follows the critique of self-esteem with a demand for humility. In essence, his complaint is about extreme self-esteem and self-indulgence. McGowan, too, has a problem with such arrogant self-importance.

Another disconnect between the two approaches is the way in which the develop the child's humility. While the Christian perspective contends that Christianity instills children with a sense of humility before God, atheists believe their worldview instills children with a sense of humility before the universe. Indeed, McGowan (2007a, 126–127) sees atheists as having an advantage over religion in terms of delivering a humble worldview: humility "is the natural consequence of religious disbelief" because it teaches children that they are not the "center of the universe." What is clear is that whereas Barna and Rosemond possess a notion of Christianity that offers ultimate, unchanging truth, the atheist tends to operate from the presumption that truth is a moving object which can only be possessed for short intervals before it must be sought after once more. This difference is driven home in the 2005 secular children's book *Humanism: What's That?* The author, Helen Bennett, a Unitarian Universalist humanist and retired teacher, directly engages children on humanist values through a fictional dialogue between an objective teacher and six inquisitive students. Through the teacher character, Mrs. Green, Bennett (2005, 37) also extols humility and the moving object of truth: "The fact is, *no one person or religion really knows the whole truth*—and that includes Humanists!"

While present in most atheist writings, humility is a trait absent from the critique proffered by new atheists. Christopher Hitchens, for example, makes the case that religion is child abuse, after visiting only its most extreme elements. Hitchens (2007b, 218) blames religion for "institutionalizing and refining the practice" of torture (with no mention of course of the United States' documented refinement of torture), promulgating both female and male genital mutilation, perpetuating 'the masturbation taboo,' and creating fertile ground for sexual abuse within the Roman Catholic Church. According to Hitchens, 'religious instruction' is responsible for much of the horrors of the world. The mistake of Hitchens critique is his use of the most extreme examples of unethical behaviour and practices to support his condemnation (see Nall 2008). Moreover, many Christians would join Hitchens in assailing many of these attitudes and practices. For his part, Richard Dawkins (2006, 339) condemns society for permitting parents to indoctrinate their children with their religious or political views: "A child is not a Christian child, not a Muslim child, but a child of Christian parents or a child of Muslim parents." Dawkins urges all parents to discern for themselves the validity or invalidity of the world's faiths; his advocacy of no religious training is to prepare children to realize the incompatibility of different religions. Dawkins echoes this parenting approach in "Good and Bad Reasons for Believing," a letter to his ten-year-old daughter Juliet, which appears in *Parenting Beyond Belief*. Here Dawkins advocates basing beliefs on evidence rather than tradition, authority, or revelation. He explains that "evidence" is "a good reason for believing something," and that scientists are "the specialists in discovering what is true about the world and the universe" (2007d, 13–14).

Clearly, any sound mind must agree with Dawkins that evidence and good reasoning, if they are to reflect some form of truth and be taken seriously, must bolster beliefs. Absent from Dawkins' suggestion here, however, is recognition of the way in which reason and evidence have been utilized to manipulate facts. Indeed, there are a number of problems with empirical and rational approaches to knowledge that New Atheists and their disciples are fast to forget. By grounding the primacy of empiricism and reason in their own system, each violates "Godel's proof, that no system is self-axiomatising" (Glynn 1991, 311–313). In short, both atheistics and religious approaches to knowledge derive their justification from within, grounding them tautologically. While it would be foolish to contend that beliefs do not require good arguments, one finds that New Atheists tend to reify reason and scientific observation, forgetting their inescapably subjective qualities. According to philosopher Simon Glynn, reason is nothing but the formal relations between facts. Our observation of facts, however, is conceptually mediated. Glynn (1991, 317) writes that "the laws of reason are indeed contextually constrained, and therefore, in this sense, relative." Moreover, the Truth of Falsity of a claim is dependent upon theoretical preconceptions, revealing that absolutist claims for reason are doomed to fail. While recommending the abandonment of the subjective vantage points inherent in religion, Dawkins and Hitchens fail to acknowledge the way in which conceptual frames influence even the non-religious scientist in discerning 'facts.' In a similar vein, even the far more open-minded atheist Dale McGowan speaks of secular parenting approaches' supreme advantage of being open to 'discovering' or pursing knowledge. Inherent in his advocacy of freethought's quest for knowledge is a failure to recognize the way in which our experience of the world is conceptually mediated. Thus, Heidegger (quoted in Glynn 1991, 313) writes, "a fact is only what it is in the light of the fundamental conception." Just as our planet's biosphere has a distinct influence on the evolution of all life on earth, so too do our concepts influence the evolution of our knowledge. The birth of certain kinds of facts is dependent upon the oxygen of a particular conceptual atmosphere. Our ability to even experience certain facts/truth is limited by the preconceptions produced by our pragmatically influenced theoretical conceptualizations of the world.

If Dawkins and Hitchens call attention to the epistemological failings, ignorance, and dangers of religion, McGowan recommends that atheists appreciate principles of democratic pluralism and empathize with believers. Indeed, McGowan sees empathy as one of the supreme virtues parents should instill in their children. Echoing Barna's exaltation of the values of mercy, patience, compassion, and love, McGowan highlights empathy as the "ultimate sign of maturity" and urges parents to continually push out "the empathy boundary" to include the "other." Rather than preaching empathy, McGowan (2007a, 128) urges parents to embody it. "Allow your children to see poverty up close… Engage other cultures and races not just to value differences but also to *recognize sameness*. It's difficult to hate when you begin to see yourself in the other." McGowan demands that atheist parents teach their children to have empathy for those who do not share their non-religious beliefs: "Too many nonbelievers shake their heads contemptuously at the very idea of religious belief, failing to recognize religion for what it is—an understandable response to the human condition. Let me repeat that: If the religious impulse seems completely incomprehensible to you, I humbly suggest that you don't fully grasp the human condition."

Atheist parents who set the wrong example will see their own intolerant vice exhibited in their children's behaviour. "You'll know you've failed at this the first time you see your kids mocking or sneering at religious belief. Be thoroughly ashamed when that happens, since they will almost certainly have learned it from you" (McGowan 2007a, 129). While McGowan insists parents have the right, indeed the obligation, to confront the kind of religiosity that proscribes "intolerance, ignorance, and fear," he also demands that atheist parents applaud those "religious people and institutions whenever charity, tolerance, empathy, honesty, and any of our other shared values are in evidence. An important part of this is recognizing that not all expressions of religion and not all religious people are alike" (2007b, 36). While his view is not necessarily common among New Atheists, McGowan (2007c, x) summarizes a common view among them: "it would be just as silly to imply that one cannot raise good, intelligent, moral, and loving children in a religious home as to imply the opposite."

While atheists are distrusted by much of America, as exemplified in previously stated data, McGowan articulates a view of atheists; honesty much agreed upon within the community: "Honesty is the essence of secularism." According to McGowan, atheists are those willing to set aside what they 'wish' the world was in preference for the truth of what it actually is. He writes that despite being consistently rated "as the least trustworthy minority in the United States," his experience finds atheists who "are often *paralyzed* by our obsession with honesty." Moreover, "most of the humanists and atheists I know are relentlessly, exhaustively honest, sometimes to a comical extent" (McGowan 2007a, 130).

Other key values McGowan insists atheists should focus on include openness, generosity, and gratitude. The virtue of openness, writes McGowan (2007a, 131), is in "recognizing our own fallibility" and keeping "our opinions and ideas open to challenge and potential disconfirmation." The atheists' commitment to 'openness' and 'humility' are manifest in the group's historical appreciation of doubt. Upon accepting the point-of-view that God does not exist, McGowan contends atheists are also faced with accepting the responsibility this void of power leaves. The specific form this realization of responsibility should take is generosity. Atheists, he writes, "have no excuse to sit passively. If atheists believe there is "no divine safety net, no universal justice, no Great Caretaker, no afterlife reward," then McGowan (2007a, 132) contends atheists "have the full responsibility to create a just world and care for the less fortunate because there's no one else to do so." Bennett (2005, 48) echoes this point in her children's book. Humanists, her protagonist explains to the students, "take responsibility for their own actions and their own lives here on earth." Another consequence of rejecting the idea of God is in reallocating 'thanks'. Indeed, McGowan sees an atheist worldview as one filled with gratitude for those who are directly responsible for the things from which we benefit. Instead of thanking God before meal time, McGowan suggests atheist families might take time out to thank the truck drivers and the produce workers who are directly involved in the process of putting food on our plates.

Finally, McGowan writes that children and parents in atheist families have good reason to value the virtue of courage. Here again we find a parallel between those extremely dedicated Christians and similarly dedicated atheists. Just as dedicated Christians feel their lifestyle is beyond the current of the mainstream, so, too, do atheist parents. As a result, atheists, like Revolutionary Parents, wish to instill courage in their children. McGowan (2007a, 129–130) writes, "It takes very little courage to live in the mainstream. As long as you embrace the norms and beliefs of the majority, you'll encounter little difficulty, little resistance." But being an atheist child requires courage, writes McGowan. He recommends parents point to examples of courageous people, such as Socrates, Martin Luther King, and Michael Newdow.

One of the most significant differences between the Christian and atheist parenting literature discussed here is in their approaches to authority. One will recall that Rosemond advocates a 'benevolent dictatorship' whereby parents do not spend their time reasoning, but instead insist that children obey on the premise that parents are vested with authority. In "Thoughts on Raising a Curious, Creative, Freethinking Child," retired psychiatrist Robert E. Kay contends that parents should teach by example rather than by mere authority. Children should not be criticized for asking questions, he says, and parents should do their best to answer them. Kay (2007, 188), however, does note that parents have the right to point out when certain questions are inappropriate or badly timed. Whereas Rosemond notes the rebelliousness of children, Kay (2007, 188) points to the fact that young children are inclined to resist orders, but tend to be co-operative: "Also remember that our cooperative instincts are far stronger than our willingness to obey."

McGowan (2007d) argues that every time "a parent raises a hand to a child, that parent is saying *you* cannot be reasoned with. In the process, the child learns that force is an acceptable substitute for reason, and that Mom and Dad have more confidence in the former than in the later." He cites research by Elizabeth Thompson Gershoff at Columbia University as having found that, as he puts it, "ten negative outcomes are strongly correlated with spanking, including a damaged parent-child relationship, increased antisocial and aggressive behavior, and the increased likelihood that the spanked child will physically abuse her/his own children" (2007d). Parents should keep a mental list of their children's favourite privileges such as video games or reading before bed and implement a policy whereby such privileges are revoked when children exhibit poor behaviour. "Choose well, and the selective granting and withholding of privileges will work better than spanking" (McGowan 2007d). In terms of when to do what kind of discipline, McGowan suggests this line of action: first, attempt to reason with the child; if reasoning fails, threaten to revoke privileges, give time-outs, or, realizing that parental disapproval is a strong and 'underrated' tool, express your dissatisfaction with particular behaviour.

Discipline and values meet in a rather novel way in the atheist literature on parenting. Compared to Rosemond, atheist parenting advice is much more accepting of 'contrarian' behaviour. Indeed, one might see speaker and writer Stu Tanquist as actually encouraging a degree of respectful dissenting intellectual activity. Tanquist (2007, 51) writes that he and his daughter have two explicit rules posted in their home: (1) Always question authority; (2) when in doubt, see rule 1. While Tanquist does not feel the need to limit questioning in the same way Barna suggests Christian parents should, he is clear to explain that he retains ultimate authority. "Inviting questioning is not the same as a complete abdication of responsibility," writes Tanquist. "As her parent and legal guardian, I obviously need to put my foot down from time to time. The point is that my daughter is encouraged to openly and freely challenge my views, without fear of consequence for the challenge" (Tanquist 2007, 51). His approach, however, attempts to counter what atheists argue is a false basis of power, one that Christian parenting literature holds in high regard. Tanquist (2007, 51) views overvaluation of authority as a threat to rational thinking and good character: "Our house rules are a recognition of the error in reasoning called the *argument from authority*. People commit this fallacy when they blindly accept statements made by people in a position of authority." This perspective deeply impacts not only the manner in which atheist parents discipline—they tend to believe their commands should be supported by good reasons which the children deserve to understand—but also results in a disdain for indoctrination. Specifically, atheist parents write that they do not want their children to merely inherit their atheism. If indeed they become atheists it should be because they have come to such a conclusion on their own, through reason.

Whereas every indication is that Christian parents are to keep children from being exposed to atheist perspectives, atheists, perhaps because they operate within a predominantly religious environment, are encouraged to openly discuss and introduce their children to the world's religions. Moreover, atheists encourage their children to utilize their reason to discover their own truth. Typifying secularist parenting, Shermer (2007, viii) wrote the following to his daughter when she transitioned from middle school to high school: "It matters less to me what your specific beliefs are than that you have carefully arrived at your beliefs through reason and evidence and thoughtful reflection." McGowan (2007c, x) seconds Shermer: "I really *do* believe I've made the best moral and intellectual choice in setting religion aside. I think the negatives of religious belief outweigh the positives, but I would never want to see someone forced to believe as I do. That includes my children. They deserve an honest chance to work things out for themselves." Here we realize that the atheist parenting approach replaces reverence for religion with reverence for reason. As analyzed earlier, exaltation of reason is not thoroughly free of value. Just as there is no view from no where, the non-religious vantage point touted by the non-religious parenting strategy is indeed a viewpoint which immediately discounts religious doctrines others believe are of absolute importance.

One of the key differences between Barna and Rosemond's parental approach advocated by the likes of Kay is that the latter seeks to expose children to ideas that the parent disagrees with. Rather than closing off his children to ideas which he disdains, Kay recommends parents introduce children "to reality, to people, to the world, and to all sorts of ideas, *especially those with which you disagree.*" Kay even encourages parents to invite children to try out the religion of their choice. He does, however, urge atheist parents to offer views on what he calls the "more toxic" elements of religious belief including the idea that "a mythical god can read your mind, or control what happens, or consign you to hell. These toxic ideas get in the way of their developing questions and opinions, so you are within your rights as a parent to head them off in advance by declaring them just plain dumb" (Kay 2007, 189). Sean P. Curley (2007, 32) also encourages parents to introduce their children to religions—all of them: "Don't be so worried about reading or telling the stories, just treat them with the same reason and skepticism you would treat any other book. They do have great things to say in many cases." One of the unique aspects of the atheist approach to parenting is that it allows children an uncommon degree of dissent and essentially encourages children, through reason, to discover their own truth. Writing in response to the rhetorical question asked by an atheist's child, "What if I don't want to be Humanist?" Curley (2007, 63) writes: "What you believe and what you practice is ultimately up to you. All I would ask is that you research the possibilities, look at all the data, and come to a reasoned and reasonable decision about who you are and what your philosophies are."

Whereas Barna and Rosemond encourage parents to allow their children to pursue their "faith, in whatever form that journey takes," the insistence is that faith is the starting point and that whatever discoveries are made should be made within the Christian faith context. Atheist parents, on the other hand, while essentially placing faith in the power of reason to lead children to a sceptical interpretation of religion, nevertheless permit their child to explore not only 'atheism' or 'faith' but truth itself, in whatever form such a journey takes. In his newest book *Raising Freethinkers* McGowan proffers as a salient tenet of good parenting the call to "*Leave kids unlabeled.*" He writes that labeling children 'Christian' or 'atheist' fundamentally conflicts with secular parenting's key goal of encouraging freedom of thought. "It is just as dishonest to label a child with a complex worldview as to call her a 'Republican' or a 'Marxist' " (2009, viii–ix). While one would be hard-pressed to disagree that such a neutral position is fairer to children, the difficulties of true objective parenting are made clear when McGowan (2009, ix) writes, just a few lines beyond his call to "leave kids unlabeled," that non-religious parents should "*Normalize disbelief.* There is no greater contribution non-religious parents can make to their children's future as freethinkers than to make religious disbelief a normal, unexceptional option in our culture." One must ask whether or not labeling one's child an atheist in this context is any less potent than normalizing disbelief and, by extension, discouraging faith. Would it matter, for instance, whether parents withheld the label of 'Christian' from their child if they proceeded to exalt the virtues of deep belief and faith? The point, simply, is that both secular and religious parents are limited in their ability to empty their parenting of its biases. Indeed, there may be no point in withholding 'atheist' or 'Christian' labels while thoroughly inculcating children in the salient principles of the respective worldviews.

Despite these differences, however, atheist parenting author Dale McGowan has no fear in acknowledging the value of some Christian parenting. According to McGowan, there isn't anything secular parents can achieve that religious parents cannot. He recognizes that both secular and religious parenting can instill in children an appreciation for critical thinking, questioning of authority, and the rejection of the traditional concept of sin. McGowan (2009, 1) also admits that in preparing to write *Raising Freethinkers* he was surprised to find that even the notably conservative Christian thinker James Dobson's work "serves up some solid parenting advice along with his unfortunate enthusiasm for corporal punishment, gender stereotypes, and homophobia." He also notes his respect for the work of Christian parenting author Dr. William Sears. McGowan does not, however, believe that secular parenting and religious parenting are the same. The difference, he writes, is that of the contextual space "in which religious parenting and nonreligious parenting happen." Indeed, McGowan reverses the argument that non-religious parenting is desperately lacking religious context; instead he argues that the time has come for liberal religious parents to recognize that they have more in common with secular parents, and perhaps more to gain by identifying with them. There is in his writing (2009, vi) a subtle hint that the liberal believers have so hollowed out traditional religion that the time has come to complete the transition and let go of it altogether.

> My hat is off to religious parents who encourage unrestrained doubt, applaud fearless questioning, and reject appeals to authority. I admire

their willingness to dissent from their group's majority. Considering the current growth in Christian fundamentalism at the expense of more moderate versions, such religious parents are salmon swimming against a mighty current. At the core of traditional monotheistic religion are the ideas that doubt is bad, that certain questions are not to be asked, and that church and scripture carry some degree of inherent authority.

In short, McGowan seems to recommend renouncing religion rather than reforming or co-opting it. He does not, however, demonize or insult liberal religious parents. His argument is that "followers of progressive religion have far more in common with the nonreligious than they do with their more conservative and literalist coreligionists" (2009, vi).

One aspect of McGowan's argument that does not appear to be fool-proof is his unsubstantiated assertion that fundamentalist interpretations of Christianity are growing significantly faster than the liberal Christian movement. Although fundamentalist Christianity enjoys one of the highest conversion rates, it also has one of the highest drop-out rates, and those who leave almost always choose more liberal versions of Christianity (Altemeyer 2006, 128–129). Moreover, we should consider the incredible growth of the United Church of Christ, one of Christianity's most liberal churches, as well as the spread of various progressive Christian groups and movements such as the Network of Spiritual Progressives, Cross Left, and The Center for Progressive Christianity. Moreover, there is no proof that literalist interpretations predominate across the entirety of Christianity. While fundamentalist Christianity may have succeeded in gaining prominence in recent years, it does not necessarily follow that the majority of Christians are literalists. In fact, as the Pew Survey (2008, 11) shows, many fail to assert affirmative beliefs in Heaven, including 15 percent of Muslims, 16 percent Protestants, 18 percent of Catholics, 49 percent of Hindus, and 62 percent of Jews. Fewer state an affirmative belief in Hell: Protestant (17 percent), Catholic (40 percent), Jewish (78 percent), Muslim (20 percent), Buddhist (74 percent), Hindu (65 percent).

CONCLUSION

This chapter has argued that negative attitudes grounded in religious sentiment towards atheists in the United States are almost entirely unfounded. As Edgell and others (2006, 230) have noted, "Americans construct the atheist as the symbolic representation of one who rejects the basis for moral solidarity and cultural membership in American society altogether." In the past, groups such as Catholics, Jews, and Communists have played the role of the symbolic villain that the American people stand united against. Typifying the way in which atheists are viewed, Edgell (2006, 227) notes that one particular respondent to the Public Agenda poll, "a Republican in her mid-sixties, told our interviewer that belief in something transcendent is necessary to move beyond 'the me,' the narrowly self-interested consumerism that she sees as rampant. This interview excerpt shows how she linked together the ideas of consumerism, arrogance, atheism, and American identity." The authors (2006, 230) concluded that "attitudes toward atheists tell us more about American society and culture than about atheists themselves" and "that in answering our questions about atheists, our survey respondents were not, on the whole, referring to actual atheists they had encountered, but were responding to 'the atheist' as a boundary-marking cultural category." In exploring atheist parenting literature, this chapter has hopefully shown this common bogeyman characterization as empirically unfounded.

The differences—as well as the similarities—between the Christian parenting model represented by Barna and Rosemond and the atheist parenting model represented by McGowan, Curley, and Kay are inescapably real. For example, one finds that in both Barna and Rosemond, a premium is put on heterosexual marriage that is not found in atheist parenting instruction. Indeed, whether one is married or not receives little or no attention in the atheist parenting book. Since Rosemond and Barna believe that Christian parents, properly informed by the Bible, are operating from a perfect point of view and authority they, particularly Rosemond, tend to discount the role of reasoning and parental explanation. This is an essential difference between the Christian and atheist parenting approach. Atheist parents offer their children the right to question them, putting a premium on reason, and believing that all good parenting must be firmly grounded in rationality, not mere authority. Discussion of the relativity of rationality, as stated earlier, is absent from the discussion. The main objective of the Christian approach is to produce a child who is a devoted Christian and one who has a deep and personal relationship with God. Children are to begin their exploration of life from the starting point of biblical truth and the validity of the Christian worldview. Whereas Christian parents are encouraged to allow their children to pursue their faith, 'in whatever form that journey takes,' the assumption is that these dis-coveries will be made within the context of the Christian faith. Atheist parents, on the other hand, while essentially placing faith in the power of reason to lead children to a sceptical interpretation of religion, nev-ertheless, permit their child to explore not only 'atheism' or 'faith' but also truth itself.

This study does show, however, that there is indeed some essential commonality between the groups. While we must acknowledge that each has in mind a rather divergent objective—godliness for Christians and religious doubt for atheists—both groups possess what seems to be a comparable interest in civility and consideration for their fellow human beings (whether one learns to first embrace humanity, or to embrace the life of Jesus, the resulting behaviour is essentially identi-cal). Just as Barna and Rosemond wish Christian parents to instill hon-esty, kindness, humility, and consistency in their children, McGowan and Kay urge atheist parents to do the same. If Rosemond critiques 'high self-esteem,' McGowan critiques arrogance and inflated self-importance. Both recommend the same antidote: humility. If Barna prepares Christian parents for a difficult breaking away from the status quo of parenting, McGowan prepares atheist parents for a similarly difficult shift. Even if we admit the gulf between commanding children to adhere to biblical truth and requiring adherence to the primacy of reason, one cannot escape that both require a resolve and commitment to systematic living.

The differences between Christian and atheist parenting advice are not merely symbolic. In the end, Barna and Rosemond have in their sights the rearing of a child who honours God by living in accord with the Bible and encouraging others to do the same. McGowan, Curley, and Kay, on the other hand, wish to see children instilled with keen reasoning skills, capable of discerning the material world without the assistance of a particular doctrine. Indeed, they hope children will be free of what they believe are superstitious constraints. And yet both sides have many substantive similarities. Barna and Rosemond put a premium on honesty, treatment of others, living a just life, being fair and respectful. The same can be said for the atheist authors. Indeed, both groups are hypersensitive to the development of strong, highly principled character in young adults. Character is a means with which each side seeks its ultimate end, be it a philosophical or a religiously devoted life; the moral Christian and the moral atheist walk parallel paths.

One must note, however, that the secular parenting model seems to have one important advantage over the Christian model. Whereas the Christian parenting model is contingent upon acceptance of Christian doctrine, the secular parenting model is open to any and all. In fact, its greatest virtue is its versatility; specifically its ability to be relevant regardless of the religious or non-religious path a child may take in life. The question facing a parenting model that is specifically Christian is this: what happens if the child decides to choose a religion different from Christianity or perhaps no religion at all? If Christian parenting's lessons about duty and morality are all centred on adherence to Christian faith, it may follow that those who reject Christianity are not bound by such moral codes. It seems, then, that a non-religious parenting model which grounds morality in humanistic ideals universally applicable rather than religious ideas, which a child may later renounce, proves more resistant to change, which is all but guaranteed.

IS GOD A HYPOTHESIS? THE NEW ATHEISM, CONTEMPORARY PHILOSOPHY OF RELIGION, AND PHILOSOPHICAL CONFUSION

Ryan C. Falcioni

In this chapter, I plan to demonstrate some of the fundamental philosophical confusions in the methodologies of the New Atheists, and their counterparts in the philosophy of religion—both theistic and atheistic—with regard to their view of religious belief. These confusions have led to bad philosophy as well as bad science, and stand as an obstacle to understanding religion in all of its varieties. The New Atheists, and others, have developed a straw man in treating religious claims as hypotheses, and thus their criticisms (and defences) miss their mark. The structure of this chapter is as follows: (1) demonstrate the relationship between The New Atheists and contemporary philosophy of religion; (2) discuss the God Hypothesis (GH) in its various forms, including its epistemology of evidentialism, and show why it is philosophically confused; and [3] address the effects of these confusions on the study of religion and analyze their ideological origins in the hope of avoiding them in the study of religion.

UNLIKELY BEDFELLOWS

I have found it particularly fascinating that in the barrage of critical literature (much of it by serious philosophers) on the New Atheists there has been a dominant mantra regarding the 'utter failure' of these authors to do justice to their alleged subject matter: religion. In a popular review of *The God Delusion* in the *London Review of Books*, Terry Eagleton (2006) remarks,

> Imagine someone holding forth on biology whose only knowledge of the subject is the Book of British Birds, and you have a rough idea of what it feels like to read Richard Dawkins on theology. Card-carrying rationalists like Dawkins, who is the nearest thing to a professional atheist we have had since Bertrand Russell, are in one sense the least well-equipped to understand what they castigate, since they don't believe there is anything there to be understood, or at least anything worth understanding.

This is why they invariably come up with vulgar caricatures of religious faith that would make a first-year theology student wince. The more they detest religion, the more ill-informed their criticisms of it tend to be.

Georgetown theologian John Haught (2008, xi) has commented that "the new atheism is so theologically unchallenging. Its engagement with theology lies at about the same level of reflection on faith that one can find in contemporary creationist and fundamentalist literature." He states also that "Their understanding of religious faith remains consistently at the same unscholarly level as the unreflective, superstitious, and literalist religiosity of those they criticize" (2008, xiii). Christian philosopher Alvin Plantinga (2007), in his critique of *The God Delusion* opined, "You might say that some of his forays into philosophy are at best sophomoric, but that would be unfair to sophomores; the fact is (grade inflation aside), many of his arguments would receive a failing grade in a sophomore philosophy class." To summarize, critics have pointed out the lack of philosophical and theological sophistication of the New Atheists, who they accuse of holding to an ill-informed conception of what religious beliefs *really* are. Furthermore, they accuse the new atheists of a self-serving, predatory selectiveness in choosing their battle partners.

The central criticism here is that New Atheists create straw men; they misunderstand the nature of religious beliefs, focus on the wrong things in religion, and generally fail to get at the real 'essence' of religious belief. Many of these critics of the new atheists say that they must look deeper to see the religious meaning that lies beyond or beneath the bad science and metaphysics, the abuses of religious leaders, the paradoxes of faith, etc. I am essentially making a similar claim; namely, that these atheist thinkers have missed their mark. However, I am taking this criticism one step further in claiming that many academic philosophers of religion (both defenders and detractors of religious belief) fall victim to the same misdirection in more or less the same way. The critics above are right in condemning the poor philosophy and theology of the new atheists, yet they fail to see that this is really an indictment of a dominant tradition in mainstream philosophy and theology itself. So the new atheists may fail to do justice to religious beliefs, but they are not entirely outside of the philosophical and theological tradition. Much of academic philosophy of religion actually supports the view of religious beliefs (as hypotheses standing in need of evidence) offered by the new atheists. There is an irony here that I hope to make more explicit as this work develops. The philosophers are (mostly willing) victims of, and contributors to, the same errors in thinking.

Both implicitly and explicitly, the philosophers give legitimacy to the kinds of claims about the nature of religious belief that these popular atheists assume and criticize in their works. So, in putting these thinkers in dialogue with each other, I hope to show that far from being an aberrant or fringe discussion on religion, the atheist critics are making claims that are consistent with, and legitimized by, deeply confused presuppositions and specific beliefs of major thinkers in contemporary philosophy.

Therefore, my central contention is that the God Hypothesis and its attending evidentialism fail to do justice to the nature of religious beliefs and that this can be remedied only through paying close attention to the role that religious beliefs play in the lives of believers. To be clear, I am not advocating a fideistic approach wherein religious beliefs are immune from criticism simply because they are believed. Furthermore, I am not claiming that religious beliefs cannot be confused, superstitious, or outright false. Religious beliefs can be and have been all of these things. But whether they are fundamentally hypotheses, metaphysical claims about the world, non-rational expressions of our deepest values, meaningless utterances, etc., must be argued for. The New Atheists and many philosophers of religion have not done this work and assume a view of the nature of religious beliefs that is incommensurate with any substantive analysis of these beliefs. Their diatribes thus rest upon a foundation of fundamental philosophical confusion. It is only through paying close attention to the forms of life in which religious claims occur that we can begin to make sense of their meaning and thus understand how best to go about analyzing or critiquing them.

The God Hypothesis

At this point, let us take a closer look at the basic features and the individual distinctives of this perplexing understanding of the nature of religious beliefs that we see amongst the New Atheists and their counterparts in contemporary philosophy of religion. The first and most significant claim made by Richard Dawkins, Sam Harris, and Victor

Stenger is that religious beliefs are hypotheses about the world.[1] This is really the seminal claim made by all of the New Atheists as well as (in some form or another) by their philosophical colleagues. Fundamentally, they all take belief in God to be a putative truth claim about the nature of reality. Dawkins lays out his case for the failure of this hypothesis in several of his texts. In *The God Delusion*, Dawkins offers a fairly sophisticated account of the origins and nature of the 'God Hypothesis.' For Dawkins, belief in God emerged during a particularly ignorant phase in human evolutionary history. He fundamentally repeats the view of religion as advocated in the intellectualist tradition in anthropology: Early humans postulated the existence of invisible powers in an effort to understand and control the natural elements.

Belief in God is in this way an explanatory hypothesis aimed at describing a feature of the world and the source of most everything that we see around us. It is thus a rival hypothesis both to the claims of other religious traditions and to naturalistic claims about reality and origins. And, like all truth claims, it is open to investigation as to its truth or falsity. It is really this 'debate' that concerns me most. It seems like most people in the English-speaking world (and elsewhere for that matter) have accepted the terms of the discussion as framed by the theists and their anti-theist counterparts. That this has been tacitly accepted is seen in the general types of responses to, and criticisms of, the works by these authors. One common concern is over how successful the polemics have been. Critics chide the atheist authors for failing to disprove the veracity of religious claims to their satisfaction, while sympathizers have claimed that these works are a substantial contribution to the cumulative case against the truth of religious belief. There has not been a substantial voice criticizing the sense of this entire enterprise of debating religious beliefs. The notion of 'debate' betrays a conception of the nature of religion and religious belief wherein religious claims are akin to some sort of hypothesis (a notion that both Harris and Dawkins utilize with great frequency). This hypothesis, or family of hypotheses, is open to the sort of investigation that the 'Great

---

[1] Now, at this point, we could entertain a most lengthy discussion about what exactly is meant by 'hypotheses' here. And, there are some worthwhile distinctions to be made in regards to the ways that each of these thinkers conceives of this notion. But, it is my contention that there is a fundamental commonality shared by all of these thinkers with regard to the nature of religious beliefs that can be fairly captured by the notion of hypothesis.

Debate' is aimed at providing. To be clear, I am convinced that this approach to religious belief is ultimately non-sense. The fact that religious beliefs are not hypotheses, natural or supernatural, can be seen through a cursory investigation into the grammar of religious beliefs. It is this cursory investigation that seems to be lacking in the works of all parties involved in this 'Great Debate.'

Dawkins (2006, 31) specifically takes the GH to be a hypothesis about origins: "there exists a superhuman, supernatural intelligence who deliberately designed and created the universe and everything in it, including us." He juxtaposes this hypothesis with a clear rebuttal, "any creative intelligence, of sufficient complexity to design anything, comes into existence only as the end product of an extended process of gradual evolution" (2006, 31). Thus, the existence of the God invoked in the GH is subject to the same natural, evolutionary processes as the rest of the universe. For Dawkins, the GH is much less probable than a simpler, natural explanation of origins. Dawkins then sets before us the two rival hypotheses: (1) The universe is the result of a designer's handiwork; or (2) the universe is the result of natural, evolutionary processes. Theism and atheism are competing hypotheses about the fundamental cause of the origins of the physical universe. After surveying various arguments for God's existence, and the 'evidence' for creationism (particularly in its latest manifestation in the Intelligent Design movement), Dawkins concludes that the hypothesis has failed. Dawkins grants that not all religious believers (or scientists) believe that religion is in the business of making scientific claims. There are less-than-fundamentalist believers, and colleagues in the sciences such as Stephen Jay Gould, who argue for the notion that religion and science are separate enterprises and should be analyzed and assessed in different ways. Put simply, science and religion do not ask the same questions and do not put forth the same types of answers. But, for Dawkins, thinkers like Gould represent an aberration in the history of religious belief. This 'new movement' is not consonant with the origin, nature, and function of the 'God Hypothesis'. Dawkins has developed his notion of 'memes' as a unit of cultural evolution. For Dawkins, religious beliefs (along with jokes, rituals, songs, poems, theories about life) are transmitted across cultures and are generally in the interest of survival of that given culture. And, religions are a particular form of toxic meme that Dawkins likens to a 'mind virus.' This mind virus is comprised of a host of false beliefs and bad habits of thought and action that threaten to kill off the human species. So, unless the memes of science replace the competing memes of religion, nothing less than the future of humanity is at stake. Like his New Atheism companions, he believes that we have an intellectual and moral duty to follow the evidence wherever it leads. As it turns out, in this case, it leads us away from the GH and indeed further from religion altogether.

For Dawkins, both hypotheses aspire to explain the universe, why we are here and the meaning of life. All of these questions are susceptible to a scientific explanation, and, religion has long been in the business of giving answers wrongly. For Dawkins, there is plenty of overlap between the discourses of science and religion, and religion just offers us a shoddy science. Dawkins (2007a) has made it clear that God's existence "is a scientific hypothesis and should be analyzed as skeptical as any other." And, it has clearly been falsified by the evidence.

Although I will not give here an extensive treatment of Harris's version of the GH, suffice it to say that he echoes this general approach throughout his writings. In one particularly clear instance, he argues that "beliefs about the way the world *is*, must be as evidentiary in spirit as any other" (Harris 2004, 63). Harris's focus is really on the propositional nature of all language. His view is a version of the 'picture theory of language' that Wittgenstein chides for being too simplistic in its failure to recognize and do justice to the various usages to which language is put. In Harris's (2004, 51) view, "Believing a given proposition is a matter of believing that it faithfully represents some state of the world…[this] reveals why we cannot help but value evidence and demand that propositions about the world logically cohere. These constraints apply equally to matters of religion." Religious claims, like all others, are aimed at picturing the world as it *really* is. And analyzing such claims comes via evidentiary investigation. Again, we are offered a view of religious belief as a competing hypothesis about the nature of reality and origins.

Physicist, philosopher, and recently deputized New Atheist, Victor Stenger, offers the most direct and consistent treatment of religious beliefs as hypotheses. Stenger makes it clear that religious beliefs are not only hypotheses, but also scientific ones that stand in need of clear and distinctively empirical evidence. In the preface to his most recent book *God: The Failed Hypotheses* he states, "My analysis will be based on the contention that God should be detectable by scientific means simply by virtue of the fact that he is supposed to play such a central role in the operation of the universe and the lives of humans" (Stenger 2007, 13). Stenger then sets out to see if God's hand is indeed detectable in a variety of scientific contexts in which we are told he has played some role. If there are "phenomena that, if observed, cannot be of material origin beyond a reasonable doubt…his presence would be signaled, beyond a reasonable doubt, by the empirical verification of such phenomena" (Stenger 2007, 14). The seeming circularity of this claim aside, it sets up an empirical standard for the verification of the GH. Stenger admits that even if one cannot detect unevidenced phenomena it is still logically possible that God exists, but the absence of evidence would count as evidence of absence in this case. For, if God's presence is not manifest in places in which it should be (according to the basic claims of religious believers), then we have good reason for doubting the existence of such a being. In short, the probability of God's existence rapidly approaches zero, as he is continually absent in places where we have good, doctrinal reasons, to suppose his presence. Both interesting and philosophically contentious in many regards, my goal here is not to critique the minutiae of Stenger's approach but rather to offer a general critique of the presuppositions behind his general approach to understanding the nature of religious beliefs that is revealed in such methods. This 'lack-of-evidence argument' is laid out as follows:

1. Hypothesize a God who plays an important role in the universe.
2. Assume that God has specific attributes that should provide objective evidence for his existence.
3. Look for such evidence with an open mind.
4. If such evidence is found, conclude that God *may* exist.
5. If such objective evidence is not found, conclude beyond a reasonable doubt that a God with these properties does *not* exist (Stenger 2007, 43).

Stenger does just what he promises. He looks for the evidence of God's work in a variety of contexts and, unsurprisingly, does not find any. The world seems to run just fine according to its initial conditions and natural laws. For Stenger, this is proof positive that God does not exist.

Atheistic philosopher, J. L. Mackie (1982, 6) offers us a similar account of the hypothetical nature of religious beliefs and the role of evidential arguments for/against religious propositions:

> All such arguments [for/against God's existence] can be seen as resting on one general principle, or sharing one basic form and purpose: they are arguments to the best explanation. The evidence supports the

conclusion, it is suggested, because if we postulate that conclusion is true—or better, perhaps, that it is at least an approximation to the truth—we get a more adequate overall explanation of the whole body of evidence, in the light of whatever considerations are cited, than would be given by any available alternative hypothesis.

For Mackie, both empirical and broadly rational evidences in the form of classical theistic arguments should be analyzed. Mackie cites Descartes and Locke as supporting the general view that we must use 'reason' in arguing for the truth of religious claims. In *The Miracle of Theism*, Mackie carefully weighs the relative merits of traditional theistic arguments, the evidence for miracles, and the evidence of religious experience and finds them insufficient to prove the existence of God. He also considers the traditional arguments against God's existence (e.g., the problem of evil) and sees them to be further, and ultimately superfluous, evidence for the non-existence of God. Mackie shares this cumulative case approach with both the New Atheists and many theistic philosophers. In summing up the case for the God hypothesis he concludes:

In the end, therefore, we can agree with what Laplace said about God: we have no need of that hypothesis. This conclusion can be reached by an examination precisely of the arguments advanced in favour of theism, without even bringing into play what have been regarded as the strongest considerations on the other side, the problem of evil and the various natural histories of religion. When these are thrown into the scales, the balance tilts still further against theism. (Mackie 1982, 253)

Theistic philosopher, Richard Swinburne, also thinks of the existence and activity of God in terms of testable hypotheses. Although he may not share a commitment to scientific naturalism with Dawkins and Stenger, he does indeed share an understanding about the epistemological nature of belief in God: that the question of God's existence is a question about the truth of a proposition, or a matter of fact, that is open to both empirical and rational investigation. Either God exists (and has done things such as creating the universe) or God does not exist. And, furthermore, the truth of this question can be assessed by a careful look at the evidence.

Dawkins and Swinburne have become unlikely bedfellows in this debate. For, as much as they are opposed to each other's conclusions, they share a distinctively probabilistic approach to fundamental religious claims. Dawkins (2007a) recently made the claim that, "Either there is or is not a God...this is a scientific question...you can put a probability on it, and that is very low." And if one has read any of Swinburne's more recent texts, it would be clear that he could make the same statement albeit with the final clause reading something more like 'and that is relatively high, or at least 50/50.' For Swinburne (1996, 2) "The very same criteria which scientists use to reach their own theories lead us to move beyond those theories to a creator God who sustains everything in existence." The existence of God can be inferred inductively through an understanding of natural phenomenon. God serves as an ultimate explanatory hypothesis for the existence and maintenance of the universe. Beyond this particular approach to the GH, Swinburne has argued evidentially and inductively for many of the central claims of Christianity (including creation and the resurrection). He has put forth a barrage of arguments aimed at demonstrating the probability of these 'events' occurring in history. He utilizes evidence from archaeology, anthropology, scriptural criticism, sociology, and psychology in making his cumulative case for the rationality and indeed probability of Christian Theism. But this concept is problematic; it betrays the attempt to reduce belief in God to a hypothesis. 'Theism' has now become a lowest common denominator name for the belief in God, a belief which now comes to us purer and simpler than the particulars of a 'god' entrenched in a specific historical tradition, or in the lives of individual believers. We now have a rather bare 'Theism' that can be independently assessed for its rationality as a general claim about the universe. As has been stated earlier, it is precisely this move that evidences a great confusion in such an understanding of God. A 'god' apart from a tradition is senseless. And, it is one of the claims of this chapter that it is precisely this senseless notion of God that is being defended and critiqued in the current debate. As stated in the introduction, belief in God is not a hypothesis. Treating it as such has been, and continues to be, problematic for the academic study of religion.

EVIDENTIALISM AND THE GOD HYPOTHESIS

As later analysis will demonstrate, religious beliefs are not hypotheses about the world. They do not function this way in the lives of believers in any noticeable way. Yet, the dominant epistemology of the New Atheists and their philosophical friends, treat them this way. And, it is this epistemological approach that distorts the meaning and value of religious beliefs. It is through an analysis of their shared evidentialism that we can most acutely see the disastrous effects of treating religious beliefs as hypotheses.

Evidentialism comes in many varieties but is essentially the view that the truth value (and relative strength) of a proposition is dependent on evidence. The evidentialist debate is at the core of epistemological discussions in contemporary philosophy of religion. Sam Harris offers a particularly lucid discussion of his epistemology. He claims that believing in God is epistemologically equivalent to believing that there is a diamond the size of a refrigerator buried in one's back yard. This belief is farfetched yet, in principle and in fact, is open to empirical and rational investigation. It is a claim for which it would make sense to speak of settling the facts. We understand that evidence is what is required to demonstrate the truth of these claims, yet evidentialism as a legitimate approach to religious epistemology only makes sense if we first hold to a conception of religious beliefs as the types of things that can or should be investigated evidentially. My goal here is not to attack evidentialism in any general sense, because hypotheses are exactly the types of things that stand in need of evidences. The question that I am addressing is not whether or not it makes sense to argue for the truth of any and all claims evidentially, but rather the narrower question of whether or not it makes sense to do so with religious claims.

To the extent that evidentialism applies, we know precisely what kind of evidences to look for. With questions about the existence of objects, a simple empirical observation could confirm/disconfirm these claims. For the New Atheists and their philosophical friends, the existence of God is fundamentally a claim of this type that can and should be assessed through an examination of the evidence. But the New Atheists are not the first to appropriate evidentialism. There are rough versions in the ancient world, modern evidentialism can be traced to Enlightenment empiricism. (The New Atheists share a strongly empirical approach to religious questions). Philosopher Linda Zagzebski (2007, 224) credits John Locke with an early and pervasive form of evidentialism wherein "we ought to proportion our beliefs to the evidence." W.K. Clifford, the most prominent evidentialist of the nineteenth century, expands Locke's notion into a moral demand that it is "irresponsible to believe anything on pragmatic grounds...and if we believe anything on insufficient evidence, we are wronging humankind" (Zagzebski 2007, 224). And, although many contemporary religious thinkers criticize evidentialism, it is still alive and well in many areas of analytic philosophy, especially, and somewhat ironically, in philosophy of religion. To be clear, not all evidentialists have this scientific approach. Many of them utilize other types of evidences from philosophy, experience, etc. Yet, a surprising amount of the literature focuses on the allegedly empirical data that can confirm/disconfirm religious claims.

PHILOSOPHICAL CONFUSION IN THE GOD HYPOTHESIS

At this point, I hope that it is sufficiently clear that the GH and its attending evidentialism is thriving in the academy and that this view is shared with the New Atheists. Forgetting my earlier comments, I imagine that many readers at this point might still be in agreement with the legitimacy of this enterprise. For, is it not the case that many claims of religious believers are of a factual sort? Is it not reasonable to conclude that many of the claims about cosmological origins, divine intervention, and even the historical Jesus are at least in part scientific claims or claims that, if true, would have empirical consequences that could be verified/falsified? Many religious believers seem to think that this is meaningful work, that their religious beliefs are, or can be, bolstered by such investigation. The current popularity of religious apologetics ministries provides ample evidence of the significance of this way of viewing religious beliefs.

Indeed many of these claims and questions have a point. It is the case that a broadly evidentialist approach to the study of religious beliefs has recently gained. Yet, as philosopher D.Z. Phillips has pointed out, we cannot do philosophy by Gallup Poll. In other words, we cannot merely ask people to give a philosophical account of their religious beliefs and then take them at face value. This would be a convenient philosophical heuristic, but we have a duty to do a conceptual investigation of such beliefs. What religious beliefs amount to must be seen in the lives of believers. This is a logical point about the nature of language that I believe is quite simple but warrants a more thorough discussion. To briefly make this point, how are we to determine the meaning of any given statement? If someone were to say, "the gods are sure angry today," how would we begin analyzing this? Could we merely begin the hunt for said gods and their alleged anger? Where would we look? And, what methods would we employ? Is godly anger detectable in the same way as human anger?

Before we could begin this or any analysis, we would necessarily have to consider who was saying it and in what context. And, as with all statements, we could imagine a variety of contexts in which this statement could be uttered. The individual making the utterance, the way in which it was uttered, and its relationship to other modes of discourse and life are all indispensable aspects of understanding the possibilities of sense for this claim. Each of these contexts would have far-reaching implications for any consequent investigation. I could make this claim in a tongue-in-cheek fashion as a way of casting blame for the current bad weather. In such a case, I would clearly not be advancing any sort of hypothesis, causal claim, or even an authentically religious one. One would only need to know me, my background in religion, and my propensity to say ridiculous things in order to understand that this was merely a poor attempt at sarcasm. But wait, my meaning might seem to be parasitic on the primary context for this claim, namely in the lives of some polytheistic culture who believed that there were gods and that they did cause things (e.g., thunder storms) to happen. The New Atheists might claim that my usage actually betrays the original meaning and is even dependent for its meager comedic value on the reality that it was rooted in a failed view of the world. This may be the case, but this view, like the view of my own usage must be shown in the lives of those that speak this way. And it seems to be the case with many polytheistic cultures that they too are not advancing any causal hypotheses when gods are cursed for various natural and social ills. It may actually be a way of just cursing in general, a way of expressing hopelessness in regard to the weather that is beyond our control, or it may be an attempt at primitive science. Yet, once again, what these beliefs amount to must be shown, not merely assumed. The only point made here is that religious beliefs may be many different things. They are not always failed hypotheses. Wittgenstein's critique of this latter 'intellectualist' view of traditional religious claims is most instructive here and will be addressed later in this discussion.

When dealing with the basic GH of the New Atheists and their philosophical friends, there is a further complication. For, as mentioned in the introduction, they often get support for their view that belief in god is really a GH by religious believers (and religious philosophers themselves). The New Atheists regularly indicate that the Gallup Poll can do philosophy. Harris's (2004, 232) tirade against religious moderates and liberals makes much use of the fact that their (less metaphysical and scientific) views are the aberration and the 'real' views are those of the devout believer for whom "religious faith is the belief in historical and metaphysical propositions without sufficient evidence...Faith is simply the license they give themselves to *keep believing when reasons fail*." It is not clear that the devout believer in fact believes in this way, there is a more important point that needs to be made here. Assuming, for the sake of argument, that many believers do in fact take their beliefs to be hypotheses, it is quite possible that they are doing bad philosophy. People who have meaningful and coherent religious beliefs and practices may give deeply confused philosophical accounts of them when asked. They may think that their religious beliefs are scientific claims and are justified by historical and empirical evidence, yet their lives show us that they cannot mean this. Whether or not their own religious beliefs are ultimately a putative hypothesis about the world and therefore a matter of evidence can only be settled by seeing the role that these beliefs play in their lives, not by the accounts that they may give if asked. As mentioned earlier, for religious beliefs to play the same (or even similar) role in their lives as do scientific claims would be an abnormal occurrence to say the least. Put simply, when we look at the nature and function of the religious claims of believers, we see that they are not hypotheses. Even a fairly perfunctory investigation into the nature of these beliefs shows us this. The New Atheists and their philosophical counterparts are guilty of a major distortion of these beliefs when they treat them as hypotheses. And again, this can only have awful consequences for the study of religion. It is a diversion that keeps them (and, tragically, many others who are influenced by them) from doing justice to the real nature, meaning, and function of religion.

In furthering this discussion of the confusion involved in the notion of the GH, I would like to ask what might seem like a rhetorical question, but I think it makes a significant point. Namely, assuming that most of us have had some experience with religion or at least have seen the way people engage in religious beliefs and practices, how could it occur to anyone to see them as hypotheses in the first place? Are there features of religious beliefs that are similar to hypotheses as advanced in the sciences? When religious believers make statements, are they advancing putative truth claims like one might do in the sciences? Maybe there are some similarities in the surface grammar of many religious claims (e.g., 'God exists' shares a grammatical structure with 'Trees exist' or 'The tree is my brother' shares a structure with 'Benjamin is my brother'). However, the differences between the two types of claims are rather deep. We are often lured into thinking that very different kinds of statements are more similar than they are, due, in part, to grammatical similarities. But we must investigate this similarity. Are we really making the same kind of claim when we utter these statements? Could we ask the same questions of the members of each pair of claims? Could we reasonably conduct the same type of investigation into their meaning and truth?

It would be fundamentally wrongheaded to go about analyzing the claim 'the tree is my brother' in the same way as the claim 'Benjamin is my brother.' This is intuitively obvious, but why is this a confused approach to understanding this claim? The concept of 'brother' used in each case carries a rather different meaning. And, we come to know this by seeing the role that this concept plays in the lives of those who use it. There is a simple, yet often overlooked, truth in Wittgenstein's maxim that 'meaning is in use.' Failure to play close attention to the role that these concepts pay in the lives of people can lead to disastrous forays into analysis. I imagine the naïve scientist, who takes all claims to be scientific hypotheses, running genetic tests between trees and men in order to prove whether or not men and trees are brothers. Of course we recognize that the claim of the tree being the man's brother is not a scientific statement and is not in need of an empirical test. To treat it as such is to demonstrate ignorance of the possibilities of meaning for this statement. The history of pseudoscience is littered with experiments grounded in such ignorance. Medieval alchemists weighing the human body pre- and post-mortem in order to establish the existence (and empirical properties) of the soul is but one poignant example. And yet it seems that many of us would still be comfortable asserting that statements of trees being brothers, souls, and the like can be meaningful. The meaning of talk about brother trees, souls, and houseplants can only be seen through a conceptual investigation of the role that these notions play in the lives of those who talk this way. We would have to see the way in which these terms are used and their relationships to other ways of speaking and living. Upon such analysis, belief in God does not seem to be a broadly scientific (or rational) hypothesis. It is not a claim about an object in the world that may be discovered or proven through an objective investigation. The problem is, as D.Z. Phillips (1993) argues, inquiring about divine reality is not like inquiring about the reality of this or that object, but rather like inquiring about the existence of objects in general. In other words, it is an inquiry into a kind of reality, not the reality of one or another element inside a kind of reality. Yet, this is what we are offered by the New Atheists and their philosophical friends. When I encountered the barrage of New Atheist literature, I was quite surprised to see a revamped version of the notion of God as a scientific hypothesis. Have the advances and boundaries cultivated over the last 200 years of philosophy and science been ignored?

Although it is not within the scope of this paper to address all of the ways in which religious claims are not like hypotheses, I would like to address a few of the fundamental differences between religious claims and broadly scientific ones. My goal here is to show that these differences are of great logical significance in understanding the meaning of religious claims, and that ignoring these differences results in philosophically confused and distorted accounts and criticisms of religious beliefs. Ingolf Dalferth (1988, 6) offers an account of this confusion in his text *Theology and Philosophy*:

> Scientific beliefs, for example, are held rationally if they are held tentatively and in proportion to the evidence available. Religious beliefs, on the contrary, are not tentative, but unconditional. Believers—as Wittgenstein has pointed out (1970, pp. 55ff)—do not hold their beliefs with conviction proportionate to evidence as is the case with scientific beliefs. Their beliefs are neither probable nor well founded in a scientific sense; and the apologetic attempt to make them look scientifically respectable is completely misconceived. For not even their indubitability would be 'enough in this case. Even if there is as much evidence as for Napoleon. Because the indubitability wouldn't be enough to make me change my whole life' (p. 57). Wittgenstein concluded from this that religious beliefs are neither reasonable nor unreasonable; they are not the sort of belief to which reasonability would apply.

Dalferth goes on to say of Wittgenstein's remark that "the conclusion, obviously, is too strong," but he does believe that there are indeed logical differences between scientific beliefs and practices, and religious ones. D. Z. Phillips makes much of these logical differences, claiming that it is not that there is no rationality to religious beliefs, but rather a different type of rationality, one that is internal to (or better yet, seen in) religious lives and practices. Whatever it is, it is not the same thing as rationality or evidence in the sciences, and if we are to take seriously the investigation into what type of rationality this is, we must actually look at the religious practices themselves.

We must also take a close look at the form of life in which such beliefs occur and endeavour to elucidate the meaning and internal rationality therein. One of the first things that is made apparent through even a cursory investigation is well captured in Wittgenstein's quote above; namely, that religious beliefs do not occupy the same space, and are not held in the same way as scientific beliefs are held. They are not tentative and are not held in proportion to evidences. A statement of religious belief is a statement about one's life, one's values, about ultimate things. The religious believer does not engage religious beliefs as hypotheses that may or may not turn out to be true. To believe in the religious sense is an act of commitment. This confessional element of religious belief is logically significant in understanding the very meaning of religious claims. By way of example, could we imagine a person who *merely* believes in the propositional truths of Christianity but thinks nothing of their significance for her life? I imagine this person stating, "Of course I believe that Jesus died on the cross for my sins, was resurrected on the third day, is God incarnate and is Lord of all, but this just does not matter to me." This may be logically possible, but what could we make of it? It does not seem to have much to do with religion. In the ordinary sense, to say that Jesus is Lord of all is an act of confession, an act of worship. The statement is not a claim about propositional truth value; it is a profound statement about one's life in relation to God. Religions demand that believers to give their lives to God, and this could never be a matter of evidence however convincing. In other words, a mere intellectual assent to the propositions of a given faith (based on evidential arguments) is not what is meant by having religious beliefs. To be a Christian is to live a certain way; to accept the demand upon your life that Christ has made. Believing in particular propositional truths is not 'believing' in the ordinary sense of religious belief. For the religious believer, "It is not a *matter of fact* God will always exist, but it *makes no sense* to say that God might not exist" (Phillips 1993, 1). As Phillips points out here, the believer's claim that God exists is not a hypothesis of any sort. It is not something that she takes to be true but could turn out to be false if that is where the evidence leads. As he states, "It makes as little sense to say, 'God's existence is not a fact' as it does to say, 'God's existence is a fact'" (1993, 2). The believer finds herself believing and living her life in a religious way. It is the religious way of life that shows us the meaning of her religious beliefs.

The New Atheists and their philosophical friends seem to have reversed the logic of this relationship. We do not first believe in religious propositions (because of their alleged evidential support) and then go about being religious. Rather, it is through our religious lives that we see what religious propositions mean. Thus, to see belief in God as a tentative hypothesis is to distort the meaning of religious belief as seen in the lives of believers. Put simply, believers do not, generally speaking, believe in God because of the soundness of the evidential proof for the GH. Their beliefs are not predicated upon any objective grounds. One of the most striking features of any descriptive account of religious beliefs is that they are not normally the types of things that we come to accept through any form of broadly rational investigation. Religious beliefs may be the least volitional of our beliefs. For most of us, we are born into a family and find ourselves a part of a religious tradition that few of us stray from. In reality, most believers neither accept nor reject this way of life. Whatever religious beliefs mean can only be understood in light of this most fundamental descriptive fact about religious life.

At this point, I anticipate an objection from the New Atheists and their philosophical friends. They undoubtedly grant the descriptive fact that many religious believers do not believe in God on the basis of evidences and that they engage with and hold these beliefs in a way that is very different from scientific ones. But, they may claim, this does not mean that such evidences do not exist or are not or should not be at the epistemological foundations of such beliefs. They state that the religious believer who holds her beliefs in the absence of evidence is a rather naïve believer who has not done justice to her alleged faith. As a rational being, she has the duty to search deeper in order to ground or prove those beliefs. Or, if she does not have a personal duty to conduct such an epistemological investigation, the foundation of her beliefs is in the hands of others who are labouring on her behalf to ground them; in this case, she is at least epistemologically (and maybe morally) indebted to such underlabourers. Either way, there is a demand for evidential justification.

Yet many things seem wrong about this move. First, where does this alleged epistemic duty come from? Secondly, what counts as evidence here? In addressing the first question, it seems clear that the alleged epistemic duty is not generally revealed in the religious practices themselves. As we saw in the earlier discussion, for many believers, religious claims are not a matter of evidence. Evidences neither compel nor repel religious beliefs. They simply play no role at all. Therefore, assertions such as William Kingdon Clifford's famous evidentialist dictum that "it is wrong always, everywhere, and for anyone, to believe anything upon insufficient evidence." Although there are several dimensions to Clifford's evidentialist mandate, it is fundamentally a moral claim that simply cannot be supported philosophically. Furthermore, this seems to be another instance of the abject failure of the alleged parallel between religious beliefs and scientific hypotheses. The epistemic duties we have as scientists are not the same as those we have as practitioners of faith.

A related issue here is about determining and defining the nature of the evidence. Even if we assume that evidence is relevant for religious beliefs, we still have the task of elucidating the grammar of 'evidence' in this case. What counts as evidence is indeed different in different investigations. For the sake of argument, let us accept Clifford's moral imperative that we are in dereliction of our epistemic duty if we believe in religious matters without basing them on evidence. Serious philosophical work must be done in order to clarify what evidence amounts to in the case of justifying religious belief. We cannot merely assume what kinds of evidences are admissible in grounding such beliefs. For what counts as evidence in one mode of inquiry may have no application in another. Take for instance the interdisciplinary differences in the sciences broadly conceived. A psychologist is not interested in the same sorts of evidences as a particle physicist. This is true even, or especially, when they are investigating the same sort of phenomenon. Both can investigate the cause(s) of a particular mental illness, yet they are engaged in observing, isolating, and testing different variables. The psychologist and the physicist are engaged in a common act of scientific investigation; yet do not recognize the same or even similar sorts of evidence. In short, what counts as evidence is determined by the nature of the practice in question.

As we have seen in the works of the New Atheists and their philosophical friends, there is rough agreement about the types of evidences that are germane to the discussion. And, oddly, they agree that scientific evidences are appropriate. Yet, the central claims of religion seem altogether removed from the scientific discourse. Even taken in a propositional way, what evidence could one offer for the claim that Jesus died for the sins of the world, that Muhammad is the seal of the prophets, or that God is love? These beliefs are at the core of their respective traditions and yet they do not seem to be amenable to scientific or even broadly evidential investigation. To even attempt to investigate the meaning or truth of these claims would evidence a gross ignorance of the type of claims that are being made. Standards of meaning and the methods of investigation that are appropriate are revealed in the religious traditions themselves. There is not a universal criterion of logic, science, or evidence that can be imposed from without. What evidence amounts to is something that can only be seen within a given practice. Christians may speak of evidence of the salvation that Christ provides on the cross, but this generally comes in the form of testimony. The evidence of the truth of the atoning work of Christ is the life transformed by Christ. This is indeed a form of evidence, but it has a different grammar than the evidence required by the sciences. What would scientific evidence for salvation look like? To confuse the two is bad for science and bad for religion.

How Did We Get Here?

So, if this view of the nature of religious beliefs is confused, why does it dominate this discourse? There are undoubtedly many historical and ideological factors involved, but one sticks out as significant. The New Atheists share some particular perspectives on the historical, evolutionary, and anthropological development of religious beliefs: they are an unfortunate intellectual remnant of our primitive past. The New Atheists tell us a story wherein religious beliefs emerged out of the noble quest for understanding the world by our early human ancestors. The problem here is that our human ancestors lacked scientific sophistication, and in its stead, they hypothesized about various supernatural explanations and causes for the phenomena that we experience.

Dawkins offers a slightly nuanced perspective that is particularly revealing. For him, religious beliefs may be the by-product of primitive survival instincts (2006, 176). Specifically, "Natural selection builds child brains with a tendency to believe whatever their parents and tribal elders tell them. Such trusting obedience is valuable for survival...But the flip side of trusting obedience is slavish gullibility. The inevitable by-product is vulnerability to infection by mind viruses." This learned trait combined with other aspects of our evolutionary psychology has led to the aforementioned hodgepodge of false supernatural attributions to natural phenomena. So we find ourselves believing in fatuously stupid and superstitious things about the world because of a peculiar detour in our evolutionary history. The mind virus of faith forced our primitive ancestors to forego reason and postulate all sorts of spirits, witches, miracles, and other pseudoscientific explanations of the world.

Yet, with our knowledge of this fact, we are no longer forced to believe such things. We do not have the excuse of belonging to an earlier, ignorant phase of human existence. For Dawkins and other New Atheists it is important that religious beliefs are both false and that they are part of our primitive past. We thus have both an intellectual and moral imperative to rise up from our lowly origins and evolve! Understanding this perspective gives the reader some insight into the evangelical fervour of much of their writings.

Is this story of religious beliefs as part of our evolutionary history a correct one? More importantly, does it do justice to the nature and function of the beliefs themselves? Early British anthropologists, Sir James Frazer and E.B. Tylor, are credited as pioneers of this 'intellectualist' view of 'primitive' religious beliefs. Frazer sees such beliefs as growing out of the primitive desire to understand the world. This view is not only patronizing of our evolutionary ancestors, but also, as numerous philosophers, anthropologists, and sociologists have pointed out, it completely misunderstands the nature of the religious beliefs that they were allegedly investigating. The critiques of this view of the nature of traditional religious beliefs are too numerous to count. Fundamentally, these views err in forcing a modern understanding of science on earlier peoples which leads to a revisionist understanding of their beliefs and practices. By way of just one brief example, many early accounts of rain dances envision the participants engaging in them because of a causal (read: proto-scientific) view of their. In short, the primitives are said to dance *because* of their belief that this will cause the rain. And, to be clear, when asked, the oft-given answer was: "We dance to bring the rain." However, the claim that they understand this in a causal way reveals a vast ignorance about the meaning of such practices as seen in the lives of the participants. They are not as ignorant as the intellectualists suppose. Such peoples clearly understand basic causality. As Wittgenstein (quoted in Clack 1999, 23) noted, "The same savage who, apparently in order to kill his enemy, sticks his knife through a picture of him, really does build his hut of wood and cuts his arrow with skill and not in effigy." Rituals to bring the sunrise only take place right before the sunrise. When they want light in the evening, they do not invoke gods, "they simply light a torch." They are not mistaken about the nature of cause and effect in any of these rituals. They are not putting forth a theory of what causes the rain, death, or the light. Merely looking reveals that this is so. Only someone bound by a theoretical commitment to what all language and ritual must be could confuse them.

It is logically significant that primitives danced during the rain season and not during the drought. They understood when nature brought the rain and they danced in celebration of what they knew would come. A simple and beautiful act of celebration can easily be distorted into a failed hypothesis if we do not take the time to look and see the meaning that it actually has in the lives of practitioners. The logical point about the different meaning of these beliefs is hopefully clear. In a particularly pointed piece of ire Wittgenstein (quoted in Clack 1999, 13–14) criticizes Frazer and his intellectualist view of primitive religion: "Frazer is much more savage than most of his savages, for these savages will not be so far from any understanding of spiritual matters as an Englishman of the twentieth century. His explanations of the primitive observances are much cruder than the sense of the observances themselves." Religious beliefs are not a primitive form of science. The intellectualist tradition of viewing religious beliefs as primitive hypotheses suffers from a simple failure to take a careful look at the phenomenon in question.

The failure to stop and look can be seen most poignantly in the contemporary battle over Intelligent Design. The New Atheists take particular umbrage with the attempts (some of them successful) to have this form of creationism taught alongside evolutionary theory in the science classroom. Fundamentalists and Darwinists alike take the religious notion of a creator to be a rival hypothesis to Darwinian evolution. Yet, both have failed to take a look at the biblical context and the role that the notion of creation plays in the lives of believers. The Bible itself does not treat the creation story as a scientific theory. Certainly, some fundamentalist versions of Christianity do in fact seek to replace much of science with a crude, literalist theology, but a literal, fundamentalist reading of scripture is in no way inherent. Most believers take a more dynamic approach, such that biblical stories teach many things: the meaning of life, the consequences of sin, gender roles, redemption, providence, etc. In this context, they are not doing science, they are learning about life, morality, and religious meaning.

These features of the nature and function of creation are logically significant for understanding the meaning of creation. I understand that the New Atheists may have no interest in excavating what is meaningful about creation and are content to accept fundamentalist views as the only view of scripture. Indeed, I can appreciate their anti-Intel-legent Design movement as a social and moral campaign against pseu-doscience. Yet as scholars who claim to study religion, all of their work is still ahead of them. Intelligent Design is deeply confused, but the New Atheists do not move beyond this confused understanding. Instead, their current works attempt to brand this confusion as the authentic religious account itself. They are intent upon showing the stupidity of all religious beliefs and are invested in clinging to the con-fused account. In treating creation as a scientific hypothesis that should be understood and evaluated in terms of empirical evidence, funda-mentalists and the New Atheists exhibit a profound failure to do justice to the religious notion of creation. They have distorted what can be very profound and meaningful. Intellectualism is alive and well in the works of the New Atheists and their philosophical friends. We would do well to revisit the historical critiques that demonstrated the mani-fest failures of intellectualism. The way out invariably involves under-standing how we got here in the first place.

AFTERWORD[1]

Mark Vernon

It was a sunny afternoon in Windsor, England, site of the famous cas-
tle, a home of the Queen. We sat in a teashop; nothing could have made
the occasion more congenial. It was spoilt by only one thing: we'd met
to talk about homosexuality.

We had been brought together because of our opposing views. I am
pro-gay, pro-civil partnerships and pro-inclusion on gay adoption. The
person with whom I was taking tea believes gay people in relationships
are in danger of burning forever in hell. The odd thing about our difference of views was that we were otherwise pretty indistinguishable.
My interlocutor was white, middle-aged, male, and British—as I am
myself. We were both well-educated; we might even have voted for the
same political party. The difference was that he was a Christian fundamentalist; I am a liberally minded agnostic.

My cognitive dissonance deepened further when, a few days later,
I read *The End of Faith* by Sam Harris. Harris is another white male,
though argues that 'the end of faith'— particularly of the fundamentalist variety—would be a good thing for humankind. And yet, when I
read his book, so soon after my encounter in Windsor, my cognitive
dissonance only increased. For in it I found an atheistic fundamentalism that repelled me almost as much as the Christian variety.

My concern rose not because I doubt Harris's faith in rationalism,
though I do: it just seems silly to me to think that all the evil in the
world is the result of bad thinking, and that good thinking will put all
the bad right. After all, in between us and the eighteenth-century
Enlightenment—when the idea first arose that religion might recede,
along with superstition and irrationalism—are the Nazi camps: clear
thinking did nothing to mitigate the horrors of the twentieth century.
Neither was it because his championing of evidence-based reason does
nothing to prevent him dismissing the fact that billions of people try to

---

[1] An earlier version of this article appeared in the *CAESAR: A Journal of Religion and Human Values*, Vol 1, 2008.

live better lives by following a religious faith—though they do. It is because the book fantasizes about violence quite as indulgently as the hellfire homophobe. On one page, Harris goes so far as to toy with the possibility of a nuclear strike against Muslims. It would kill millions of innocents, he muses, but might be the only option 'we' have, in the face of the threat 'they' represent to us.

Others in this book have dived into the arguments behind such points of view, to explore what is at stake in them. Here, then, let us take a step back and ask another question. What kind of world do we live in when otherwise indistinguishable individuals—white males, in this case—can espouse such diametrically, diabolically opposed positions, both believing that nothing less than the future flourishing of humankind requires adherence to their version of the truth?

Welcome to the secular age. This is a place in which every day it is possible to rub up against people with very different worldviews to your own—theistic, atheistic, agnostic, and of every variation on the theme. It is a different world from the one anticipated by secularists from the eighteenth century right up to recent times. They assumed that religion was on the wane; as science advanced, the need for religion would disappear. However, in the 1990s sociologists began to realize that something at once more fascinating and alarming was occurring. The new view was given voice when the leading sociologist of religion, Peter Berger (1999, 2), wrote, "The assumption that we live in a secularized world is false. The world is as furiously religious as it ever was" (see also Micklethwait and Wooldridge 2009). What he'd realized is that modernity is not the midwife of atheism: "What it does lead to, necessarily, is pluralism," he explained.

It is a predicament thoroughly analyzed by Charles Taylor in *A Secular Age* (2007). He draws together all the threads of the debate about secularization and explores the dominant feature of contemporary secularity, namely its radical pluralism. The ease with which we can encounter massively opposing views would in itself mark our age out as challenging. It becomes threatening because in the secular age it is also quite possible to imagine yourself changing worldviews. Before modern times, a Christian might have met atheists, but they would and quite possibly could no more thought of becoming one than, say, changing their gender. Today, such radical changes are entirely viable. These 'cross-pressures,' as Taylor calls them, are a defining characteristic of the contemporary sense of self. It is why secular and religious polemicists alike desire to lambaste their perceived opponents, and sustain their followers, with evangelical zeal. This is surely what explains the success of books like those of Harris, and others by Richard Dawkins and Christopher Hitchens. The need to write such tomes is not premised on the dominance of atheism, for if that were so there would be no need to defend it; but rather that atheism is now just one theological option amongst others.

Taylor wants to understand how this situation has arisen, and to do so he develops a new theory of secularization. First, it requires dumping the old 'subtraction' theory of secularization—the idea that what science and reason have achieved in the modern world is a stripping away of needless, primitive superstitions revealing the essential, rational core of humankind. Second, he sees secularization as a paradigm shift, the origins of which lie within religion itself. At the time of the Reformation, there arose a desire to collapse the difference between the 'higher flourishing' implicit in the religious lives of monks and priests and the 'lower flourishing' of lay people engaged in the humdrum tasks and aspirations of everyday life. Martin Luther (2002) wrote: "The works of monks and priests, be they never so holy and arduous, differ no whit in the sight of God from the works of the rustic toiling in the field or the woman going about her household tasks."

Lower flourishing is anthropocentric and during the eighteenth century this immanent dimension to life came to dominate, not least with the rise of deism. It conceives of human beings as living in a benign moral order designed by God. It was this theology that subsequently lay behind the optimistic philosophy of the Enlightenment; it enabled the French historian Chastellux to declare that his was the happiest century yet. The central ethic of contemporary humanism— that rational individuals can constructively engage in a society of mutual benefit—is the direct successor of this optimism. And modern atheism comes about because the distant God of deism is easy to drop in the embrace of a materialist worldview. However, as Kant pointed out, an age of enlightenment is not necessarily itself enlightened; at best, it is probably only on the way to enlightenment. The lesson of recent history is that violence follows revolution, as night follows day. Thus the threat of violence is still with us, be it this- or other-worldly, actual or imagined. It is negotiating this threat that Taylor identifies as the key issue for those with enough faith to still seek enlightenment in the secular age.

In particular, he believes that the confrontation between atheistic humanism and religious belief is not only a source of more violence but is also misconstrued. Many of the faults that one side finds in the other—such as that atheism is empty, or that theism is primitive—actually conceal the same faults in the side being defended. In short, both sides can exhibit bad faith, taking potshots at their opponents in order to bolster their own position. It is a game that ultimately neither side can win, since both sides have their strong points, and both have their weaknesses. Religion is clearly implicated with much that is foul in the world; though it also has the capacity to draw out the very best in humanity. Atheism too is closely associated with the worst ideologies of recent times—Stalinism and Maoism being the obvious examples, though atheists are also able to enjoy the tremendous success of science. Thus armed, both sides can perpetuate the knock-about indefinitely. This is the risk of the current confrontation: if it sets the agenda for too long, then everyone feels compelled to follow the protagonists up an intellectual cul-de-sac. To put it another way, the secular age is a context with which all people are trying to grapple. The persistent pluralism of our times is evidence that no one worldview is satisfactory. The evidence says that this pluralism is not going to disappear any time soon.

Taylor (2007b) addressed the issue directly in the speech he made after winning the Templeton Prize: "Both sides (religious believers and secular atheists) need to be wrenched out of their complacent dream, and see that no-one, just in virtue of having the right beliefs, is immune from being recruited to group violence," he said. "We urgently need to understand what makes whole groups of people ready to be swept up into this kind of project…for the best-intentioned efforts to put human history on a new, and more humane footing, have often turned this history into a slaughter bench, in Hegel's memorable phrase."

So what might we, personally, do about it? How are we, as individuals, to live peaceably in the secular age? One feature that seems to be common to the fantasies of violence against others is precisely that: 'othering' them. They are removed from the sphere of beings for which one should have compassion, and rendered as barely human—barely rational, in the case of the atheistic critique of believers; barely humane, in the case of the religious critique of atheists.

Thus, the Christian fundamentalist with whom I conversed simply could not see that the reason homosexuality exists is because sometimes people of the same sex love each other; he refused gayness as a manifestation of love, for all that he claimed to speak for a God of love. Instead, he could only envisage a future of eternal torture for same-sex couples. Similarly, to my mind, Sam Harris perverts humanist philosophy when he writes things like the following: "Some propositions are so dangerous that it may even be ethical to kill people for believing them." In the name of reason he would condemn people for thought crimes. So a first suggestion: as these debates continue, watch out for 'othering.'

Second, we might turn to the two greatest minds of the Enlightenment—David Hume and Immanuel Kant—and ask how they handled the ambivalences of the age in which they lived. For Hume, scepticism was the natural position for the Enlightenment thinker—scepticism about religion for sure, but scepticism about the fundamentals of science, too. Alternatively, Hume objected to what he called 'enthusiasm,' a kind of blindness that he defined as 'presumption arising from success.' That could apply to triumphalist rationalism as much as much as religion.

Kant found Hume's scepticism profoundly unsettling; he famously said it awoke him from his dogmatic slumbers. He wanted to put things on a firmer foundation. And he did so, but only by writing 'critiques.' In his Critiques, the key issue was understanding the limits of human knowledge; when Kant said that enlightenment was maturity, this is what he meant. It led him to a profound examination of different kinds of knowledge in an effort to see what reason can and cannot achieve. He summarized his task in three basic questions: what can I know, what ought I to do, and what may I hope for? They can be summed up in a fourth: what is man? Kant (1781, A11) wrote: "It is a call to reason to undertake anew the most difficult of all its tasks, namely, that of self-knowledge." So, secondly, we have enlightenment as scepticism or consciousness of human limitations.

This leads to a third attitude to nurture in the secular age. If scepticism is the philosophical approach that questions dogmatic worldviews—be they religious or scientistic—then there is a theological equivalent; it is called apophaticism. Apophaticism means 'proceeding by negation.' It is a way of approaching what is ultimately unknown by identifying what that unknown cannot be. So it is that approach to belief which says that God is not mortal (immortal), or not visible (invisible). Its spirit is captured in the biblical story of Moses climbing the mountain: as he ascended and symbolically got nearer to God, he did not find himself in greater light and clarity, but in deeper cloud and unknowing. In this way, apophatic theology is similar to the philosophy of the Enlightenment thinkers like Hume and Kant: both identify limits and seek intuitions of what lies beyond. All learn to live with uncertainty, not by 'othering' but by embracing their own doubt.

To put it another way, this is to advocate what might be called an agnostic spirit. T. H. Huxley, 'Darwin's bulldog,' invented the word agnosticism to describe his position of neither asserting, nor denying, that for which there is not enough proof to either assert or deny. He sought to run with the discoveries of science as far as they would take him, but strictly no further. Indeed, it was because he could run with them so far that his commitment to agnosticism became so profound: it was the opposite of sitting on the fence; it was to be awake to limits. Such an attitude may sound strange today, perhaps because we are so much more conscious of the pluralism that surrounds us and so fear that it implies a hopeless relativism. But it doesn't, I think.

Rather it is to recall the insight of Socrates, as Huxley (1894) himself does: "[Agnosticism] is of great antiquity; it is as old as Socrates; as old as the writer who said, 'Try all things, hold fast by that which is good'; it is the foundation of the Reformation, which simply illustrated the axiom that every man should be able to give a reason for the faith that is in him, it is the great principle of Descartes; it is the fundamental axiom of modern science." Socrates knew that the key to wisdom is in understanding the extent of your ignorance. He was agnostic in not asserting dogmas, and instead went around ancient Athens asking searching questions.

In fact, it is striking how, having begun his adult life as a soldier noted for his bravery in the Peloponnesian War, Socrates' subsequent philosophical life was marked by an opposition to violence. In Plato we read teachings, for example, that the followers of Socrates should love not just their friends but also their enemies. In Xenophon we read the argument that wise people use persuasion rather than violence, since violence produces only hatred whereas persuasion produces allies.

Alternatively, we can turn to another famous agnostic, if one who called himself 'atheistically inclined,' namely Bertrand Russell. Towards the end of his *History of Western Philosophy*, he reflects on how human beings across the centuries have related to their potential and powers. Sometimes, he believes, they have been too humble. In other periods, too hubristic. And today, in a secular age? He worries that we are at risk of thinking of ourselves as gods: "In all this I feel a grave danger, the danger of what might be called cosmic impiety. The concept of 'truth' as something dependent upon facts largely outside human control has been one of the ways in which philosophy hitherto has inculcated the necessary element of humility. When this check on pride is removed, a further step is taken on the road towards a certain kind of madness—the intoxication with power—to which modern man, whether philosophers or not, are prone. I am persuaded that this intoxication is the greatest danger of our time, and that any philosophy which, however unintentionally, contributes to it is increasing the danger of vast social disaster" (Russell 2004, 737).

This 'impiety', the greatest danger of his time, shows no sign of passing. It is surely an imperative in a secular age to resist it.

ABOUT THE AUTHORS

Amarnath Amarasingam is a doctoral candidate in the Laurier-Waterloo Ph.D. in Religious Studies. His research interests are in the sociology of religion, religion and the media, religion and science, as well as religious diversity in North America. He has published articles in the *Journal of Contemporary Religion*, the *Journal of Religion and Film*, and *Mental Health, Religion, and Culture*.

Reza Aslan is professor of Creative Writing at the University of California, Riverside and Senior Fellow at the Orfalea Center for Global and International Studies at UC Santa Barbara. His bestselling books include *No god but God: The Origins, Evolution, and Future of Islam*, which has been translated into thirteen languages, *How to Win A Cosmic War: Confronting Religious Fundamentalism*, and *Tablet & Pen: Literary Landscapes from the Modern Middle East*.

William Sims Bainbridge is a world-renowned sociologist who has published more than 200 articles and eleven books ranging from the sociology of religion to psychology to cognitive science. He is currently co-director of Human-Centered Computing at the National Science Foundation and he also teaches sociology at George Mason University.

Michael Ian Borer is Assistant Professor of Sociology at the University of Nevada, Las Vegas. He is the author of *Faithful to Fenway: Believing in Boston, Baseball, and America's Most Beloved Ballpark* (New York University Press, 2008) and has published articles in the *Journal of Popular Culture, Religion and American Culture, City & Community*, and *Symbolic Interaction*. Interested in the ways that popular culture blurs the boundaries between the sacred and the profane, he is conducting research on the dialectics of vice and virtue within the negotiated moral order of Las Vegas.

Stephen Bullivant is a Research Fellow at Wolfson College, University of Oxford. He completed his doctorate in theology, exploring the Catholic engagement with atheism, in 2009. He is a founding member and co-director of the international and interdisciplinary Non-religion and Secularity Research Network (www.nsrn.co.uk). In addition to his theological work, he has conducted empirical research on the sociology of unbelief in Britain, and the phenomenon of 'irreligious' experience. His theological and social-scientific articles have appeared in *Journal of Contemporary Religion, Implicit Religion, Literature and Theology, New Blackfriars,* and *Theology.*

Richard Cimino holds a Ph.D. in sociology from the New School for Social Research in 2008. He is currently a research fellow for the ChangingSEA Project at Catholic University of America, studying the religious lives of emerging adults. He is the editor of *Lutherans Today: American Lutheran Identity in the 21st Century,* author of *Trusting The Spirit: Reform and Renewal in American Religion,* and *Against The Stream: The Adoption of Traditional Christian Faiths by Young Adults,* and co-author (with Don Lattin) of *Shopping for Faith: American Religion in the New Millennium.* He is also currently the editor of *Religion Watch,* a newsletter reporting on trends in contemporary religion. His research interests include sociology of religion, secularism, and ethnography.

Rory Dickson is a doctoral candidate in the Laurier-Waterloo Ph.D. in Religious Studies. His research interests are Islam and Sufism in North America. He has published articles in the *Journal of Contemporary Islam,* and *ARC: The Journal of the Faculty of Religious Studies, McGill University.*

Ryan Falcioni is Associate Professor of Philosophy at Chaffey College in Southern California. His research and writing deals with issues in contemporary philosophy of religion, philosophy of language and cultural theory. He is also a final-year Ph.D. student in Philosophy of Religion and Theology at Claremont Graduate University where his dissertation offers a critique of some dominant trends in religious epistemology.

Steve Fuller is Professor of Sociology at the University of Warwick. Originally trained in History and Philosophy of Science (Ph.D., Pittsburgh, 1985), he is best known for his work in the field of 'social epistemology,' which addresses normative philosophical questions about organized knowledge by historical and social scientific means. 'Social epistemology' is also the name of a quarterly journal he founded in 1987 and the first of his sixteen books. Among his books that have addressed the relationship between science and religion are *Science vs. Religion?* (Polity, 2007) and *Dissent over Descent* (Icon, 2008). His most recently published book is *The Sociology of Intellectual Life: The Career* *of the Mind in and around the Academy* (Sage, 2009). Fuller has completed a book on science as an 'art of living,' published by Acumen in 2010. In 2007, Fuller was awarded a 'higher doctorate' (D.Litt.) by Warwick for long-term major contributions to scholarship. In 2008, he served as President of the Sociology and Social Policy section of the British Association for the Advancement of Science. Fuller's work has been translated into twenty languages.

Richard Harries was Bishop of Oxford from 1987–2006. On his retirement he was made a Life Peer (Lord Harries of Pentregarth). He is currently Gresham Professor of Divinity and an Honorary Professor of Theology at King's College, London. He has written books on a range of subjects, with two coming out in 2010: *Faith in politics? Rediscovering the Christian Roots of Our Political Values* and *Questions of Life and Death.*

Jeff Nall is a doctoral candidate in Comparative Studies at Florida Atlantic University (FAU), Boca Raton, Florida. He holds a Master of Liberal Studies from Rollins College and a Graduate Certificate in Women's Studies from FAU. His interests include the interdisciplinary analysis of men and masculinity, atheism, and peace activism. He has an essay in *Beyond Burning Bras: Feminist Activism for Everyone,* edited by Laura Finley and Emily Reynolds Stringer (ABC-CLIO, 2010). He has published scholarly articles in *Humanity & Society, Essays in the Philosophy of Humanism,* and *The Journal of Graduate Liberal Studies*; and regularly contributes to popular publications including *Z magazine, Toward Freedom,* and the *Humanist Network News.*

Gregory R. Peterson is Associate Professor of Philosophy and Religion at South Dakota State University, where he currently serves as program coordinator. His primary area of research is in religion and science, and ethical theory, with special attention devoted to the biological and cognitive sciences and their implications for religious and philosophical approaches to human nature. He is the author of *Minding God: Theology and Cognitive Science* (Fortress, 2002), as well as over thirty articles on religion and science in books, encyclopedias, and journals.

Robert Platzner is Professor Emeritus in the Department of Humanities and Religious Studies at California State University in Sacramento. He is an expert on Judeo-Christian history and scripture, and is well known for the textbook (co-authored with Stephen Harris) entitled *The Old Testament: An Introduction to the Hebrew Bible.*

Jeffrey Robbins is Associate Professor of Religion and Philosophy at Lebanon Valley College, where he is also the director of the American Studies Program and the College Colloquium. He is the Associate Editor of the *Journal for Cultural and Religious Theory* and co-editor of the Columbia University Press book series, "Insurrections: Critical Studies in Religion, Culture, and Politics." He has edited two books and authored three, including the forthcoming, *Radical Democracy and Political Theology*.

Christopher D. Rodkey is Pastor of Zion "Goshert's" United Church of Christ, Lebanon, PA, and teaches at Lebanon Valley College, Annville, PA. He holds a D.Min. in pastoral ministry from Meadville Lombard Theological School (Chicago, IL) and a Ph.D. in philosophy and theology from Drew University (Madison, NJ).

Christopher Smith is an independent scholar based in New York. He has authored articles in *Sociology of Religion*, among other publications. His research interests include social theory, secularism, and media theory.

William A. Stahl is professor of sociology at Luther College, University of Regina, in Regina, Saskatchewan. He is the author of the award-winning *God and the Chip: Religion and the Culture of Technology*, and co-author of *Webs of Reality: Social Perspectives on Science and Religion*.

Mark Vernon is a writer and journalist. His recent books include *The Meaning of Friendship* (Palgrave Macmillan), *After Atheism: Science, Religion and the Meaning of Life* (Palgrave Macmillan), *Chambers Dictionary of Beliefs and Religions* (Chambers Harrap, editor in chief), *Plato's Podcasts: The Ancients' Guide to Modern Living* (Oneworld), as well as *Wellbeing* (Acumen), which is part of the "Art of Living" series that he edits. He writes for *The Guardian* and *The Times Literary Supplement* amongst others, is on the faculty at The School of Life, London, and is an Honorary Research Fellow at Birkbeck College, London. He has degrees in physics and theology and a Ph.D. in philosophy, and used to be a priest in the Church of England. He is a keen blogger with a website at www.markvernon.com.

REFERENCES

Ackerknecht, Erwin H. 1943. Psychopathology, Primitive Medicine and Primitive Culture. *Bulletin of the History of Medicine* 14: 30–67.

Aikman, David. 2008. *The Delusion of Disbelief*. Wheaton, IL: Tyndale.

Al-Akiti, Muhammad Afifi. 2005. *Defending the Transgressed by Censuring the Reckless against the Killing of Civilians*. UK: Aqsa Press. Also available at: http://www.warda .info/Defending.pdf

Alexander, Richard. 1987. *The Biology of Moral Systems*. New York: A. de Gruyter.

Allen, Norm. 2007. In Defense of Radicalism. *Free Inquiry* (June/July): 52.

Altemeyer, Bob. 2006. *The Authoritarians*. Winnepeg: University of Manitoba.

Altizer, Thomas. 1967. *The Gospel of Christian Atheism*. London: Collins.

——. 1970. *The Descent into Hell*. Philadelphia: Lippincott.

——. 1977. *The Self-Embodiment of God*. New York: Harper.

——. 1980. *Total Presence*. New York: Seabury.

——. 1985. *History as Apocalypse*. Albany, NY: SUNY Press.

——. 1990. *Genesis and Apocalypse*. Louisville, KY: Westminster.

——. 1993. *The Genesis of God*. Louisville, KY: Westminster.

——. 1997. *The Contemporary Jesus*. Albany, NY: SUNY Press.

——. 2002. *The New Gospel of Christian Atheism*. Aurora, CO: Davies.

——. 2003. *Godhead and the Nothing*. Albany, NY: SUNY Press.

——. 2006. *Living the Death of God*. Albany, NY: SUNY Press.

Aquinas, Thomas. 1965. *Summa Theologiae, Vol 3*. Eds. T. Gilby and T.C. O'Brien. London: Blackfriars.

Armstrong, Karen. 2000. *The Battle for God: A History of Fundamentalism*. New York: The Random House.

Arthur, John. 2007. Famine Relief and the Ideal Moral Code. In *Ethics in Practice*, ed. Hugh LaFollette, 582–590. Malden: Blackwell.

Asad, Talal. 1993. *Genealogies of Religion*. Baltimore: Johns Hopkins Univ. Press.

Associated Press/Ipsos. 2005. Religious Attitudes Poll. June. http://wid.ap.org/polls/ 050606religion.html (accessed June 9, 2005).

Atran, Scott. 2002. *In Gods We Trust: The Evolutionary Landscape of Religion*. New York: Oxford Univ. Press.

Augustine. 1992. *Confessions*. Ed. Henry Chadwick. Toronto: Oxford.

Baggini, Julian. 2003. *Atheism: A Very Short Introduction*. Oxford: Oxford Univ. Press.

Baggini, Julian. 2007. Toward a More Mannerly Secularism. *Free Inquiry* (February/ March): 41–44.

Bainbridge, William Sims and Rodney Stark. 1979. Cult Formation: Three Compatible Models. *Sociological Analysis* 40: 285–295.

——. 1985. *The Future of Religion: Secularization, Revival, and Cult Formation*. Berkeley: University of California Press.

Bainbridge, William Sims. 1984. Religious Insanity in America: The Official Nineteenth-century Theory. *Sociological Analysis* 45: 223–240.

——. 1987. *Sociology Laboratory*. California: Wadsworth.

——. 1995. Neural Network Models of Religious Belief. *Sociological Perspectives* 38: 483–495.

——. 2006. *God from the Machine: Artificial Intelligence Models of Religious Cognition*. California: AltaMira.

——. 2007. *Across the Secular Abyss*. Maryland: Lexington.

Bakan, David. 1958. *Sigmund Freud and the Jewish Mystical Tradition*. Princeton: Van Nostrand.

Ballen, Kenneth. 2007. The Myth of Muslim support for terror. *Christian Science Monitor*. (February 23): 9.

Barna, George. 2007. *Revolutionary Parenting: What the Research Shows Really Works*. Illinois: Tyndale.

Barrett, Justin L. 2004. *Why Would Anyone Believe in God?* California: AltaMira.

Baylor ISR. 2006. *American Piety in the 21st Century: New Insights to the Depth and Complexity of Religion in the US*. Waco, TX: Baylor Univ.

BBC. 2007. Blair feared faith "nutter" label. *BBC News*, November 25. http://news.bbc .co.uk/1/hi/uk_politics/7111620.stm.

Bellah, Robert N. 1971. Between Religion and Social Science. In *The Culture of Unbelief*, eds. Rocco Caporale and Antonio Grummelli. Berkeley: University of California Press.

Bellah, Robert. 1970. Religion and Belief: The Historical Background of 'Non-belief.' In *Beyond Belief*. New York: Harper & Row.

Benedict, Ruth. 1934. *Patterns of Culture*. Boston: Houghton Mifflin.

Bennett, Helen. 2005. *Humanism, What's That? A Book for Curious Kids*. New York: Prometheus Books.

Berger, Peter. 1999. The Desecularization of the World: A Global Overview. In Peter Berger, ed. *The Desecularization of the World: Resurgent Religion and World Politics*. Washington: William B. Eerdmans.

Berlinski, David. 2008. *The Devil's Delusion: Atheism and its Scientific Pretensions*. New York: Crown Forum.

Bernstein, Richard. 1983. *Beyond Objectivism and Relativism*. Philadelphia: University of Pennsylvania Press.

Bibby, Reginald. 2002. *Restless Gods*. Don Mills, ON: Stoddart.

Bice, John. 2007. Taking Atheism out of the Closet. *American Atheist* (August): 21–23.

Black, Alan W. 1983. Organised Irreligion: The New South Wales Humanist Society. In *Practice and Belief: Studies in the Sociology of Australian Religion*, eds. Alan W. Black and Peter E.

Glasner, 154–166. Sydney and Hemel Hempstead: Allen & Unwin.

Bloom, Paul. 2004a. *Descartes' Baby: How the Science of Child Development Explains what Makes Us Human*. New York: Basic Books.

———. 2004b. The Duel between Body and Soul. *New York Times*. September 10, sec. A23.

Boyd, Robert, Herbert Gintis, Samuel Bowles, and Peter J. Richerson. 2003. The Evolution of Altruistic Punishment. *Proceedings of the National Academy of Sciences of the United States of America* 100, no. 6: 3531–3535.

Boyer, Pascal. 2001. *Religion Explained: The Evolutionary Origins of Religious Thought*. New York: Basic Books.

Brague, Rémi. 2007. *The Law of God: The Philosophical History of an Idea*. Chicago: University of Chicago Press.

Brierley, Peter. 2000. *The Tide is Running Out: What the English Church Attendance Survey Reveals*. London: Christian Research

———. 2006. *Pulling out of the Nosedive: A Contemporary Picture of Churchgoing: What the 2005 English Church Census Reveals*. London: Christian Research.

Bruce, Steve. 1993. Religion and Rational Choice: A Critique of Economic Explanations of Religious Behavior. *Sociology of Religion* 54: 193–205.

———. 1996. *Religion in the Modern World: From Cathedrals to Cults*. New York: Oxford Univ. Press.

———. 2002. *God is Dead: Secularization in the West*. Massachusetts: Blackwell.

Bullivant, Stephen. 2008a. Introducing Irreligious Experiences. *Implicit Religion* 11, No. 1 (April): 7–24.

———. 2008b. Research Note: Sociology and the Study of Atheism. *Journal of Contemporary Religion* 23, no. 3 (October): 363–368.

Bunting, Madeline. 2006. Why the intelligent design lobby thanks God for Richard Dawkins. *The Guardian*, March 27. http://www.guardian.co.uk/print/0,,329443427,00.html.

Campbell, Colin. 1971. *Toward a Sociology of Irreligion*. London: Macmillan.

Caputo, John, and Gianni Vattimo. 2007. *After the Death of God*. Ed. Jeffrey Robbins. New York: Columbia Univ. Press.

Caputo, John. 2001. *On Religion*. New York: Routledge.

Caroll, Lewis. 1916. *Alice in Wonderland*. New York: Gabriel.

Carpignano, Paolo, Robin Andersen, Stanley Aronowitz, and William DiFazio. 1993. Chatter in the Age of Electronic Reproduction: Talk Television and the 'Public Mind.' In *The Phantom Public Sphere*, ed. Bruce Robbins, 93–120. Minneapolis: University of Minnesota Press.

Carpignano, Paolo. 1999. The Shape of the Sphere: The Public Sphere and the Materiality of Communication. *Constellations* 6: 177–189.

Casanova, José. 1994. *Public Religions in the Modern World*. Chicago: University of Chicago Press.

Chadarevian, Soraya de. 2007. The Selfish Gene at 30: The Origin and Career of a Book and its Title. *Notes & Records of the Royal* Society 61, no. 1 (January): 31–38.

Chaves, Mark. 1994. Secularization as Declining Religious Authority. *Social Forces* 72: 755–757.

Cimino, Richard and Christopher Smith. 2007. Secular Humanism and Atheism Beyond Progressive Secularism. *Sociology of Religion* 68, no. 4 (Winter): 407–424.

Cipolla, Benedicta. 2007. Is Atheism Just a Rant Against Religion? *The Washington Post*, May 26, sec. B09.

Clack, Brian. 1999. *Wittgenstein, Frazer, and Religion*. New York: St. Martin's Press.

Coppedge, James F. 1973. *Evolution: Possible or Impossible?* Grand Rapids, MI: Zondervan.

Curley, Sean P. 2007. *Humanism for Parents: Parenting without Religion*. United States: no publisher given.

Dalai Lama. 2005. *The Universe in a Single Atom: The Convergence of Science and Spirituality*. New York: Broadway.

Dalferth, Ingolf U. 1988. *Theology and Philosophy*. Oxford: Blackwell.

Daly, Mary. 1984. *Pure Lust*. New York: Harper San Francisco.

Davie, Grace. 1994. *Religion in Britain since 1945: Believing without Belonging*. Cambridge: Blackwell.

———. 2002. *Europe: The Exceptional Case: Parameters of Faith and Society in the Modern World*. London: Darton, Longman & Todd.

———. 2006. A Papal Funeral and a Royal Wedding: Reconfiguring Religion in the Twenty-first Century. In *Redefining Christian Britain: Post 1945 Perspectives*, ed. Jane Garnett et al, 106–112. London: SCM Press.

Dawkins, Richard. 1982. *The Extended Phenotype*. Oxford: Oxford Univ. Press.

———. 1983. Universal Darwinism. In *The Philosophy of Biology*, eds D. Hull and M. Ruse, 15–35. Oxford: Oxford Univ. Press.

———. 1986. *The Blind Watchmaker*. New York: Norton.

———. 1989. *The Selfish Gene*. New York: Oxford Univ. Press.

———. 1997. Obscurantism to the Rescue. *Quarterly Review of Biology* 72, no. 4: 397–399.

———. 2003. Now Here's an Idea. *Free Inquiry* (October/November): 12–13.

———. 2006. *The God Delusion*. New York: Houghton Mifflin.

———. 2007a. An Argument for Atheism. Fresh Air with Terry Gross. National Public Radio. March 28.

———. 2007b. Atheists for Jesus. In *The Portable Atheist*, ed. Christopher Hitchens. 307–310. Philadelphia: Da Capo.

——. 2007c. Darwinism and Unbelief. In *The New Encyclopedia of Unbelief*, ed. Tom Flynn, 230–235. New York: Prometheus Books.

——. 2007d. Good and Bad Reasons for Believing. In *Parenting Beyond Belief: On Raising Ethical, Caring Kids Without Religion*, ed. Dale McGowan, 13–19. New York: AMACOM.

——. 2007e. Science and the New Atheism. *Point of Inquiry Podcast*. December 7. http://www.pointofinquiry.org/richard_dawkins_science_and_the_new_atheism.

Della Rocca, Michael. 2008. *Spinoza*. London: Routledge.

Demerath, III, N. J. 1995. Rational Paradigms, A-Rational Religion, and the Debate over Secularization. *Journal for the Scientific Study of Religion*, 34: 105–112.

Dennett, Daniel C. 1995. *Darwin's Dangerous Idea*. New York: Simon & Schuster.

Dennett, Daniel C. 2003. *Freedom Evolves*. New York: Vikings.

Dennett, Daniel. 2006. *Breaking the Spell: Religion as a Natural Phenomenon*. New York: Penguin.

Denny, Frederick Mathewson. 1994. *An Introduction to Islam*. New York: Macmillan.

Desmond, Adrian and James Moore. 2009. *Darwin's Sacred Cause: Race, Slavery and the Quest for Human Origins*. London: Allen Lane.

Dickson, Rory. 2008. A Contest of Grammar: Religion and Knowledge in the Thought of Ibn Arabi and Ibn Taymiyyah. *ARC: The Journal of the Faculty of Religious Studies* 36: 35–51.

Dobbelaere, Karel. 1981. Secularization: A Multi-dimensional Concept. *Current Sociology* 29: 1–213.

Dogan, Mattei. 2002. Dissatisfaction and Mistrust in West European Democracies. *European Review* 10, no. 1 (February): 91–114.

Douglas, Mary. 1982. The Effects of Modernization on Religious Change. In *Religion and America: Spirituality in a Secular Age*, eds. Mary Douglas and Steven M. Tipton. Boston: Beacon Press.

Downey, Allen B. 2007. The Godless Freshman. *Free Inquiry* 27, no. 5 (Aug./Sept): 56–57.

Eagleton, Terry. 2006. Lunging, Flailing, Mispunching. Review of *The God Delusion* by Richard Dawkins. London *Review of Books* 28, no. 20 (October 19): 32–34.

Eagleton, Terry. 2009. *Reason, Faith, and Revolution: Reflections on the God Debate*. New Haven: Yale Univ. Press.

Edgell, Penny, Joseph Gerteis and Douglas Hartmann. 2006. Atheists as "Other": Moral Boundaries and Cultural Membership in American Society. *American Sociological Review* 71, no. 2 (April): 211–234.

Edgerton, Robert B. 1966. Conceptions of Psychosis in Four East African Societies. *American Anthropologist* 68: 408–424.

Ernst, Carl W. 1997. *The Shambhala Guide to Sufism*. Boston: Shambhala.

Esposito, John L. and Dalia Mogahed. 2007. *Who Speaks for Islam? What a Billion Muslims Really Think*. New York: Gallup Press.

Evans, Gillian. 2003. *A Brief History of Heresy*. Oxford: Blackwell.

Falwell, Jerry. 1980. *Listen, America!* New York: Bantam Books.

Febvre, Lucien. 1982. *The Problem of Unbelief in the Sixteenth Century*. Cambridge: Harvard Univ. Press.

Feser, Edward. 2008. *The Last Superstition: A Refutation of the New Atheism*. Indiana: St. Augustine's Press.

Finke, Roger and Rodney Stark. 1992. *The Churching of America, 1776–1990*. New Brunswick: Rutgers Univ. Press.

Flanagan, Owen. 2002. *The Problem of the Soul: Two Visions of Mind and How to Reconcile Them*. New York: Basic Books.

Flanagan, Owen. 2007. *The Really Hard Problem: Meaning in a Material World*. Cambridge, MA: MIT Press.

Flynn, Tom. 2007. Tour De Force. *Free Inquiry* (April/May): 57–58.

Free Inquiry. 2006. Dawkins, Dennett, and Haack Win Forkosch Awards. August/ September, 9.

Freud, Sigmund. 1961. *The Future of an Illusion.* Garden City, NY: Doubleday.

Friedman, Daniel. 1995. Defining Our Jewish Heritage. In *Judaism in a Secular Age: An Anthology of Secular Humanistic Jewish Thought,* eds. R. Kogel and Z. Katz, 257–259. New York: KTAV.

Fuller, Steve. 2000. *Social Epistemology.* Bloomington: Indiana Univ. Press.

——. 2006. *The New Sociological Imagination.* London: Sage.

——. 2008. *Dissent over Descent: Intelligent Design's Challenge to Darwinism.* Cambridge, UK: Icon.

Funnell, Margaret G., Paul M. Corballis, and Michael S. Gazzaniga. 2003. Temporal Discrimination in the Split Brain. *Brain and Cognition* 53: 218–222.

Garrison, Becky. 2008. *The New Atheist Crusaders and their Unholy Grail.* Nashville: Thomas Nelson.

Gau, Nathan. 2005. *An Examination of Both the Cultural Phenomenon of* The Da Vinci Code *and the Evangelical Responses To It.* MA Thesis, Trinity Evangelical Divinity School.

Gazzaniga, Michael S. 1998. The Split Brain Revisited. *Scientific American* 279, no. 1 (July): 50–55.

Giannetti, Jason. 2008. Richard Dawkins: *Vox Populi. Journal of Liberal Religion* 8, no. 1: http://meadville.edu/journal/LL_JLR_v8_n1_Giannetti.pdf.

Giddens, Anthony. 1990. *The Consequences of Modernity.* Stanford: Stanford Univ. Press.

——. 1991. *Modernity and Self-identity: Self and Society in the Late Modern Age.* Stanford: Stanford Univ. Press.

——. 1994. Living a Post-traditional Society. In *Reflexive Modernization.* Cambridge: Polity Press.

Glynn, Simon. 1991 The De-con-struction of Reason. *Man and World* 24: 311–320.

Goetz, Stewart, and Charles Taliaferro. 2008. *Naturalism.* Grand Rapids, MI: William B. Eerdman's.

Goldstein, Warren S. 2009. Secularization Patterns in the Old Paradigm. *Sociology of Religion,* 70: 157–178.

Gould, Stephen Jay. 1999. *Rocks of Ages.* New York: Ballantine.

Greeley, Andrew. 2004. *Religion in Europe at the End of the Second Millennium: A Sociological Profile.* New Brunswick, NJ: Transaction.

Greene, Joshua D. 2001. An fMRI Investigation of Emotional Engagement in Moral Judgment. *Science* 293: 2105–2108.

Guadia, Gil. 2008. God is Not Great. *American Atheist* (September): 29–30.

Gunaratna, Rohan. 2002. *Inside Al Qaeda: Global Network of Terror.* New York: Columbia University Press.

Habermas, Jürgen. 1990. *Moral Consciousness and Communicative Action.* Trans. Christian Lenhardt and Shierry Nicholsen. Cambridge: MIT Press.

Hacking, Ian. 1990. *The Taming of Chance.* Cambridge, UK: Cambridge Univ. Press.

Hadden, Jeffrey K. 1987. Toward Desacralizing Secularization Theory. *Social Forces* 65, no. 3 (March): 587–611.

Hallaq, Wael B. 2005. *The Origins and Evolution of Islamic Law.* Cambridge, UK: Cambridge Univ, Press.

Halman, Loek. 2001. *The European Values Study: A Third Wave.* University of Tilburg.

Ham, Ken. 1999. Creation: 'Where's the Proof?' *Creation* 22, no. 1: 39–42. http://www .answersingenesis.org/creation/v22/i1/creation.asp.

Ham, Ken. 2003. Searching for the 'magic bullet': Why do creation-defenders often seem to be too quick to jump onto the latest 'evidences'? *Creation* 25, no. 2: 34–37. http://www.answersingenesis.org/creation/v25/i2/bullet.asp.

Hanegraff, Hank. 2008. L-I-G-H-T-S to the Word of God. *Christian Research Institute,* statement DB010. http://www.equip.org/site/c.muI1LaMNJrE/b.2634609/k.AFFC/ DB010.

Haraway, Donna. 1990. *Simians, Cyborgs, Women.* London: Free Association Books.

Harris Poll. 2003. While Most Americans Believe in God, Only 36% Attend a Religious Service Once a Month or More Often. No. 59. October.

Harris, Sam. 2004. *The End of Faith: Religion, Terror, and the Future of Reason.* New York: W. W. Norton.

Harris, Sam. 2008. *Letter to a Christian Nation.* New York: Vintage Books.

Hartung, John. 1995. Love Thy Neighbor: The Evolution of In-group Morality. *Skeptic* 3, no. 4: 86–100.

Haught, John F. 2008. *God and the New Atheism: A Critical Response to Dawkins, Harris, and Hitchens.* Louisville: Westminster John Knox.

Hauser, Marc. 2006. *Moral Minds: The Nature of Right and Wrong.* New York: Harper Perennial.

Hecht, Jennifer Michael. 2003a. *The End of the Soul.* New York: Columbia Univ. Press.

———. 2003b. *Doubt: A History.* San Francisco: Harper.

Heck, Paul L. 2007. Sufism – What Is It Exactly? *Religion Compass* 1: 148–164.

Hedges, Chris. 2006. *American Fascists: The Christian Right and the War on America.* New York: Free Press.

Heider, Fritz. 1958. *The Psychology of Interpersonal Relations.* New York: Wiley.

Herberg, Will. 1955. *Protestant-Catholic-Jew.* New York: Anchor Books.

Herrmann, Benedikt, Christian Thöni, and Simon Gächter. 2008. Antisocial Punishment Across Societies. *Science* 319: 1362–1366.

Hitchens, Christopher, ed. 2007d. *The Portable Atheist.* London: Perseus.

Hitchens, Christopher. 2005. Confessions of a Dangerous Mind. *Slate,* June 13. http://www.slate.com/id/2120810/.

———. 2007a. Bullshitting about Atheism. *Free Inquiry* 27, no. 4 (June/July): 24–25.

———. 2007b. *God is not Great: How Religion Poisons Everything.* Toronto: McClelland & Stewart.

———. 2007c. God is Not Great. *Point of Inquiry Podcast.* July 6. http://www.pointofin quiry.org/christopher_hitchens_god_is_not_great/.

———. 2007e. The *Zeitgeist* Shifts. *Free Inquiry* 27, no. 5 (Aug/Sept): 17–18.

Hoelzl, Michael and Graham Ward, eds. 2008. Introduction. In *The New Visibility of Religion: Studies in Religion and Cultural Hermeneutics,* 1–11. London: Continuum.

Hoffmann, R.J. 2006. Spiritual Libertarians. *Free Inquiry* (October/November): 25–27.

———. 2007. Subject the Sacred to Scrutiny. *Free Inquiry* (December/January): 62–63.

Hout, Michael and Claude S. Fischer. 2002. Why More Americans Have No Religious Preference. *American Sociological Review* 67, no. 2 (April): 165–190.

Hunsberger, Bruce E. and Bob Altemeyer. 2006. *Atheists: A Groundbreaking Study of America's Nonbelievers.* Amherst, NY: Prometheus Books.

Huxley, Thomas Henry. 1893. Evolution and Ethics – The Romanes Lecture. *Collected Essays IX.* http://aleph0.clarku.edu/huxley/CE9/E-E.html.

Huxley, Thomas Henry. 1894. *Science and Christian Tradition.* New York: D. Appleton.

Iannoconne, Lawrence. R. 1995. Voodoo Economics? Reviewing the Rational Choice Approach to Religion. *Journal of the Scientific Study of Religion* 34: 76–89.

Jackson, Sherman. 2007. Jihad and the Modern World. In *Islam in Transition: Muslim Perspectives,* ed. John L. Esposito and John J. Donohue. 394–408. New York: Oxford Univ. Press.

James, William. 1896. The Will to Believe. An address to the philosophical clubs of Yale and Brown universities. http://falcon.jmu.edu/~omearawm/ph101willto believe.html.

———. 1902. *The Varieties of Religious Experience.* New York: Longmans.

——. 1948. *Essays in Pragmatism*. New York: Hafner.

Johnson, Ellen. 2008. Enlighten The Vote. *American Atheist* (January): 4.

Johnson, Steven. 2008. *The Invention of Air*. New York: Penguin.

Jones, Edward E., David E. Kanhouse, Harold H. Kelley, Richard E. Nisbett, Stuart Valins, and Bernard Weiner. 1972. *Attribution: Perceiving the Causes of Behavior*. Morristown, NJ: General Learning Press.

Kant, Immanuel. 1993. *Critique of Practical Reason*. Trans. Lewis White Beck. 3rd Edition. Upper Saddle River, NJ: Prentice Hall.

Kant, Immanuel. 1996. *Critique of Pure Reason*. Trans.Werner Pluhar. Indiana: Hackett.

Kaplan, Mordecai. 1991. *Dynamic Judaism: The Essential Writings of Mordecai M. Kaplan*. New York: Fordham Univ. Press.

Kaplan, Mordecai. 1994. *The Meaning of God in Modern Jewish Religion*. Detroit: Wayne State Univ. Press.

Kaufman, William E. 1992. *Contemporary Jewish Philosophies*. Detroit: Wayne State Univ. Press.

Kay, Robert E. 2007. Thoughts on Raising a Curious, Creative, Freethinking Child. In *Parenting Beyond Belief: On Raising Ethical, Caring Kids Without Religion*, ed. Dale McGowan, 186–190. New York: AMACOM.

Keller, Nuh Ha Mim. 2006. Who or what is a Salafi? Is their approach valid? *The Q-News Articles* (November 2): http://www.masud.co.uk/ISLAM/nuh/salafi.htm.

Keysar, Ariela. 2001. *American Religious Identification Survey*. New York. The Graduate Center of the City University of New York.

Keysar, Ariela. 2003. No Religion: A Profile of America's Unchurched. *Public Perspective* (January/February): 40–44.

Knight, David. 2004. *Science and Spirituality: The Volatile Connection*. London: Routledge.

Koproske, Colin. 2006. The Secular Stigma. *Free Inquiry* 27, no. 1 (December): 49–50.

Kosmin, Barry A., Egon Mayer and Ariela Keysar. 2001. *American Religious Identification Survey 2001*. New York: Graduate Center of the City University of New York.

Kosmin, Barry and Ariela Keysar, eds. 2007. *Secularism and Secularity*. Hartford, CT: ISSSC.

Kurtz, Paul. 2007a. The New Atheism and Secular Humanism. *Point of Inquiry Podcast*. September 14. http://www.pointofinquiry.org/paul_kurtz_the_new_atheism_and _secular_humanism/.

——. 2007b. 'Yes' to Naturalism, Secularism, and Humanism. *Free Inquiry* (April/ May): 4–5.

——. 2007c. Are 'Evangelical Atheists' Too Outspoken? *Free Inquiry* (Feb/Mar): 4–5.

Larner, Christina. 1984. *Witchcraft and Religion*. New York: Blackwell.

Layton, David. 2007. A Fresh Look At Atheism And The Enlightenment. *Free Inquiry* (June/July): 64–65.

Levitt, Mairi. 1996. 'Nice when they are Young': Contemporary Christianity in Families and Schools. Aldershot: Avebury.

Lewis, Bernard. 2003. *The Assassins: A Radical Sect in Islam*. New York: Basic Books.

Lewis, C. S. 1952. *Mere Christianity*. San Francisco: HarperSanFrancisco.

Linker, Damon. 2008. In Godless books, mindless arguments. *National Post*. January 7.

Lubarsky, Sandra B. 1996. Judaism and Process Thought. In *Jewish Theology and Process Thought: Between Naturalism and Supernaturalism*. Eds. Sandra B. Lubarsky and David Ray Griffin, 47–57. Albany: State University of New York.

Luther, Martin. 2002. *A Prelude by Martin Luther on the Babylonian Captivity of the Church*. http://www.ctsfw.edu/etext/luther/babylonian/babylonian.htm

Mackie, J. L. 1982. *The Miracle of Theism : Arguments for and against the Existence of God*. New York: Oxford Univ. Press.

244

REFERENCES

Maher, Bill. 2005. *Scarborough Country*. Interview by Joe Scarborough, MSNBC, June 15. http://www.msnbc.msn.com/id/6980984

Maher, Bill. 2008. God love him. In *Famous*. Interview by Marni Weisz. October.

Mahmoud, Saba. 2005. *Politics of Piety: The Islamic Revival and the Feminist Subject*. Princeton: Princeton University Press.

Marcuse, Herbert. 1964. *One-dimensional Man*. Boston: Beacon Press.

Marshall, David. 2007. *The Truth Behind the New Atheism*. Oregon: Harvest House.

Martin, David A. 1969. Toward Eliminating the Concept of Secularisation. In *The Religious and the Secular*, ed. David Martin. London: Routledge.

Masuzawa, Tomoko. 2006. *The Invention of World Religions*. Chicago: University of Chicago Press.

McEwan, Ian. 2009. Root of All Evil? Interview with Richard Dawkins. February 2. http://richarddawkins.net/articles/3573.

McGowan Dale. 2007b. Living with Religion. In *Parenting Beyond Belief: On Raising Ethical, Caring Kids Without Religion*, ed. Dale McGowan, 35–38. New York: AMACOM.

——, ed. 2009. *Raising Freethinkers: A Practical Guide for Parenting Beyond Belief*. New York: AMACOM.

——. 2007a. Seven Secular Virtues: Humility, Empathy, Courage, Honesty, Openness, Generosity, and Gratitude. In *Parenting Beyond Belief: On Raising Ethical, Caring Kids Without Religion*, ed. Dale McGowan, 126–134. New York: AMACOM.

——. 2007c. Preface. In *Parenting Beyond Belief: On Raising Ethical, Caring Kids Without Religion*, ed. Dale McGowan, ix-xiv. New York: AMACOM.

——. 2007d. Parenting Beyond Belief: Reason vs. the Rod. *Humanist Network News*. October 17. http://humaniststudies.org/enews/?id=319&article=3.

McGrath, Alister and Joanna Collicutt McGrath. 2007. *The Dawkins Delusion? Atheist Fundamentalism and the Denial of the Divine*. Illinois: IVP Books.

McGrath, Alister. 2004. *The Twilight of Atheism: The Rise and Fall of Disbelief in the Modern World*. London: Rider.

McGrath, Alister. 2009. Root of All Evil?. Interview with Richard Dawkins. Upper Branch Productions, 2008. http://debunkingchristianity.blogspot.com/2007/07/richard-dawkins-interviews-alister.html.

——. 2007. *Dawkins' God: Genes, Memes, and the Meaning of Life*. Massachusetts: Blackwell.

McPherson, Miller, Lynn Smith-Lovin & Matthew E. Brashears. 2006. Social Isolation in America: Changes in Core Discussion Networks over Two Decades. *American Sociological Review* 71 (June): 353–375.

Mennell, Stephen. 2007. *The American Civilizing Process*. Cambridge: Polity Press.

Meyrowitz, Joshua and John Maguire. 1993. Media, Place, and Multiculturalism. *Society*, 41–48.

Meyrowitz, Joshua. 1985. *No Sense of Place: The Impact of Electronic Media on Social Behavior*. New York: Oxford Univ. Press.

——. 1994. Medium Theory. In *Communication Theory Today*, ed. David Crowley and David Mitchell, 50–77. Stanford: Stanford Univ. Press.

——. 2000. Multiple Media Literacies. In *Television: The Critical View*, ed. Horace Newcomb, 425–438. New York: Oxford Univ. Press.

Micklethwait, John and Adrian Wooldridge. 2009. *God is Back: How the Global Revival of Faith is Changing the World*. New York: Penguin.

Milgram, Stanley. 1963. Behavioral Study of Obedience. *Journal of Abnormal and Social Psychology* 67: 371–378.

Miller, Elliot. 1985. The Christian and Authority. *Forward* 8, no. 1 and 2 (Spring and Summer). http://web.archive.org/web/20040215181018/http://www.equip.org.

Miller, George A. 1956. The Magical Number Seven, Plus or Minus Two: Some Limits on our Capacity for Processing Information. *Psychological Review* 63: 81–97.

Minsky, Marvin, and Seymour Papert. 1969. *Perceptrons*. Cambridge: MIT Press.

Minsky, Marvin. 2006. *The Emotion Machine*. New York: Simon & Schuster.

Mohler, R. Albert. 2008. *Atheism Remix*. Wheaton, IL: Crossway.

Morris, Simon Conway. 2003. *Life's Solution*. Cambridge: Cambridge Univ. Press.

Nall, Jeff. 2008. Fundamentalist Atheism and its Intellectual Failures. *Humanity & Society* 32, no 3: 45–62.

Nanda, Meera. 2008. Trading Faith for Spirituality. *American Atheist* (February): 20–25.

Nelkin, Dorothy. 2004. God Talk: Confusion between Science and Religion. *Science, Technology and Human Values* 29, no. 2: 139–152.

Nietzsche, Friedrich. 1999. *Thus Spake Zarathustra*. Trans. Thomas Common. Mineola, NY: Dover Publications.

Nietzsche, Friedrich. 1961. *Thus Spoke Zarathustra*. Trans. R. J. Hollingdale. Baltimore: Penguin Books.

Nietzsche, Friedrich. 2003. *Writings from the Late Notebooks*. Ed. Rüdiger Bittner. Cambridge: Cambridge Univ. Press.

Norenzayan, Ara, and Azim F. Shariff. 2008. The Origin and Evolution of Religious Prosociality. *Science* 332, no. 58: 58–62.

O'Donnell, James J. 1979. The Demise of Paganism. *Traditio* 35: 45–88.

Onfray, Michel. 2007. *Atheist Manifesto: The Case Against Christianity, Judaism, and Islam*. Trans. Jeremy Leggatt. New York: Arcade.

Ou, Wanmei, Matti S. Hämäläinen, and Polina Golland. 2009. A Distributed Spatiotemporal EEG/MEG Inverse Solver. *NeuroImage* 44: 932–946.

Pape, Robert A. 2006. *Dying to Win: The Strategic Logic of Suicide Terrorism*. New York: Random House.

Parsons, Keith M. 2008. Atheism: Twilight or Dawn? In *The Future of Atheism: Alister McGrath & Daniel Dennett in Dialogue*, ed. Robert B. Stewart, 51–65. London: SPCK.

Pascal, Blaise. 1961. *Pensés*. New York: Doubleday.

Peters, Ted. 2008. The God Hypothesis in the Future of Atheism. In *The Future of Atheism*, ed. Robert Stewart. 163–182. Minneapolis: Fortress Press.

Pew Forum on Religion & Public Life. 2008. U.S. Religious Landscape Survey. Religious Beliefs and Practices: Diverse and Politically Relevant. Washington, DC: The Pew Forum on Religion & Public Life. http://religions.pewforum.org/pdf/report2-religious-landscape-study-full.pdf.

Phillips, D. Z. 1993. *Wittgenstein and Religion*. New York: St. Martin's Press.

Phillips, D.Z. 1994. *Wittgenstein and Religion*. London: Palgrave Macmillan.

Pigliucci, Massimo. 2008. Is Dawkins Deluded? *American Atheist* (May/June): 16–18.

Pinker, Steven. 1997. *How the Mind Works*. New York: Norton.

——. 2008. The Stupidity of Dignity. *The New Republic*, 28 May.

Plantinga, Alvin. 2007. The Dawkins Confusion: Naturalism ad absurdum. *Books & Culture*. www.christianitytoday.com/bc/2007/002/1.21.html.

Plato. *Euthyphro*. Trans. Benjamin Jowett. The Internet Classics Archive. http://classics.mit.edu/Plato/euthyfro.html.

Pollitt, Katha. 2008. Onward Secular Soldiers. *Free Inquiry* (December/January): 20–21.

Pomeroy, Keenan. 2008. Going Beyond God, and Discovering a Religion: An Atheistic Approach to Being Religious. *Journal of Liberal Religion* 8, no 1.

Poupard, Paul. 2004. *Where Is Your God? Responding to the Challenge of Unbelief and Religious Indifference Today*. Chicago, IL: Liturgy Training Publications.

Proctor, Robert. 1988. *Racial Hygiene*. Cambridge, MA: Harvard Univ. Press.

Prothero, Stephen. 2007. *Religious Literacy: What Every American Needs to Know – and Doesn't*. New York: HarperCollins.

Putnam, Robert D. 2000. *Bowling Alone: The Collapse and Revival of American Community*. New York: Simon & Schuster.

Rand, Ayn. 1989. *The Virtue of Selfishness*. New York: Penguin.

Rawls, John. 1971. *A Theory of Justice*. Cambridge, MA: Harvard Univ. Press.

Reisz, Matthew. 2008. Losing Our Religion? *Times Higher Education*, January 24. http://www.timeshighereducation.co.uk/story.asp?storyCode=400261&section code=26.

Robbins, Jeffrey. 2003. *Between Faith and Thought: An Essay on the Ontotheological Condition*. Charlottesville: University of Virginia Press.

Robertson, John Mackinnon. 1929. *A History of Freethought in the Nineteenth Century*. London: Watts & Co.

Robinson, John. 1963. *Honest to God*. Philadelphia: Westminster.

Roheim, Geza. 1955. *Magic and Schizophrenia*. Bloomington: Indiana University Press.

Rollins, Peter. 2006. *How (Not) to Speak of God*. Brewster, MA: Paraclete.

Rollins, Peter. 2008. *The Fidelity of Betrayal*. Brewster, MA: Paraclete.

Rose, Hilary and Steven Rose, eds. 2000. *Alas, Poor Darwin*. New York: Harmony Books.

Rosemond, John. 2007. *Parenting by The Book: Biblical Wisdom for Raising Your Child*. New York: Howard Books.

Roy, Olivier. 1994. *The Failure of Political Islam*. Cambridge, MA: Harvard Univ. Press.

Roy, Olivier. 2004. *Globalized Islam: The Search for a New Ummah*. New York: Columbia Univ. Press.

Rubenstein, Richard L. 1992. *After Auschwitz: History, Theology, and Contemporary Judaism*. Baltimore: Johns Hopkins Univ. Press.

Rumelhart, D. E. and J. L. McClelland. 1986. *Parallel Distributed Processing*. Cambridge: MIT Press.

Ruse, Michael. 1999. *Mystery of Mysteries*. Cambridge, MA: Harvard University Press.

Rushkoff, Douglas. 2003. *Nothing Sacred: The Truth About Judaism*. New York: Crown Publishers.

Russell, Bertrand. 1957. *Why I Am Not a Christian and Other Essays*. London: Allen & Unwin.

Russell, Bertrand. 2004. *History of Western Philosophy*. London: Routledge.

Ruthven, Malise. 2004. *Fundamentalism: The Search for Meaning*. Oxford: Oxford Univ. Press.

Safi, Omid. 2006. *The Politics of Knowledge in Premodern Islam: Negotiating Ideology and Religious Inquiry*. Chapel Hill: The University of North Carolina Press.

Sarfati, Jonathan. 1998. Loving God with All Your Mind: Logic and Creation. *Creation ex nihilo Technical Journal* 12, no. 2 (August): 142–151. http://www.answersin genisis.org/tj/v12/i2/logic.asp.

Schimmel, Annemarie. 1975. *Mystical Dimensions of Islam*. Chapel Hill: University of North Carolina Press.

Schnädelbach, Herbert. 1984. *Philosophy in Germany, 1831–1933*. Cambridge: Cambridge Univ. Press.

Schneewind, Jerome. 1984. The Divine Corporation and the History of Ethics. In *Philosophy in History*, eds. Richard Rorty, J. Schneewind and Q. Skinner, 173–192. Cambridge: Cambridge Univ. Press.

Scola, Angelo, and Paolo Flores D'Arcais. 2008. *Dio? Ateismo della ragione e ragioni della fede*. Venezia: Marsilio Editori.

Segerstrale, Ullica. 2000. *Defenders of the Truth: The Sociobiology Debate*. Oxford: Oxford University Press.

Seid, Judith. 2001. *God-Optional Judaism: Alternatives for Cultural Jews Who Love Their History, Heritage, and Community*. New York: Citadel.

Shermer, Michael. 2006. *The Science of Good and Evil: Why People Cheat, Gossip, Care, Share, and Follow the Golden Rule*. New York: Holt.

Shermer, Michael. 2007. Foreword to *Parenting Beyond Belief: On Raising Ethical, Caring Kids Without Religion*, ed. Dale McGowan, vii–viii. New York: AMACOM.

Shiner, Larry. 1967. The Concept of Secularization in Empirical Research. *Journal for the Scientific Study of Religion* 6: 207–220.

Singer, Peter. 1981. *The Expanding Circle: Ethics and Sociobiology*. New York: Farrar, Straus & Giroux.

——. 1999. *A Darwinian Left*. London: Nicolson and Weidenfeld.

——. 2002. *One World: The Ethics of Globalization*. New Haven: Yale Univ. Press.

Sirriyeh, Elizabeth. 1999. *Sufis and Anti-Sufis: The Defence, Rethinking and Rejection of Sufism in the Modern World*. Richmond: Curzon Press.

Smith, Christian. 1998. *American Evangelicalism: Embattled And Thriving*. Chicago: University of Chicago Press.

Smith, Huston. 2003. Winnowing the Wisdom Traditions: An Interview with Mark Kenaston. In *The Way Things Are: Conversations with Huston Smith on the Spiritual Life*, ed. Phil Cousineau, 59–74. Berkeley: Univ. of California Press.

Sober, Elliott, and David Sloan Wilson. 1998. *Unto Others: The Evolution and Psychology of Unselfish Behavior*. Cambridge, MA: Harvard Univ. Press.

Sober, Elliott. 2008. *Evidence and Evolution*. Cambridge, UK: Cambridge Univ. Press.

Sosis, Richard. 2007. Breaking the Wrong Spell. *Free Inquiry* (December/January): 59–60.

Spinoza, Baruch. 1996. *Ethics*. London: Penguin Books.

Stark, Rodney and Roger Finke. 2000. *Acts of Faith: Explaining the Human Side of Religion*. Berkeley: University of California Press.

Stark, Rodney and William Sims Bainbridge. 1985. *The Future of Religion: Secularization, Revival and Cult Formation*. Berkeley: University of California Press.

Stark, Rodney and William Sims Bainbridge. 1987. *A Theory of Religion*. New York: Peter Lang.

Stenger, Victor J. 2007. *God: the Failed Hypothesis; How Science Shows that God Does Not Exist*. Amherst, NY: Prometheus Books.

Sterelny, Kim. 2001. *Dawkins vs. Gould: Survival of the Fittest*. Cambridge: Icon.

Stewart, Matthew. 2006. *The Courtier and the Heretic: Leibniz, Spinoza, and the Fate of God in the Modern World*. New York: W.W. Norton.

Stewart, Robert B. 2008. The Future of Atheism: An Introductory Appraisal. In *Future of Atheism: Alister McGrath & Daniel Dennett in Dialogue*, ed. Robert B. Stewart, 1–16. London: SPCK.

Suellentrop, Chris. 2006. Abdullah Azzam, The Godfather of Jihad. *Slate*, November 2. http://www.slate.com/id/2064385/

Swatos, William Jr. and Kevin Chistiano. 1999. Secularization Theory: The Course of a Concept. *Sociology of Religion* 60: 209–228.

Swinburne, Richard. 1996. *Is There a God?* New York: Oxford Univ. Press.

Tanquist, Stu. 2007. Choosing Your Battles. In *Parenting Beyond Belief: On Raising Ethical, Caring Kids Without Religion*, ed. Dale McGowan, 49–56. New York: AMACOM.

Tarde, Gabriel. 1969. *On Communication and Social Influence*. Chicago: University of Chicago Press.

Taylor, Charles. 1991. *The Malaise of Modernity*. Toronto: Anansi.

——. 2007. *A Secular Age*. Cambridge: Harvard University Press.

——. 2007b. Statement at the Templeton Prize News Conference. http://www.metanexus.net/magazine/tabid/68/id/9827/Default.aspx.

Taylor, Mark C. 1984. *Erring: A Postmodern A/theology*. Chicago: University of Chicago Press.

Thagard, Paul. 2007. Cognitive Science. In *Stanford Encyclopedia of Philosophy*. http://plato.stanford.edu/entries/cognitive-science/ (accessed June 5, 2009).

Thoburn, Nicholas. 2003. *Deleuze, Marx and Politics*. London: Routledge.

Tillich, Paul. 1951. *Systematic Theology*. Vol. 1. Chicago: University of Chicago Press.
——. 1952. *The Courage to Be*. New Haven, CT: Yale Univ. Press.
——. 1964. *Theology of Culture*. Ed. Robert Kimball. London: Oxford.
——. 1996. *The Irrelevance and Relevance of the Christian Message*. Cleveland: Pilgrim.
Times. 2006. Authors enjoying "enormous" sales boost from *Da Vinci Code* case. *Times Online*, March 9. http://entertainment.timesonline.co.uk/tol/arts_and_entertainment/books/article739299.ece.
Trimingham, J. Spencer. 1971. *The Sufi Orders in Islam*. London: Oxford Univ. Press.
Tschannen, Olivier. 1991. The Secularization Paradigm: A Systematization. *Journal for the Scientific Study of Religion* 30: 395–415.
Turk, D. J., T. F. Heatherton, W. M Kelley, M. G. Funnell, M. S. Gazzaniga, and C. N. Macrae. 2002. Mike or Me? Self-recognition in a Split-brain Patient. *Nature Neuroscience* 5: 841–842.
Turner, James C. 1985. *Without God, Without Creed: The Origins of Unbelief in America*. Baltimore, MD: Johns Hopkins Univ. Press.
Urbach, Ephraim E. 1987. *The Sages: Their Concepts and Beliefs*. Trans. I. Abrahams. Cambridge, MA: Harvard Univ. Press.
van Bruinessen, Martin and Julia Day Howell, eds. 2007. *Sufism and the 'Modern' in Islam*. New York: I.B. Taurus.
Varghese, Roy. 2007. The 'New Atheism': A Critical Appraisal of Dawkins, Dennett, Wolpert, Harris, and Stenger. *There is a God* by Anthony Flew, 161–183. New York: Harper One.
al-Muhajabah. 2006. Muslims Condemn Terrorist Attacks. 2 November. http://www.muhajabah.com/otherscondemn.php
Vattimo, Gianni. 1999. *Belief*. Stanford: Stanford Univ. Press.
——. 2002. *After Christianity*. New York: Columbia Univ. Press.
Voas, David and Alasdair Crockett. 2005. Religion in Britain: Neither Believing nor Belonging. *Sociology* 39, no. 1 (February): 11–28.
Voas, David. 2008. Forthcoming. The Rise and Fall of Fuzzy Fidelity in Europe. *European Sociological Review*.
Wallace, Anthony F. C. 1959. The Institutionalization of Cathartic and Control Strategies in Iroquois Religious Psychotherapy. In *Culture and Mental Health*, ed. Marvin Opler, 63–96. New York: Macmillan.
Warner, R. Stephen. 1993. Work in Progress toward a New Paradigm for the Sociological Study of Religion in the United States. *American Journal of Sociology* 98: 1044–1093.
Warren, Elizabeth. 2006. The Middle Class on the Precipice: Rising financial risks for American families. *The Harvard Magazine*. January-February, http://harvardmagazine.com/2006/01/p-the-middle-class-on-the.html
Weber, Max. 1946. Science as a Vocation. In *From Max Weber, Essays in Sociology*, ed. H. H. Gerth and C. Wright Mills, 129–156. New York: Oxford Univ. Press.
Weinberg, Steven. 1992. *Dreams of a Final Theory*. New York: Atheneum.
Weinberg, Steven. 2008. Without God. *New York Review of Books*. September 25.
Wilber, Ken. 2001. *Eye to Eye: The Quest for the New Paradigm*. Boston: Shambhala.
Wilson, Bryan. 1976. Aspects of Secularization in the West. *Japanese Journal of Religious Studies* 3: 259–276.
Wilson, Bryan. 1982. *Religion in Sociological Perspective*. Oxford: Oxford Univ. Press
Wilson, Edward. 1978. *On Human Nature*. Cambridge, MA: Harvard Univ. Press.
Wine, Sherwin. 1995a. The Meaning of Jewish History. In *Judaism in a Secular Age: An Anthology of Secular Humanistic Jewish Thought*, eds. R. Kogel and Z. Bauer, 228–234. New York: KTAV.
Wine, Sherwin. 1995b. Intermarriage. In *Judaism in a Secular Age: An Anthology of Secular Humanistic Jewish Thought*, eds. R. Kogel and Z. Bauer, 245–250. New York: KTAV.

Winter, T. J. 2007. The Poverty of Fanaticism. In *Islam in Transition: Muslim Perspectives*, eds. John L. Esposito and John J. Donohue. 382–392. New York: Oxford Univ. Press.

Wootton, David. 1988. Lucien Febvre and the Problem of Unbelief in the Early Modern Period. *The Journal of Modern History* 60: 695–730.

World Values Survey. 1999. www.worldvaluessurvey.org

Zagzebski, Linda Trinkaus. 2007. *Philosophy of Religion: An Historical Introduction*. Fundamentals of philosophy, vol. 3. Malden, MA: Blackwell Pub.

Zak, Paul, Angela A. Stanton, and Sheila Ahmadi. 2007. Oxytocin Increases Generosity in Humans. *PLoS One* 2, no. 11: e1128. doi:101371/journal.pone.0001128.

Zeki, Semir. 2003. The Disunity of Consciousness. *Trends in Cognitive Sciences* 7: 214–218.

INDEX